China Inside and Out

China Inside and Out

Politics and Policies in a Turbulent World

Mel Gurtov

BLOOMSBURY ACADEMIC
NEW YORK • LONDON • OXFORD • NEW DELHI • SYDNEY

BLOOMSBURY ACADEMIC

Bloomsbury Publishing Inc, 1359 Broadway, New York, NY 10018, USA
Bloomsbury Publishing Plc, 50 Bedford Square, London, WC1B 3DP, UK
Bloomsbury Publishing Ireland, 29 Earlsfort Terrace, Dublin 2, D02 AY28, Ireland

BLOOMSBURY, BLOOMSBURY ACADEMIC and the Diana logo are trademarks of
Bloomsbury Publishing Plc

Copyright © Mel Gurtov 2025

Cover design: Chloe Batch
Cover image: Pacific Ocean Bloom from Oceans Blooming Series,
2016, by Shu-Ju Wang

All rights reserved. No part of this publication may be: i) reproduced or transmitted in any form, electronic or mechanical, including photocopying, recording or by means of any information storage or retrieval system without prior permission in writing from the publishers; or ii) used or reproduced in any way for the training, development or operation of artificial intelligence (AI) technologies, including generative AI technologies. The rights holders expressly reserve this publication from the text and data mining exception as per Article 4(3) of the Digital Single Market Directive (EU) 2019/790.

Bloomsbury Publishing Inc does not have any control over, or responsibility for, any third-party websites referred to or in this book. All internet addresses given in this book were correct at the time of going to press. The author and publisher regret any inconvenience caused if addresses have changed or sites have ceased to exist, but can accept no responsibility for any such changes.

ISBN: HB: 979-8-2163-6592-1
PB: 979-8-2163-6593-8
ePUB: 979-8-2163-6594-5
ePDF: 979-8-2163-6595-2

Typeset by Deanta Global Publishing Services, Chennai, India
Printed and bound in the United States of America

For product safety related questions contact productsafety@bloomsbury.com.

To find out more about our authors and books visit www.bloomsbury.com and sign up for our newsletters.

CONTENTS

List of Charts vi
Map vii
About the Author viii
Foreword ix

PART I China and the World

1 US-China Relations: Policy and Diplomacy 3

2 US-China Relations: The Strategic Competition 43

3 China's Relations with Russia and Europe 77

4 China and the Global South 95

5 China's Relations with Its Near Neighbors 125

PART II Inside China

6 Politics and Society 153

7 The Economy and Environment 173

8 Human Rights 193

PART III

9 For Further Reflection 223

Notes 229

CHARTS

1.1 US Trade with China, 1985–2018 18
2.1 China and US Military Spending Since 2000 51
2.2 Members of the Pacific Islands Forum 67
5.1 A Snapshot of Japan-China Economic Relations 139
7.1 Comparative Economic Strength of the US and China 175
7.2 Estimated Breakdown of China's GDP Composition Over Time 177
7.3 The Leading Greenhouse Gas Emitters 183

ABOUT THE AUTHOR

Mel Gurtov is Professor Emeritus of Political Science at Portland State University and Senior Editor of *Asian Perspective*. He has published over thirty books on China, US foreign policy, and international politics from a global-citizen perspective. He blogs at https://melgurtov.com and has a podcast at https://melgurtov.substack.com. He lives in Deadwood, Oregon.

FOREWORD

This book seeks to provide students of international affairs, whether specifically interested in China or not, with a way to keep abreast of the latest information and analysis that is different from the usual textbook. Rather than a chronological narrative of China's evolution, I provide brief, focused readings that offer insights into the most important recent developments in China's international relations and domestic affairs. The readings and opinion draw from my lifelong research on China, my blog, and an array of Chinese and Western news sources. A documents section at the end of each chapter consists of official speeches and statements from China and other countries. The final chapter has questions for students that require analysis and, perhaps, debate.

Intentionally, the book devotes the first two (and longest) chapters to the US-China relationship, which has become the most important in international affairs. At this moment, opinion polls consistently show that Americans regard China as a major threat, both economically and strategically, while Chinese regard the United States as determined to contain China and impede its development. Tensions between the two countries remain high, over issues that have been around for over a decade: human rights, trade, Taiwan, the South China Sea, military budgets. Other issues have arisen that add to the mix, such as the war in Ukraine, educational exchanges, nuclear weapons, the fentanyl trade, and the future of artificial intelligence. In past times, all these points of contention would not have impeded the search for common ground through diplomatic engagement, in common recognition that constant friction can have calamitous consequences. Now, however, interest in finding common ground is less than it has been in a very long time.

In the classic study of a Chinese village on the verge of dramatic change in the late 1940s, *Fanshen*, William Hinton wrote that "without understanding the Revolution in China one cannot understand today's world." Now, understanding *everything* about China is essential to understanding today's world. I hope that these readings will help you, the student, to do so. I invite anyone who wants to delve deeper into international politics, China, and US foreign policy to subscribe (it's free) to my blog, https://melgurtov.com or my podcast, https://melgurtov.substack.com.

This book would not have been possible—indeed, would not have occurred to me—but for Mark Selden, who didn't believe me when I said I had written my last book. Mark persuaded me to consider bringing together my blogs on China, and once I did, I saw what he saw. And so did Ashley Dodge at Rowman & Littlefield, whose support for my last two books I greatly appreciate. Thanks also to my wife Jodi, my family, and my friends. They didn't bat an eye when I said I was writing another book. They didn't believe my last was my last either.

Mel Gurtov
Deadwood, Oregon

PART I

China and the World

1

US-China Relations

Policy and Diplomacy

Introduction

Ever since the United States and China normalized relations in 1971 with President Richard Nixon's famous trip to Beijing, the road to finding common ground has been rocky. In this chapter, we look at attempts at engagement through direct communications between leaders and through exchanges, such as trade and people-to-people programs. Three US presidents—Barack Obama, Donald Trump, and Joseph Biden—have had a total of eleven face-to-face meetings with Chinese leader Xi Jinping as of spring 2025. Those meetings took place at official summits and international gatherings, with two in Beijing and four in the United States. Two telephone "virtual summits" also took place. The meetings typically ended with announcements of agreement to cooperate, such as on climate change, pandemic research, drug trafficking, educational exchanges (**Selection 5**), trade and investment, and military-to-military communication (**Selection 4**). But breakthroughs on contentious core issues, such as (for the United States) on human rights or on Taiwan (for China), have yet to occur and may be a bridge too far.

US-China policy differences, as revealed in **Selections 1 and 3**, stem from sharply different understandings of "partnership or rivalry" and national security. Until Donald Trump's first election in 2016, US policy had consistently been to "manage" relations with China, seeking to avoid direct conflict by both competing and cooperating within a "rules-based international order" (**Selection 10** and **Document 1**). Xi Jinping agrees that management is necessary, and he says that it is best carried out by US partnership with China. He means that there should be no US interference in what China regards as its internal affairs (Taiwan, Tibet, human rights). As for a rules-based order, the Chinese point to US domination of international rule-making bodies and (in their view) to consistent US violations of the rules.

Trump's two administrations have jettisoned the traditional approach in favor of a China policy based on a combination of trade pressure and ideological dogma (**Selection 2**). But the trade war in his first term was nothing compared with what happened in the second—a tit-for-tat series of tariff increases, initiated by Trump, that threatened to reduce economic relations with China to near-zero (**Selection 11**).

How to balance partnership and rivalry is the overriding challenge for both nations, and **Selection 12** offers the author's suggestions on how the challenge might be handled. But in 2024, a US presidential election year, politics prevailed. That was reflected in multiple ways: Trump's major tariff increases (**Selection 10 and Document 2**); public opinion polls in both countries (**Document 3**); the so-called China Initiative in the United States (**Selection 6**); and the Republican House majority's "China Week" agenda (**Selection 9**).

Despite growing differences over trade and investment, US-China commercial interactions remain central to their relationship and to the world economy. The US-China goods trade is one of the world's largest, with total trade of around $734 billion in 2024. US imports were valued at $439 billion and exports to China at $144 billion. The US deficit thus came to about $295 billion, the largest goods trade deficit with any country. The deficit was much smaller than it used to be as both the Trump and Biden administrations imposed restrictions on exports to and investments in China, citing national security concerns. China retaliated with trade and investment restrictions of its own. A trade and chips war ensued, with bipartisan support in the US Congress (**Selections 8 and 10**).

Nevertheless, China is wedded to economic globalization, and its officials appealed to the second Trump administration to accept the view that trading and investing with China is a win for both sides (see **Selection 7, Document 5**, and Chapter 7 on the economy). But with Trump moving aggressively toward a tariff war with China, two Chinese experts believe high technology will be "the core of Sino-US competition." They are convinced that China can survive the pressure (**Documents 5 and 6**).

(1) Finding Common Ground with China (2021)

Managing Relations

"It seems clear to me we need to establish some common-sense guardrails," President Joe Biden told President Xi Jinping in their November 16, 2021 virtual summit. Xi reportedly replied to his "old friend" with a metaphor about boats finding their way together through rough waters. This was not the usual summit: no preliminary fanfare, no final communiqué, no evident agreements on the most contentious issues in US-China relations. Yet it was an important event.

Amidst all the wrangling between the United States and China about human rights, trade, Taiwan, and a host of other issues, a central concern both countries share is how to *manage* the relationship. What is the most effective structure for ensuring that conflict over issues doesn't spill over into armed conflict? Are there areas of agreement that can be solidified with proactive projects involving the two nations and others? In the Barack Obama era (2009–17), the answer was around sixty US-China working groups focused on specific issues, such as environmental protection and military-to-military communication. In Donald Trump's first term (2017–21), these were largely abandoned, without sustained diplomacy to replace them. Biden did not restore the dialogue groups. His national security team was made up of people who believed that engagement with China had not produced significant results.

Biden's comment about establishing "common-sense guardrails" is self-evidently correct, as is Xi's opening comment that the two countries need a "sound and steady" relationship. But how to structure relations remained the burning question. No substitute was found for the Obama-era working groups which, even if they didn't produce dramatic results, did help foster improved communications and a spirit of cooperation. As a result, trade and exchanges in technology and education back then were not the burning issues they later became.

Engaging China

I submit that the way forward is to make engagement with China a US strategic objective. The reasons are simple: China is one of the two most important challenges for US national security—first, because of its global economic and political influence, which comes at a time of high US tensions with Russia and the growing risk of nuclear war; second, because of the climate crisis, to which both countries are the leading contributors. Thus, engaging China is in the national interest, as the Obama era demonstrated. Other advantages of engagement for the United States include avoidance of dangerous confrontations and decreased likelihood of misperceptions and miscommunications; recruitment of scientific talent from China; reduction of tariff barriers; opportunities to reduce military spending from force reductions in Asia and avoidance of an arms race; more opportunities for people-to-people exchanges, including tourism; participation in each other's trade networks and a variety of other multilateral fora; promotion of public health research and climate change mitigation; wider cooperation in UN peacekeeping operations and other programs; opportunities for reducing nuclear weapons arsenals; a greatly improved security climate across Asia; and cooperative efforts on aid to developing countries. Most of these US advantages are also positives for global security.

One has to ask: Are US national security objectives served by *not* engaging China and ramping up across-the-board conflict? Does forming a coalition of states to confront China on its human rights violations or its militarization of the South China Sea islands induce positive changes in Chinese policy? Do high tariffs on Chinese exports change their trade policies or their technological progress? Does upgrading relations with Taiwan add to its security? To be clear, naming and shaming China's repression of human rights, refusing to abide by its unilateral takeover of some South China Sea islands, seeking to reduce the trade deficit with China, and maintaining "strategic ambiguity" on defense of Taiwan if attacked are all appropriate policies. But many of these aims are not served, and in fact are undermined, by pressure tactics. The Chinese will respond with pressure of their own, raising tensions and the risk of violent confrontations.

Chinese Views

Some high-level Chinese commentaries suggest that engagement would be welcome in Beijing. The Chinese foreign ministry, in its response to the Biden-Xi meeting, had this to say: "The key is that both sides should meet each other halfway and use actions to create a good atmosphere to ensure that the meeting achieves positive results. . . . China is open to all options that are conducive to the development of Sino-US relations." Notably, that statement was from the ministry's so-called "wolf warrior," Zhao Lijian; who is usually associated with vitriolic comments on US policies. I suspect that he and the ministry were told to reflect Xi's position on striving for "coexistence" and "win-win" solutions. China's veteran America watcher, Wang Jisi, a longtime proponent of US-China engagement, offered the opinion that the best hope for resolving US-China differences was to address their different "mindsets." He wrote in March 2021: "Whereas the Chinese insist on identifying principles, the Americans want action on immediate issues. The Chinese believe in first 'finding common ground while reserving differences,' which means agreement on a set of principles, including mutual respect and win-win cooperation."[1]

Bridging the US-China divide is a huge challenge, but Professor Wang's advice offers a starting point: finding common ground. The climate crisis is surely just such an opportunity, and one that would "create a good atmosphere" for further progress in reducing tensions and building trust.

(2) Trump 1.0 and China (2020)

The Trump administration's orchestrated attack on China is a dramatic departure from his once-fulsome praise of Xi Jinping's leadership. But that was before the Covid pandemic. Now, official statements on China are uniformly critical and alarmist. With Secretary of State Mike Pompeo taking the lead, the criticism has escalated to the ideological level. Pompeo condemns not "China" but the Chinese Communist Party, using Cold War-era talking points that are reminiscent of the 1950s–1960s, when some US experts on the Soviet Union explained its behavior as due to Marxism-Leninism rather than national interest calculations.

In fact, Donald Trump never bought the 2017 National Security Council's designation of both Russia and China as America's chief security threats. China has been in his sights since the late 1980s, almost exclusively over trade. So long as the possibility existed of a major trade deal with China that Trump could proclaim a big win, he was willing to treat Xi Jinping the same way he treated Putin—as a dear friend doing his best in difficult circumstances. With the onset of the coronavirus and the disruption to a trade deal, Trump unleashed the voices around him hostile to China, from economic adviser Peter Navarro and Pompeo to Senators Tom Cotton and Ted Cruz.

Thus began the lengthy list of anti-China measures—restrictions on technology transactions; closure of the US consulate in Wuhan; pressure on Chinese students and visiting scholars to return home; harassment of American scientists of Chinese descent as well as Chinese scientists collaborating with Americans (the so-called China Initiative—see **Selection 6**); termination of the Peace Corps and public health cooperation with China; limitations on Chinese journalists and news organizations; sanctions on Chinese officials in Hong Kong and those involved with military projects in the South China Sea; and (successful) threats to withdraw Defense Department funds from any US university that hosted a Confucius Institute—a project of the Chinese education ministry to provide free language instruction and cultural programs to US schools at all levels. (See **Selection 5** for details.) Most of these steps prompted Chinese counteractions, bringing the relationship to its lowest point in over fifty years.

Nothing of the sort happened in US relations with Russia. The Trump administration haphazardly implemented sanctions voted by Congress but failed to confront Russian support of breakaway forces in Ukraine's east. Meantime, the Vladimir Putin regime carried out state terrorism with another brazen Novichok nerve gas attack, this time on his main political opponent, Aleksei Navalny. Neither Trump nor any US official said a word about that attack or any other assault on Putin's critics. Nor did Trump say anything about well-documented Russian interference in the US electoral process.

(3) Biden and Xi Seek Coexistence (2023)

The first face-to-face meeting in a year between Presidents Joe Biden and Xi Jinping went about as expected: some potentially meaningful agreements, some continuing disagreements, some controversies unexplored, and plenty of avowals to get along. Bottom line: No breakthroughs, but none expected.

Bridging Some Gaps

Xi's message for the United States was plain. He wanted to convey the foundational idea that China, with its stunning economic and commercial advances since the 1980s, was on par with the United States as a world leader, has interests that must be respected, and seeks a cooperative relationship with the United States to achieve global stability and increased prosperity. With an eye to his domestic audience, Xi appeared relaxed and very much the equal of Biden—at least as portrayed by the Chinese media. Biden's message for China was not much different from Xi's: The United States and China have a global obligation to work together, and if Xi is prepared to meet some US concerns, the two countries can overcome tensions that have led to predictions of inevitable conflict.

The two leaders did seem to have successfully addressed three issues that were harming relations: the fentanyl trade, the climate crisis, and military talks. Xi agreed to target Chinese companies that export to Mexico the precursor chemicals used in the production of fentanyl. The US readout of the meeting noted the "establishment of a working group for ongoing communication and law enforcement coordination on counternarcotics issues."[2] Xi and Biden also reached agreement to "pursue efforts to triple renewable energy capacity globally by 2030." And—a very important turnabout by China—Xi agreed to resume three channels of military-to-military discussions as well as "telephone conversations between theater commanders." Restoring these military interactions was essential because of the dangerous situation in the South China Sea and Taiwan, where close encounters between Chinese and US aircraft and ships had raised the risk of a violent confrontation.

Staking Out Interests

According to the US readout of the meeting, Biden reaffirmed the importance of the US security system that was expanding in the so-called Indo-Pacific region—the system the Chinese consider a reversion to containment. Biden "emphasized the United States' enduring commitment to freedom of navigation, adherence to international law, maintaining peace and stability in the South China Sea and East China Sea, and the complete denuclearization of the Korean Peninsula." He reiterated the US commitment to defense of Ukraine and Israel—raised concerns regarding PRC human rights abuses, including in Xinjiang, Tibet, and Hong Kong; and reassured Xi that the US continued to support "one China," meaning that Taiwan is a part of China. Biden insisted that Taiwan-China differences could be settled peacefully, and he "called for restraint in the PRC's use of military activity in and around the Taiwan Strait." On trade, Biden restated US concerns about China's "unfair trade practices" and said the US "will continue to take necessary actions to prevent advanced U.S. technologies from being used to undermine our own national security, without unduly limiting trade and investment."

The official Chinese press account reported Xi's insistence that the fundamental choice facing China and the United States came down to either "zero-sum thinking" and competition that would mean a turbulent world, or increased cooperation to tackle the world's problems. "The world can accommodate both China and the United States. China and the United States' respective successes are opportunities for each other," Xi said. He repeated what he had told Biden at Bali, Indonesia, in November 2022, that China was pursuing its own road of development, was not out to displace the United States, but would not tolerate pressure tactics. Xi proposed five "pillars" of the relationship: mutual understanding and respect; establishment of effective avenues for dialogue; increase in cooperative undertakings, such as on climate change and artificial intelligence; acceptance of great-power responsibilities in regional and international organizations; and an increase in all kinds of exchanges, such as air traffic and people-to-people.[3]

Xi directly addressed the Taiwan issue, which he described as the "most important and most sensitive issue" in relations with the United States. He urged the United States to take "concrete actions" to ease tensions over Taiwan, including stopping arms sales. Those sales had increased significantly under Biden as the result of bipartisan Congressional legislation. And on trade, Xi said that unfair US policies were "harming China's just interests" and "constraining China's high-quality development." But the Chinese account did report favorably on Biden's comments on the global importance of US-China cooperation and his reiteration of support for the One-China principle.

After their meeting, Biden was asked if he still thought Xi was a dictator, referring to a previous time when Biden had called him that. Biden replied this time: "Well, look, he is." That gaffe was, as far as I can tell, the only complication in what seems to have been a rather successful summit, exemplified by China's pledge to expand people-to-people exchanges, increase the number of senior-level contacts, and work (in the words of the US readout) toward "finding a way to live alongside each other peacefully." Of course, the devil is in the details, but for now, a start had been made toward resetting US-China relations.

(4) Military-to-Military Communication Resumes (2024)

The Long Path to Reconvening

Direct US-China military talks date to 2009, when a Strategic and Economic Dialogue was established. Those talks evolved into three channels for military discussions: annual talks between senior officials, the Military Maritime Consultative Agreement on aerial issues, and the Defense Policy Coordination Talks on crisis management. Military-to-military talks are essential for mutual security among major powers and in regional hot spots. Without them, a violent incident is more likely to happen. But in 2023, China rejected a military-to-military visit between the two countries' defense chiefs, citing US weapons and training aid to Taiwan. The US Defense Secretary, Lloyd Austin, underscored the central importance of conflict management in the Taiwan Strait, saying: "The whole world has a stake in maintaining peace and stability in the Taiwan Strait. The security of commercial shipping lanes and global supply chains depends on it. And so does freedom of navigation worldwide. Make no mistake: conflict in the Taiwan Strait would be devastating."[4] Austin deplored China's unwillingness to "engage more seriously on better mechanisms for crisis management."

Prospects for such talks improved with Foreign Minister Wang Yi's visit to Washington ahead of Xi's visit in November 2023. President Biden said the two countries "need to manage competition in the relationship responsibly and maintain open lines of communication." Wang Yi said his goal was to "stabilize China-US relations," but also said that would not be easy. US-China military-to-military communications did resume following the Biden-Xi summit, which took place outside San Francisco. "There is a stabler momentum in the overall and defense relations between China and the US . . . [due to] high-level strategic communication, policy communication, institutionalized dialogues and exchanges in specialized fields," a Chinese defense ministry spokesperson told reporters.

A Multitude of Formats

Four meetings between the two countries' militaries took place following the San Francisco summit. A particularly important one occurred in April 2024: the Military Maritime Consultative Agreement Working Group, which resumed in Honolulu after a three-year hiatus. The subject was operational air and naval safety. In 2023, the Pentagon listed over 180 times in the previous two years during which US and Chinese jets narrowly avoided collisions, all due—the Pentagon said—to "coercive and risky" maneuvering by the Chinese.⁵ The Chinese disputed the charge, noting that these near accidents took place close to China's borders and Taiwan. But they did agree with the American assessment at the April meeting that "open, direct and clear communications with the PLA [People's Liberation Army, China's armed forces] and with all other military forces in the region is of utmost importance to avoid accidents and miscommunication."

The other meetings that took place during Biden's tenure were: Chairman of the Joint Chiefs of Staff and Air Force General CQ Brown, Jr. meeting with PLA General Liu Zhenli (December 2023); US-China Defense Policy Coordination Talks at the Pentagon between senior US and Chinese military officials (January 2024), a resumption of talks that had not taken place since September 2021; and, in April 2024, Secretary of Defense Lloyd Austin meeting with China's new Minister of Defense, Admiral Dong Jun—the first such conversation since November 2022. Of all these talks, the working group has apparently been the most useful. According to one US military spokesman, "We've observed a reduction in unsafe behavior between us and PLA aircraft and vessels over the last several months. So, we're encouraged by that." However, he also cited "dangerous and unlawful" Chinese acts against the Philippines.

(5) The Rise and Fall of US-China Exchange Programs

Starting in the 1980s and continuing to the onset of the Covid pandemic and the first Trump administration, US-China collaboration was all the rage in Washington and Beijing. Whether the subject was medical research, economic and social research, or physics, exchanges between US and Chinese academic institutions, commercial entities, and even military and legislative bodies were almost universally encouraged. Colleges and universities in both countries jumped at the opportunity to establish joint programs and robust student and teacher exchanges. But by 2020, exchange relationships of all kinds were being cut back or terminated. This was due largely to the "China threat" being pushed in Congress, the highly unfavorable view of China in American media and public opinion, and Chinese upset with the US "Cold War mentality" predicated on containment of China. Then came the second Trump administration's targeting of foreign students who had protested against Israel over its war in Gaza. Over one thousand students had their visas revoked; at least several were deported without a hearing despite having not committed any illegal act. The threat of removal cast a chill over the lives of all international students.⁶

In this selection, we look at four kinds of US-China exchanges that have become politicized as bilateral relations worsened. All four raise the question of whether, and to what extent, US "national security" is helped or hurt by cuts in exchange programs.

Educational Exchanges

Talks between US and Chinese leaders in 2024 were notable for the common ground they found on increasing people-to-people exchanges, particularly in education. Presidents Biden and Xi both mentioned the importance of these exchanges at their 2023 summit meeting, and Secretary of State Antony Blinken, during his April trip to China, gave a talk to American students there on how critical study in China is for cross-cultural understanding and prevention of misperceptions between governments. But the positive rhetoric was overtaken by politics.

In May 2024, the Department of Defense suddenly announced termination of all but one West Coast "flagship" language program in Chinese, citing funding cuts by Congress. The University of Oregon and the University of Washington were among the affected schools. The decision caught language teachers by surprise; they had every reason to think Chinese-language programs would be strongly supported in the national interest. Flagship programs offer substantial financial support for rigorous training in neglected languages that are considered of national security import, including Arabic and Persian as well as Chinese. Following the Defense Department's decision, only nineteen of thirty universities that hosted flagship programs remained. A significant falloff in student enrollment in Chinese occurred, just when fluency was most needed in and out of government service. US students in China totaled fewer than 1,000; only about 400 went to China for study in 2023—far fewer than the "50,000 in five years" proposed by Xi Jinping.

On the other hand, roughly 277,000 Chinese students were enrolled in US schools in 2024, second only to Indian students. Yet official Chinese complaints about the treatment of students were increasing. A foreign ministry official said:

> the US side keeps overstretching the concept of national security and has arbitrarily canceled Chinese students' visas, forbidden their entry and forcibly repatriated them without any conclusive evidence, causing enormous harm to relevant students. The inspection rooms at some US airports have become a nightmare for Chinese students. What the US side is doing contradicts its statement about facilitating and supporting people-to-people exchanges between the two countries.

That claim gained support when US Secretary of State Marco Rubio announced in late May 2025 that the US will "aggressively revoke" the visas of Chinese students in the US who have ties to the CCP or work in "critical fields."

Officials emphasized the lack of safety for travelers in each other's country. The US State Department put out a travel advisory for students and others. China responded with a travel warning of its own and a personal warning from its ambassador to the United States. An article in *Latitudes*, the newsletter of the Chronicle of Higher Education, said:

> Ambassador Xie Feng held a 'Safety Journey in the U.S.' event, cautioning about risks to Chinese students and other travelers, including "harassment" and potential deportation when entering the country, anti-Asian discrimination, and government interference with people-to-people exchanges. Xie also accused American leaders of "poisoning the public-opinion environment" and harming the relationship between the two countries. The Chinese embassy later posted a pamphlet online with safety tips for navigating the United States.

US policy is redirecting Chinese language training toward Taiwan. And the number of students from Taiwan is increasing. In the academic year 2023–2024, Taiwan was the fifth-largest source of international students in the United States, behind India, China, South Korea, and Canada. The number is just over 23,000, a rise of 6.1 percent from a year earlier.[7]

Cultural Exchanges: The Case of Confucius Institutes in the US

Symptomatic of the official unease with any kind of people-to-people exchange with China is the attack on Confucius Institutes (CIs) based at US educational institutions. The institutes' funding agency was Hanban, the Office of Chinese Language Council under the Chinese education ministry. Starting in 2004, Hanban provided teachers and textbooks free of charge to schools at every level, from K-12 to universities. Less than fifteen years later, an increasing number of US officials and Congress members concluded that the CIs were not simply an element of China's soft power; they were a Communist Party plot to corrupt the minds of American youth and even engage in espionage. These attacks were successful: CIs in the United States that once numbered over 100 are now fewer than five. The rapid decline mainly occurred for two reasons: threats by the Defense Department to deny funds to schools that hosted CIs, and denial of visas to Chinese teachers hoping to go to the United States on CI missions.[8]

I was co-author of a study, paid for by Hanban, that evaluated—without any Chinese interference with the research, I must add—how well the CIs delivered on cultural learning. I participated in nearly 100 interviews of American directors of CIs, university officers and staff, and American teachers in communities with CI-funded classes. No one mentioned Chinese political interference. Academic freedom was not violated, financial dependence on China was not created, and China was not presented one-sidedly by its teachers. In short, CIs performed exactly as promised. Besides promoting Chinese language and cultural learning in communities small and large across the country, each CI took on some additional or more specialized role, such as partnering with other community organizations on cultural themes, teaching noncredit online classes in addition to K-12 classes, or providing study abroad opportunities. The American interviewees uniformly expressed gratitude for their CI's contributions to the community's cultural awareness and students' international competency. (See Lee Lu, Mel Gurtov, and Dale Cope, *Confucius Institutes in the U.S.: Final Report*, November 2020.)

Guilt by association essentially did away with CIs in the United States and in several other countries. But this amounted to cutting off our nose to spite our face—denying communities and schools opportunities for cultural enrichment, people-to-people interaction, and mutual US-China understanding precisely at a moment when these were desperately needed. In past years—I would say, from soon after the opening of US-China relations in the 1970s—China was accepted as an economic partner despite its communist system. Now we are back to McCarthyism. Strange to have to make an argument about the value of learning a foreign language and knowing more about another country's culture. And to think that just a few decades ago, "internationalizing" college curricula was all the rage, as US educators came together on the importance of helping students become more competitive in the global marketplace.

Research Exchanges

China's military-industrial complex is said to have benefited from hundreds of millions of dollars in federal funding to US research projects that included Chinese researchers, a year-long joint probe by the House Select Committee on China and the House Education and Workforce Committee concluded in 2024.

> Through nearly 9,000 joint research publications, funded by the Department of Defense or the Intelligence Community, the lawmakers discovered that Americans worked with Chinese researchers on strategic technology research . . . [on] topics like high-performance explosives, tracking of targets, and drone operation networks, nuclear and high-energy physics, artificial intelligence, quantum technology, and hypersonics—the kind of technology that the Chinese military could use against the US military in the event of a conflict,

the investigation concluded. The panel recommended significantly curtailing the ability of researchers who receive US grants to work with Chinese universities and companies that have military ties.[9]

Part of the report focused on several joint China-based institutes established between Chinese and American universities, including one with the University of California, Berkeley, and another with the Georgia Institute of Technology. Both Berkeley and Georgia Tech disputed many of the report's findings. But in a statement to the *New York Times*, Berkeley said it had decided to terminate its ownership in the Chinese institute in part because of its lack of visibility into research being conducted there by affiliates of other institutions. Georgia Tech announced that it would discontinue participation in its joint institute and work to end its degree programs in China, saying the inclusion of its Chinese partner on a restricted US trade list had made the cooperation "untenable."[10]

What needs highlighting here is how exchange programs with China that might relate to US national security have become political targets along with all other kinds of exchanges. It is not at all certain that China's strategic technology programs were helped by US researchers, much less that the Chinese military had acquired technology that it "could use against the US military in the event of a conflict." The termination of academic ties to China at Berkeley and Georgia Tech was the result of the implied threat of loss of federal funds, not agreement on the House committees' findings or denial of the mutual benefits of collaboration.

Scientific Exchanges

If there is one area of US-China relations that has clearly been mutually beneficial, it's scientific cooperation. In 1979, when US-China relations were officially normalized, the very first agreement was on scientific cooperation. By the time the agreement was renewed in 2011, scientific cooperation had expanded dramatically to include agricultural science, high-energy physics, clean energy, and biomedical research.[11] The US-China Agreement on Cooperation in Science and Technology (SAT), its official name, was on the verge of expiring in President Biden's last year in office as the anti-China crowd in Congress argued that China systematically violated intellectual property rights and used collaborative research to support its military.

Supporters of the SAT acknowledged that cooperation could be abused, but they pointed to the far greater benefits to both parties, and to the world. The benefits included the window provided into Chinese research and the opportunity to engage the Chinese on US concerns. The agreement helped China transition from ozone-depleting chlorofluorocarbons (CFCs) and enabled the sharing of influenza data used to devise vaccines. It also facilitated data sharing about satellites, climate, and seismic activities, as well as fusion and subatomic particle experiments. Chinese scientists and engineers formed a significant proportion of all new PhDs from US universities: 17 percent in 2020. China became a science superpower if one judges from the scientific papers its scientists publish. Its scientists have out-published US scientists in scientific and technological journals. Moreover, scientific papers co-authored by US and Chinese scientists outnumbered any other collaborative papers by a wide margin. "Chinese-born researchers, whether working in China or the United States, are key to international academic collaborations between the two countries," wrote Karin Fischer, citing a study published by the National Bureau of Economic Research. "Seventy-nine percent of collaborative papers in 2018 had at least one author who was of Chinese descent working in the United States or who had previously worked or studied in America before returning to China."[12]

Put simply, the research of Chinese scientists has become crucial to international scientific collaboration. And the patents they create, the collaborative work they do, and (yes) the fees and living costs they pay are major contributions to American science and the institutions that give them a home.

China wanted to continue the SAT. An embassy spokesman in Washington said in 2024: "China is ready to discuss the content and form of the agreement with the United States on the basis of equality and mutual benefit." Harvard's John Holdren, who signed the initial SAT when he served as Obama's director of the Office of Science and Technology Policy, agreed: The SAT signing gave "a form of permission for lab-to-lab, university-to-university, scientist-to-scientist cooperation. It legitimized the whole notion that collaboration was respectable."[13]

The SAT was renewed for five years in December 2024. To satisfy critics in Congress, the agreement was amended to exclude "critical or emerging technologies."[14] That limitation, on national security grounds, was in line with the view under both Biden and Trump that advanced technologies should not be exported to China.

(6) The China Initiative Profiles Chinese Americans

Scientific research exchanges were badly set back by the so-called China Initiative, which started in President Trump's first term and continued for a while under President Biden. That program, run by the Department of Justice, sought—with outstanding failure—to weed out Chinese scientists, including Chinese Americans, who were supposedly committing economic espionage. Only four professors from China or of Chinese descent were ever convicted, none for espionage. The University of Michigan's president was among many major university leaders and Congress members who wrote to the US attorney general to criticize the unfairness of the China Initiative, saying it amounted to racial profiling, lacked evidence of wrongdoing, and put pressure on the university to "investigate researchers who are singled out only because of their personal or professional connections with China."

Mainly as a result of the political pressure, about 1,400 top Chinese scientists gave up their US positions and returned to China.[15] To be sure, some were enticed home by China's "Thousand Talents" program, which offered returning scientists lucrative academic and research positions. But the China Initiative clearly was the primary cause. Before Biden ended it, the careers of several prominent scientists of Chinese descent in the United States were ruined or set back. Fear stalked Chinese visitors and citizens alike; many experienced insults and animosity. A 2022 survey of 1,300 scientists of Chinese descent at American universities found

> a strong sense of uneasiness and fear: 35 percent of respondents feel unwelcome in the United States, and 72 percent do not feel safe as an academic researcher; 42 percent are fearful of conducting research; 65 percent are worried about collaborations with China; and a remarkable 86 percent perceive that it is harder to recruit top international students now compared to 5 years ago.[16]

Thus, 61 percent of the Chinese scientists reported considering leaving the United States for another country even though "an overwhelming majority (89 percent) of our respondents indicated their desire to contribute to the US leadership in science and technology."

As the Michigan letter states, Chinese scientists are crucial to "the future of the US STEM [science-technology-engineering-math] workforce." Moreover: "Many of our most challenging global problems, including climate change and sustainability, and current and future pandemics, require international engagement. Without an open and inclusive environment that attracts the best talents in all areas, the United States cannot retain its world leading position in science and technology." "So much of our intellectual technological power is from immigrants," said Steven Chu, one of the signers, a Nobel Prize-winning physicist at Stanford University and a former US secretary of energy. "We're shooting ourselves not in the foot but in something close to the head."

In 2024–2025, Chinese science and math students and researchers were returning to China in increasing numbers. In all, their numbers in the US declined by 4 percent from 2023. India's international students took the top spot among international students for the first time.[17] See Chapter 6 for further discussion.

(7) Trade Politics

Trade Becomes a National Security Matter

As Chart 1.1 shows, the US-China trade has been characterized by consistent and substantial US deficits. The deficits began to be especially large in 2000 (about $84 billion), grew to over $270 billion in 2010, and peaked in 2018 at nearly $420 billion. Since then, they have become much smaller, shrinking to around $220 billion by 2023, due mainly to the Trump administration's high tariff policy in his first term. Biden sustained and extended that policy, with additional controls on high-technology exports to China. US trade generally was redirected to other parts of East Asia as well as to Europe, Mexico, and Canada. (China's trade pattern likewise changed, as indicated below). Trade tensions with China led to much talk in the Biden years about decoupling economic ties. Senior officials in the Biden administration assured Beijing that decoupling was not US policy. But "derisking" and "diversifying" were. Secretary of the Treasury Janet Yellen was the main official to carry that message. In trips to Beijing, she called for restoring "constructive relations," but qualified that aim by saying: "Even as our targeted actions may have economic impacts, they are motivated solely by our concerns about our security and values." On trade, she said on one trip, the US sought "healthy

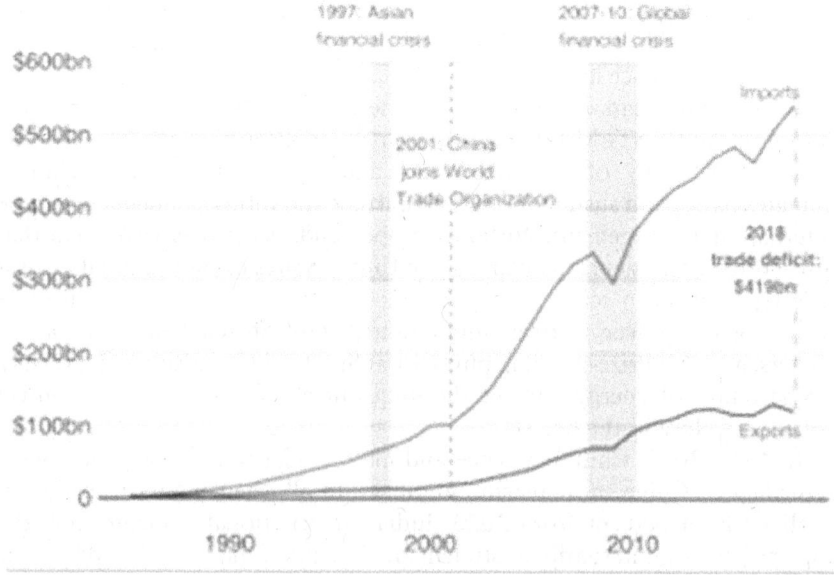

CHART 1.1 *US Trade with China, 1985–2018.* Source: US Bureau of the Census

competition" with China and supported its economic progress—so long as China "plays by the rules."

Behind the seemingly neutral language was a concerted effort by the Biden administration to deprive China of advanced computer chips. The action took place on two fronts. Domestically, the government subsidized building more semiconductor facilities at home, barred the export of advanced semiconductor technology to China, stopped any US company that might benefit from government subsidies of its chip making from investing in China, and restricted Chinese companies' access to US cloud computing services to curtail China's use of advanced chips for artificial intelligence. In October 2024, Biden issued regulations to forbid US investments in Chinese firms that were developing artificial intelligence (AI), quantum information technologies, and microelectronics and semiconductors that could have military applications. On the international front, the United States urged (i.e., pressured) companies in allied nations to refrain from providing China with advanced technology. The Netherlands responded by banning high-tech machinery sales to China. Japan and South Korea enacted restrictions on other high-technology exports to China. Taiwan Semiconductor Manufacturing Company (TSMC), the world leader in advanced chip manufacturing, was pressured to stop selling to China. The United States also imposed sanctions on Chinese companies that were exporting so-called dual-use goods to Russia, such as machine tools, which (according to Secretary of State Blinken) "fill critical gaps in Russia's military-industrial base."

The Biden administration also imposed restrictions on financial movements into China, specifically on private equity and venture capital firms that invested in Chinese companies working on semiconductors, AI, and quantum computing. US investments in China were a drop in the bucket—about 5 percent of total foreign investment in China—but restricting investments added to the bad news for China's economy in 2024. What we need to keep in mind, however, is that China's economic woes have become a global problem. Its economy represents around 22 percent of global economic growth, which means a dramatic slowdown adversely impacts other economies' trade, investment, and consumerism. Nevertheless, as soon as Trump took office again early in 2025, he issued an executive order that expanded on Biden's restrictions list for Chinese investments in the United States as well as on US high-technology investments in China.

China's Response

The Chinese aren't fooled by shifts in language. Decouple, derisk, diversify—they're all code words for actions directed at them. "Targeted actions" by the United States mean export and investment controls on advanced technology, such as semiconductors. "Economic impacts" are certain; the Chinese charge that export controls on high technology hinder China's economic development. Reference to "our security and values" are not persuasive to the Chinese, who see the US controls as linked less to security than to false notions of a China threat. And "playing by the rules" surely rankles China, since the rules—embedded in the World Bank, the International Monetary Fund, and the World Trade Organization—have always been determined by the US and its Western partners, which have the majority voting power.

China put up a vigorous defense of its trade policy, using arguments that used to belong exclusively to Western leaders and economists. For example, the official *Renmin ribao* (People's Daily) published an editorial on May 16, 2024, that accused "some American politicians" of using a false argument—that China is exporting factory overcapacity—to justify trade protectionism. "Fundamentally, the United States is protecting its excess low-end capacity," the editorial stated. "From a global perspective, free and open international trade and investment can boost competitiveness of industries across the world."

China has various ways to retaliate when it is being targeted. In the Netherlands case, China stopped exporting two minerals, gallium and germanium, that are important in chip manufacture. Those export controls, which began in August 2023, were later applied to the United States as well as to other countries that went along with the Netherlands, such as Japan and South Korea. In response to rising US tariffs, the Chinese reduced exports to the United States and turned to the Global South (see Chapter 4), especially Mexico, from which Chinese goods can be re-exported to the United States. China also shifted imports of agricultural products from the US to Brazil and other developing-country sources. Chinese foreign investment policy also changed, away from the US and Europe to Southeast and South Asia and other developing economies. To be sure, China's excessive reliance on exports for economic growth is a vulnerability. But nationalism is a strong motive force, and foreign "bullying" has a long, unforgotten history in China.[18]

Within China, retaliation against foreign firms is another option. Post-Covid, China put the welcome mat out to foreign businesses. But under US trade pressure, Chinese authorities turned to investigating and harassing some of them, US firms in particular. Two US consulting firms were hit, enough to warrant an unusual warning from the head of the US Chamber of Commerce in Beijing to consider the risks of investing. China's clampdown seemed to be motivated by the same concern—national security—that Xi Jinping used in dealing with domestic troublemakers. Beijing issued new counter-espionage laws that authorized the Ministry of State Security to raid corporate offices in search of just about any documents and data it believed would reveal a company's competitive strategy and links to other firms in

China. An exit ban, mainly intended to prevent Chinese from leaving the country, was also briefly applied to foreign executives. Finally, China, like the United States, compiled a list of companies that it barred from doing business there. In December 2024, after the Biden administration expanded export controls on chip-making technology, China's foreign affairs ministry announced sanctions on thirteen US defense firms and six executives, freezing their assets, stopping Chinese firms from doing business with them, and forbidding visits to China.[19]

"National security" has become China's watchword in trade, just as it has in US trade policy. That means more restrictions. As China's security minister wrote: "The scope of national security is constantly expanding." Nevertheless, numerous Chinese sources have made clear that the preference is for conducting trade in a normal manner rather than becoming embroiled in a tit-for-tat cycle of tariffs that slash international trade. Common interests should be the guideline, these sources say, pointing to the rising number of trade exhibitions and business-to-business exchanges. For example, the authoritative "Zhong Sheng" (The Bell, an editorial collective) wrote:

> In the current situation, China-US common interests are not decreasing but increasing. This is the common aspiration of the great majority of firms and people. It is also the important basis for both sides to move forward and open mutually advantage cooperation. . . . Cooperation between companies on both sides show that so long as they keep to mutual respect, mutual benefit, equal consultation, adherence to economic rules and market regulations when doing business, and expansion and deepening of mutually beneficial cooperation in economy and trade, China and the US can absolutely realize mutual gain.[20]

(8) Chips War: Advantage China?

Preventing China from acquiring the most advanced semiconductor chips, and simultaneously building up US chip capacity, are huge undertakings. The former aim requires plugging holes in the global supply chain and gaining the cooperation of the major chip manufacturers, starting with Nvidia. The latter aim requires a huge investment commitment by the chip makers, such as Intel, TSMC, and Microsoft—in the hundreds of billions of dollars, subsidized by the US government under the CHIPS and Science Act.

Both aims have been difficult to achieve. The first—to attract chipmaking to the United States—was thought to have been met when TSMC, Taiwan's premier semiconductor industry, committed in 2020 to building a $65-billion plant outside Phoenix. The Biden administration gave the company a $6.6

billion subsidy under the CHIPS Act. TSMC had yet to produce any chips in the United States. The reasons are the same as those that have troubled Chinese investors from the People's Republic: cultural clashes between Taiwan and American workplace practices. The Taiwanese simply work harder and longer than American workers. And training the most skilled engineers takes many months. If you've ever seen the movie, *American Factory*, you know what this is about.

Trump's election put TSMC in a bind. He assailed the Biden subsidy deal with TSMC, arguing that Taiwan would ultimately keep control of chip making.[21] TSMC's leadership responded by upping its commitment to new plant construction by $100 billion for a total promise of $165 billion, by far its largest overseas investment. But will the promise be fulfilled?

Globalization—that is, the worldwide supply chain—is also defeating the US chips war with China. A lively chips market has developed in China despite US national security bans on exports. Although Nvidia's advanced AI chips have been kept from being exported to China,

> The [*New York*] *Times* spoke with representatives of 11 companies in China that said they sold or transported banned Nvidia chips, and found dozens more businesses offering them online. Several vendors in a vast, mazelike market in Shenzhen reported deals involving hundreds or thousands of chips . . . the *Times* also found procurement documents showing that more than a dozen [Chinese] state-affiliated entities purchased restricted chips, including organizations under sanctions for modernizing the Chinese military.

In a word, the global supply chain makes it all too easy to get around US export controls, and the profit motive is outpacing national security considerations.[22]

Most importantly, China, led by Huawei Technologies, is determined to become as self-reliant as possible in advanced semiconductor technology. The more China is targeted in what looks like a trade war, the more certain it is that China will pull out all the stops to reduce dependence on foreign sources. As a foreign ministry spokesman said in 2024, with specific reference to US export controls on semiconductor chips: "The real purpose is to hold back China's high-quality development and deprive China of its legitimate right to development." Then came China's answer to large-scale US investments in artificial intelligence: DeepSeek, an open-source alternative to the AI models of Nvidia, Meta, and other corporations, and apparently using far less sophisticated chips. It's become all the rage in China, with DeepSeek executives being hailed as heroes. China's ability to overcome US export controls on advanced computer chips has led to much soul-searching in the US AI community.[23]

(9) The Republicans' "China Week" (2024)

"China Week" sounds like a time for celebrating Chinese culture and food. But for Republicans in the House of Representatives, it was all about politics. They seemed to think that targeting China would play well in the elections, so they went all out with over two dozen pieces of legislation in 2024. Democrats joined them on some votes. Voting to punish China is a safe bet. "The best way to get something done in Washington is to frame it" on China or national security, said Rory Murphy, who had served as vice president of government affairs at the US-China Business Council. "There's no political consequence to being too tough on China," he added.

The primary purpose of the bills was to demonstrate that the Republican Party was the only one that could be trusted to confront China and defend national security. House Speaker Mike Johnson of Louisiana previewed the bills in a speech in July 2024, saying China posed "the greatest threat to global peace" and that "Congress must keep our focus on countering China with every tool at our disposal." But all the bills had to pass in the Senate to become law. When Trump won reelection in November 2024 and Republicans took control of Congress, most of the bills were introduced as part of a major economic decoupling from China, justified by an exaggeration of the China threat.

Here are the main bills that passed in the House in 2024:

- The Biosecurity Act, to prevent US federal agencies from contracting with five Chinese biotech companies and their clients. It would also establish an inter-agency process for identifying additional companies. Biotech executives argued that decoupling from the firms would contribute to widespread US drug shortages. The House therefore extended the deadline to January 2032 for halting existing contracts with those Chinese firms.
- The Hong Kong Economic and Trade Certification Act intended to support Hong Kong's representative offices in the United States. In a nearly unanimous vote, the House decided to show solidarity with pro-democracy protesters in Hong Kong by closing these trade promotion offices.
- A bill requiring Senate ratification of any World Health Organization agreement on pandemic preparedness. (The United States withdrew from the WHO on Trump's reelection.)
- Revival of the China Initiative (see **Selection 6**).
- A bill to restrict the sale of agricultural land to foreign nationals from China, as well as from Russia, North Korea, and Iran.

- A bill to restrict federal funding of the few remaining colleges that hosted Confucius Institutes.
- Still other bills to prevent government purchases of Chinese-made batteries and drone equipment.

The Chinese embassy called the bills a "new McCarthyism" that "interfere in China's internal affairs, infringe upon China's sovereignty, and smear China's image." The embassy spokesperson said in a statement that passage of that legislation "will cause serious interference to China-US relations ... and will inevitably damage the US' own interests, image, and credibility."

(10) Trump 2.0 and China: The Rocky Road Ahead (2024)

Beijing on the Virtues of Cooperation

On November 7, 2024, Xi Jinping sent a congratulatory message to President-elect Trump that said:

> A stable, healthy, sustainably developing China-US relationship fits with the common interests of the two countries and with the expectations of international society. I hope the two sides will keep to the principles of mutual respect, peaceful coexistence, and win-win cooperation, strengthen channels of dialogue, improve control over differences, expand mutually beneficial cooperation, and move down the road of correctly getting along in a new period, with prosperity for both countries and benefits to the world.

Subsequently, other Chinese sources, as well as Xi in his final meeting with President Biden at the Asia-Pacific Economic Cooperation summit on November 16, repeated this line of thought: China wants more rather than less cooperation with the United States. An article in the *People's Daily* the day after Xi's message by the editorial collective "Zhong Sheng" reinforced it, saying: "Win-win cooperation is the trend of the times and should be the bottom line of China-US relations." The article reminded readers of China-US economic interdependence:

> Today, China is the third-largest export market for U.S. goods, and the US is China's third-largest trading partner. Over 70,000 US companies invest and operate in China, and exports to China alone support 930,000 US jobs. Last year, 1,920 new US companies were established in China,

and 80 percent of US companies in China plan to reinvest their profits this year.

The commentary cited achievements of China-US cooperation in diplomacy, finance, climate change, and military-to-military communication. Thus, wrote Zhong Sheng, "whether promoting world economic recovery or resolving international and regional hotspot issues, China-US coordination and cooperation are needed."

Subsequent Chinese commentaries were directed at Elon Musk, then Trump's unofficial second in command and owner of Tesla. The commentaries noted that Tesla sales in China had skyrocketed, providing a perfect example of the mutual benefits of China-US trade.

A Steep Slope

Coordination and cooperation are very unlikely to be realized, however, because of probably insuperable obstacles each country has set. The second Trump administration will not merely reject engagement, as Biden's did; this time around, relations with China will be on a much steeper slope. Under Trump, we will no longer hear about "managing" relations, competing with China, or looking for shared interests. Stabilizing the US-China relationship, which drew praise from Xi at his final meeting with Biden—"The [China-US] relationship has remained stable on the whole," Xi said—will no longer be important to Washington. There are several already clear reasons for this conclusion: Trump's announced determination to impose very high tariffs on Chinese goods, his appointment of China hawks to key national security positions, the bipartisan hostility toward China in Congress, China's highly unfavorable rating in American public opinion, and the advice Trump has received from previous appointees in the Project 2025 report. Moreover, as I discuss below, Trump, unlike Biden, will not be distracted from his China policy by overseas conflicts.

As for China, the emphasis on points of actual and potential collaboration with the United States is just one piece of its America policy. Xi qualifies cooperation in important ways—by saying that the United States must have a "correct strategic perception" of China, must adhere to the three principles mentioned in Xi's message to Trump, and must choose between "partnership or rivalry." When Xi met Biden at their final meeting in 2024, Xi consolidated the choice in terms of "four red lines [that] must not be challenged": "The Taiwan question, democracy and human rights, China's path and system, and China's development right."[24] Those qualifications aimed at specific elements of US policy: security alliances directed at the "China threat," military and political support of Taiwan, and denial of semiconductor and other high-tech exports to China. US presidents, Donald

Trump least of all, have not been moved by Chinese appeals to principle. Nor have they been open to "correcting" their perceptions of China to suit Beijing.

Making a Deal

Nevertheless, it is worth examining where room for a China-US deal might exist. A major caveat is in order, however: Donald Trump's modus operandi which, as Bob Woodward has said in his various books on Trump, centers on fear and winning. In Trump's transactional framework, the "art of the deal" is to instill fear in the opponent, never fold, and win, which means getting a "good return on investment," not compromising for short-term gain and most certainly not making concessions to promote trust. In his first administration, Trump had to deal with advisers who were not all in on Trump's style—policy managers who valued diplomacy as an alternative to confrontation. With few guardrails to restrain him in his second term, Trump dominates the policymaking scene as never before. His appointments of loyalists, some of whom are viscerally hostile to China and others of whom are vastly inexperienced, virtually ensure that Trump's word and whim will be unquestioningly followed.

There were three early signs of the China hawks' intentions. In the House of Representatives, the Republicans' "China Week" agenda was being readied for approval with some Democrats' support (**Selection 9**). The bipartisan US-China Economic and Security Review Commission's annual report to Congress recommended even more provocative steps, such as revoking China's bilateral free trade privileges, barring the import of technologies from China, and—in a direct challenge to a Chinese priority—creating a Manhattan Project to achieve artificial intelligence capable of surpassing human cognition. A third sign came from the Project 2025 report, with its theme of the ubiquitous China threat (see **Document 2**).

What might a good return on investment look like to Trump? Since his top priority is trade, he would aim at a major increase in Chinese purchases of US goods to reduce the trade deficit (even though that didn't work the first time around) and improved conditions for US investments, all while retaining sharp restrictions on advanced technology exports to China. In return, Trump might be willing to lower US tariffs on Chinese imports. He also might induce Xi by promising to reduce US arms aid and high-level visits to Taiwan, though he might get pushback from strongly pro-Taiwan officials such as Marco Rubio, the Secretary of State and National Security Adviser.

There is a wildcard issue here: the fentanyl trade. Trump made control of fentanyl central to his imposition of higher tariffs on trade with Mexico and Canada in 2025. He seemed bent on doing the same with China (see **Selection 11**). In a Senate hearing, John Ratcliffe, the CIA director, was asked if China could do more to control fentanyl production. Ratcliffe said China could crack down. "One of the reasons that they don't is that there are more than 600 [China]-related companies that produce those precursor chemicals and an industry that generates $1.5 trillion."[25] Yet fentanyl seemed to be merely an excuse for imposing higher tariffs on Canada and China.

Trump would be far less interested in making a deal on China's military aid to Russia, climate change, scientific and other exchanges, or human rights. Some of those issues *are* important to some Republicans, but they rank low (if at all) among Trump's priorities. Nor would strategic issues that have bipartisan and Pentagon concern necessarily get Trump's attention: the South China Sea disputes (including protection of Philippines ships), US security coalitions in Asia (the Quad Security Dialogue group—India, Japan, Australia, US—and AUKUS—Australia-United Kingdom-US), and competition with China in the Pacific Island microstates. In Trump's mind, these involvements soak up US resources and risk unacceptable levels of commitment. But they could be bargaining chips. Trump might be willing to backtrack on US security commitments in Asia, bilateral and multilateral, if a winning commercial deal proved attainable.

Trump's Strategy

But China might, as happened in Trump's first term, prefer a trade war to a deal on tariffs. That may move him to weaponize tariffs—which is what he did in April 2025, and again in October 2025. Trump's strategy seemed to be that once the United States removed itself from Israel's wars on Hamas and Hezbollah—reflected in his advice to Prime Minister Benjamin Netanyahu to finish business quickly—and from Vladimir Putin's war on Ukraine—by selling a "peace" plan under which aid to Ukraine becomes a European responsibility and Russia accepts its territorial gains in Ukraine—Trump would be free to wield tariffs to hammer China. Trump can claim support for hostility toward China from nearly everyone in official Washington, and from a majority of the public that believes (according to polls by the Chicago Council on Global Affairs) that the United States should actively work to limit China's power and that trade with China mainly weakens US national security (see **Document 3** below).

One thing is clear: The Chinese are not going to kowtow to Trump over tariffs or any other element of economic decoupling. In the first place, China is already shifting export markets to countries that have signed onto China's Belt and Road loan initiative. Second, the Chinese government is finally recognizing the limitations of an export-driven economy and has introduced the first of perhaps several financial stimuli designed to meet consumer demands. But another purpose of strengthening the economy might be to make US strategists think twice about trying to take advantage of a weakened China. Third, if Trump carries out a tariff war with China, the Chinese will respond just as they did the first time around—by raising their own tariffs on US goods. (They did so immediately after Trump's April announcement.) They can also be expected to impose restrictions, as before, on US firms doing business in China and deny US manufacturers access to critical resources, notably rare earth minerals.

Fourth, Trump's decoupling from China—which would expand upon the Biden policy of restricting advanced technology exports to and investment in China—is moving China further in the direction of self-reliance. As always, nationalism is a powerful force in Chinese politics. Their leaders have made very clear that they are not going to let the US get away with interfering in China's development (see **Document 5**). And they apparently have popular support in addition to technology: see **Document 3**.

(11) Trump's Tariff War in 2025

Tariffs Without Limit

In the first months of 2025, speculation was rife about Trump's plans for tariffs on Chinese imports. The question was: How high would he go? The thinking in Washington, as best I can surmise, was that high tariffs would complicate China's already serious economic situation, since Beijing's economy depends heavily on exports. Close off the US market, as Project 2025 proposed (**Document 2**), and Xi Jinping would not only be in political trouble at home; he would have to give the US a new trade deal—and give Trump a major political victory at home.

Trump imposed 10 percent tariffs on China twice in February and March, and then—on the same day (April 2, 2025) that he shocked world markets with tariff increases on about sixty countries—hit China with a further 34-percent reciprocal tariff. When Beijing retaliated, Trump imposed an additional 50-percent tariff, bringing the total tariff on Chinese goods to 104 percent. China, predictably, raised its tariff rate on US goods to 84 percent. When China did not buckle, Trump raised the tariff rate to 125 percent and then 145 percent; China stopped at 125 percent. What was Trump's overall aim? His public argument for raising tariffs was two-fold: force US trade partners with the highest surpluses to lower their tariffs on US exports, and convince United States and other multinational firms to move their manufacturing to the United States to avoid the US tariffs. Both aims mainly had China in mind.

Advantage China?

China's foreign ministry had warned that a tariff war with the United States would "hurt the one who launched it." In its first response to Trump's tariffs, China's commerce ministry issued a statement that read in part: "The United States has drawn the so-called 'reciprocal tariffs' based on subjective and unilateral assessments, which is inconsistent with international trade rules and seriously damages the legitimate rights and interests of relevant parties." There was no mention of a summit meeting with Trump. Instead, China not only matched Trump's tariffs. Beijing added ten US companies to its "Unreliable Entities List" on the grounds that those companies had conducted military business with Taiwan. China again stopped exports to the United States of rare earth minerals, using the same argument as the United States: national security. These minerals are essential to the manufacture of a wide range of technologies, and China has near-monopoly control of their processing.[26] China also imposed controls on dual-use (civilian/military) exports to twenty-eight major US companies, including General Dynamics, Boeing, and Lockheed Martin. Beijing issued a white paper on economic and trade relations that accused Washington of "isolationist and coercive" behavior. But the paper also defended free trade principles and once again proposed dialogue to resolve differences.[27]

Ordinarily, China would shift manufacturing to Southeast Asia, where China in 2024 had a total trade with the ten Association of Southeast Asian Nations (ASEAN) countries of about $900 billion. From there, China would ship their products to the United States. Trump made that option less attractive by imposing very high tariffs on those countries as well—such as 46 percent on Vietnam, 49 percent on Cambodia, 24 percent on Malaysia, and 36 percent on Thailand. Their economies depend heavily on exports, hence the US tariffs are painful—hardly a way to treat countries friendly to the US and wary of China's economic power. The new US tariffs may well turn out to be a strategic blunder. Xi visited Vietnam, Cambodia, and Malaysia in mid-April, emphasizing solidarity against US "unilateralism and hegemonism." He signed multiple trade deals. Malaysia's Prime Minister Anwar Ibrahim told Xi: "In the face of [US] unilateralism, Malaysia wishes to strengthen cooperation with China and together deal with risks and challenges. The ASEAN cannot approve of any unilateral method of imposing tariffs."[28] In 2025, Southeast Asian leaders are urging closer regional ties to offset Trump's tariffs.

China may benefit from Trump's decision in two other ways. Some international companies, jolted by the unpredictability of US trade policy, found that staying in China was their safest option.[29] Others, like Apple, moved production elsewhere (to India, in Apple's case) rather than back to the United States. Moreover, China might use Trump's tariff war as an opportunity to make needed domestic policy changes, such as, increasing self-reliance in goods it typically imports and investing more in household consumption.

A Ceasefire, Not a "Reset"

Thus, Beijing may defeat two aims of Trump's trade war: boxing China in, and bringing corporate investment and production back to the US. But Trump was unmoved. "China played it wrong, they panicked—the one thing they cannot afford to do," Trump messages on April 4. Perhaps it was he who panicked. Apparently responding to cries of alarm on Wall Street, and concerns in his cabinet, Trump on April 9 halted reciprocal tariffs on all countries for ninety days, though not on China. Then, as the largest businesses and business lobbies complained about the tariffs and consumer prices started to rise, Trump agreed in mid-May to meet Chinese officials in Geneva for trade talks. Trump hinted that he might drop the tariff rate on China to 80 percent. Instead, the two sides reached agreement on a ninety-day suspension of their tariff rates while negotiations continued under a trade consultation mechanism. The US tariff on Chinese goods was reduced to 30 percent, and China reduced its rate on US goods to 10 percent. Trade talks did take place in London in June 2024, but only a "framework" agreement was reached. China consented to restart rare earth exports to the United States, and the United States agreed to export unspecified advanced technology to China. That deal collapsed in October 2025, leading Trump to impose a 100 percent tariff on Chinese goods.

It is hard to know whether or when a firm US-China tariff and trade agreement will occur. Talks might go on for some time. China has made the most of the controversy, using it to promote patriotism, as though the country is at war. Perhaps most revealing about the trade talks is that China succeeded in gaining US acceptance of the principles of equality and mutual benefit while resisting "pressure and threats," as one Chinese scholar put it.

Among China's America watchers, Trump's decision-making was cause for head shaking. As the dean of that group, Professor Wang Jisi, said: "The dizzying changes in Trump's foreign policy since he took office reflect a lack of international perspective and diplomatic experience. His strategic direction is chaotic and incoherent, lacking long-term planning or systematic policy thinking, and is often reactive and improvised in response to immediate developments."[30]

(12) The Way Forward (2024)

The large array of divisive issues in US-China relations would appear to doom any chance of a reset. Though agreement on some of those issues may yet be reached, such as on trade, most others are either nonnegotiable (such as on Taiwan and human rights) or not subject to independent monitoring (such as on climate change, control of the fentanyl trade, and hacking). In a word, long-term friction and difficult negotiations are facts of life in this relationship. Both sides say they are searching for a "way to get along." What will it take?

I suggest that three changes need to happen for US-China relations to realize a productive reset: agreement on guiding principles, redefinition of security by both parties, and increasing incentives to cooperate.

First in importance is bridging the gap between the two governments in the way they deal with one another. The United States stresses the need to *manage* the competition and sustain dialogue. That modest ambition has been stated many times, for example in a US statement following a meeting between Wang Yi and Blinken on the sidelines of the Munich Security Conference in March 2024: "ongoing efforts to maintain open lines of communication and responsibly manage competition in the relationship." US diplomats recite assurances of respect for China's interests but are results-oriented: They want to see progress on specific issues that impact US national security and political values. The Chinese, as I argue in my book *Engaging China*, tend to react defensively to the US setting the agenda—such as by reminding the United States of China's "red lines" on sovereignty and security, and by arguing that the US has failed to live up to promises made to China. Therefore, agreement on principles should precede discussion of policies: "The finer details will fall into place when they are aligned with the bigger picture," Xi has said.

The Chinese insist that the most important principle the United States must accept is partnership rather than rivalry. When US national security adviser Jake Sullivan visited Beijing in August 2024, Xi told him that the two countries "need to first and foremost find a good answer to the overarching question: Are China and the United States rivals or partners?" So long as the United States regards China chiefly as a rival, Wang Yi said to Blinken, "relations are bound to remain fraught with troubles and problems." The way forward for China is to set differences aside and not provoke confrontations over them—which is what Xi and other officials mean by "seeking common ground while reserving differences" (*qiutong cunyi*).

China's insistence on principles is linked to concerns about security. National security in China means above all *state (or regime)* security. As has become evident in recent years, Xi has been obsessed about multiple internal security issues—in the party, the provinces, the environment, technology, the professions, police, the military, and above all, the economy. "High quality of development can only be achieved in a highly secure environment." These days, economic insecurity looms large: household income trails GDP growth, the real estate bubble has burst, youth unemployment is very high, the population is aging and shrinking, investment capital is moving from

China to Japan and elsewhere, and consumer spending has tightened. Some China watchers see a country that has peaked socially and economically, its people gripped by malaise and the economy by stagnation. Insecurity breeds instability and, as Premier Li Qiang said, "stability is of overall importance, as it is the basis for everything we do." From Mao to Xi, economic performance has always been central to regime stability and legitimacy. Failure to deliver on the economy invites "disturbances," as occurred under the zero-Covid policy. And when there are disturbances, China is vulnerable to foreign interference—the historically informed idea that "when there is chaos within, there is calamity without" (*neiluan waihuan*).

The United States operates on a different security concept: globalism. A worldwide network of security relationships, aid programs, trade and investment arrangements, and political ties to strategically located countries, are intended to keep America safe from ideological and military adversaries. Threats to the American way of life are primarily external, not internal: Russia at one time, then terrorism, now China. Hence the attraction of the containment doctrine, of nuclear deterrence, of counterterrorism, and of maintaining a military "second to none." To a greater extent than China, US leaders feel compelled to become involved, directly or indirectly, in just about any conflict abroad that might threaten global or regional stability.

These contrasting views of security are difficult to reconcile. Every US policy that China complains about, whether human rights or trade sanctions, rubs up against China's conception of state security—just as US "national security" is used to justify every element of its China policy. Leaderships in both countries therefore need to adjust their notions of security if partnership is to have real meaning. For China, that might mean retreating from tight alignment with Russia, and dropping exaggerated accusations of US interference in Hong Kong, while for the US it might mean modifying its export controls on high-tech and halting the militarization of Asia policy that targets China. (Janet Yellen's advice is well worth taking: "We should not make the mistake of becoming so consumed with our competition with China that we become defined by it.") In a world in which US-China relations rest on stable, friendly bonds, such policy revisions seem attainable.

Incentives to cooperate—the third change—flow from mutual acceptance of the goal of *competitive coexistence*: competition in commerce and political influence, but a search for specific ways to build common security and peaceful relations. Eliminating demonizing language, such as the constant talk in the US about the "China challenge" and the "China threat," and in China about the United States "Cold War, zero-sum mentality," would help. Removing barriers to exchanges of talent, technology, and capital is another step. Joint action on global issues—for example, humanitarian aid in the Middle East and Africa, and a more ambitious common agenda on climate change—would also incentivize tension reduction.

These three areas of needed change would take the United States and China beyond the current period of useful, but still somewhat ritualistic, dialogue. This is not to minimize the value of the bilateral agreements reached at San Francisco or since. Cooperation on climate change, resumption of military talks (potentially including nuclear weapons), targeting of fentanyl-related chemical plants, collaboration on scientific research, and fulsome exchange programs can all work to build trust and expand the agenda. As Ambassador Burns has concluded, "We do want to live in peace with China. No person in their right mind should want this relationship to end up in conflict or war." But there are people who want to push China to the brink, making it imperative that the US and China seize the moment and take more ambitious steps. As Xi told Blinken, "No progress is regress."

Documents

Document 1. Xi Jinping and US National Security Adviser Jake Sullivan Discuss Partnership versus Rivalry

(*Background:* Sullivan met with Xi Jinping in Beijing in August 2024. Xi and other top leaders emphasized the essential need for the United States to develop "a right strategic perception" of China, whereas Sullivan called for managing the relationship responsibly so as to avoid direct conflict. Below is an account of their meeting as reported by Xinhua, the official Chinese news agency.)

Source: Xinhua, August 29, 2024, https://english.news.cn/20240829/160 1450bb7014590aa945eabbb372207/c.html. The US readout of the meeting is US Embassy, Beijing, https://china.usembassy-china.org.cn/readout-of -national-security-advisor-jake-sullivans-meeting-with-president-xi-jinping -of-the-peoples-republic-of-china/

Xi pointed out that in this changing and turbulent world, countries need solidarity and coordination, not division or confrontation. People want openness and progress, not exclusion or regress. As two major countries, China and the United States should be responsible for history, for the people and for the world, and should be a source of stability for world peace and a propeller for common development. Xi stressed that when China and the United States, two major countries, engage with each other, the No. 1 issue is to develop a right strategic perception, and they need to first and foremost find a good answer to the overarching question: Are China and the United States rivals or partners?

China's foreign policy is open and transparent and its strategic intentions are aboveboard, both of which have been highly consistent and stable, Xi said, adding that China is focused on managing its own affairs well and will continue deepening reform comprehensively to further improve and develop the system of socialism with Chinese characteristics that suits its national conditions.

China follows a path of peaceful development. While realizing its own development, China is also ready to work with other countries for common development and to jointly build a community with a shared future for mankind, he said.

Xi pointed out that China's U.S. policy is highly consistent. While great changes have taken place in the two countries and in China-U.S. relations, China's commitment to the goal of a stable, healthy and sustainable China-U.S. relationship remains unchanged, its principle in handling the relationship based on mutual respect, peaceful coexistence and win-win cooperation remains unchanged, its position of firmly safeguarding the country's sovereignty, security and development interests remains unchanged, and its efforts to carry forward the traditional friendship between the Chinese and American people remain unchanged, he said.

Xi expressed the hope that the United States will work in the same direction with China, view China and its development in a positive and rational light, see each other's development as an opportunity rather than a challenge, work with China to find a right way for China and the United States—two countries with different civilizations, systems and paths—to coexist in peace and achieve common development on this planet, and work to maintain the stability of China-U.S. relations and, on that basis, improve and take forward the relationship.

Sullivan conveyed the regards of President Joe Biden to President Xi, and thanked President Xi for meeting him. He said that since the San Francisco summit meeting between the two presidents, the two sides have earnestly implemented their common understandings and achieved positive progress. This round of strategic communication in China was in-depth, candid, substantive and constructive.

He reiterated that the United States does not seek a new Cold War, it does not seek to change China's system, the revitalization of U.S. alliances is not against China, the United States does not support "Taiwan independence," and it does not seek conflict with China. The one-China policy of the United States has not changed, and it has no intention to use Taiwan as a tool to contain China.

The United States hopes to maintain strategic communication with China and find a way for the United States and China to coexist in peace and for U.S.-China relations to develop in a sustainable way. President Biden looks forward to having communication again with President Xi soon, Sullivan added.

Xi asked Sullivan to pass on his regards to Biden, and expressed readiness to stay in touch with Biden to guide and steer the development of China-U.S. relations.

Document 2. Project 2025's Recommendations for US China Policy
(*Background:* Project 2025 was an ambitious policy planning guide for the second Trump administration. Published as *Mandate for Leadership: The Conservative Promise*, it was a design for dismantling the "Deep State" and carrying out an authoritarian agenda unrestrained by Constitutional and legal limits. Trump's campaign, concerned about the bad press Project 2025 was getting, ordered that it be disconnected from it. But while Trump may have distanced himself from some of the project's recommendations, his subsequent executive orders clearly showed that he was closely following them. CNN counted at least 140 people who worked on the Project 2025 document and who previously worked for the Trump administration. They include the two authors whose chapters are below.)

(From Chapter 6, "Department of State," by Kiron K. Skinner)

The designs of the People's Republic of China (PRC) and the Chinese Communist Party, which runs the PRC, are serious and dangerous. This tyrannical country with a population of more than 1 billion people has the vision, resources, and patience to achieve its objectives. Protecting the United States from the PRC's designs requires an unambiguous offensive-defensive mix, including protecting American citizens and their interests, as well as U.S. allies, from PRC attacks and abuse that undermine U.S. competitiveness, security, and prosperity.

The United States must have a cost-imposing strategic response to make Beijing's aggression unaffordable, even as the American economy and U.S. power grow. This stance will require real, sustained, near-unprecedented U.S. growth; stronger partnerships; synchronized economic and security policies; and American energy independence—but above all, it will require a very honest perspective about the nature and designs of the PRC as more of a threat than a competitor. The next President should use the State Department and its array of resources to reassess and lead this effort, just as it did during the Cold War. The U.S. government needs an Article X for China, and it should be a presidential mandate. Along with the National Security Council, the State Department should draft an Article X, which should be a deeply philosophical look at the China challenge.

Many foreign policy professionals and national leaders, both in government and the private sector, are reluctant to take decisive action regarding China. Many are vested in an unshakable faith in the international system and global norms. They are so enamored with them they cannot brook any criticisms or reforms, let alone acknowledge their potential for being abused by the PRC. Others refuse to acknowledge Beijing's malign activities and often pass off criticism as conspiracy theories. For instance, many were quick to dismiss even the possibility that COVID-19 escaped from a Chinese research laboratory. The reality, however, is that the PRC's actions often do sound like conspiracy theories—because they are conspiracies. In addition, some knowingly or not parrot the Communist line: Global leaders including President Joe Biden, have tried to normalize or even laud Chinese behavior. In some cases, these voices, like the global corporate giants BlackRock and Disney, directly benefit from doing business with Beijing.

On the other hand, others acknowledge the dangers posed by the PRC, but believe in a moderating approach to accommodate its rise, a policy of "compete where we must, but cooperate where we can," including on issues like climate change. This strategy has demonstrably failed.

As with all global struggles with Communist and other tyrannical regimes, the issue should never be with the Chinese people but with the Communist dictatorship that oppresses them and threatens the well-being of nations across the globe. That said, the nature of Chinese power today is the product of history, ideology, and the institutions that have governed China during the course of five millennia, inherited by the present Chinese leaders from the preceding generations of the CCP. In short, the PRC challenge is rooted in China's strategic culture and not just the Marxism–Leninism of the CCP, meaning that internal culture and civil society will never deliver a more normative nation. The PRC's aggressive behavior can only be curbed through external pressure

(from Chapter 26, "The Case for Fair Trade," by Peter Navarro. Navarro also served in Trump's second administration as senior counselor for trade and manufacturing. The tariff war with China was largely his idea.)

The Chinese Communist Party's policy goal is to propel the Chinese economy, but its broader goal is to strengthen Communist China's defense industrial base and associated warfighting capabilities. That China unabashedly seeks to supplant America as the world's dominant economic and military power is not in dispute. Rather, it is a prominent feature of Communist Chinese dictator Xi Jinping's rhetoric Xi has promised that the deed will be done by 2049, the 100-year anniversary of the Communist takeover of the Mainland.

In light of Communist China's broader geopolitical and military agenda, the American President who takes office in January 2025 must view the U.S.–China trade relationship and associated policy reforms within the context of the broader existential threat posed by Communist China. The question is whether that next President should seek to decouple economically and financially from Communist China as America's first best response to China's unrelenting aggression or continue efforts to negotiate with an authoritarian country and brutal dictatorship with a well-established reputation for failing to abide by any agreements it enters. . . .

Viewed as a whole, the extent of Communist China's aggression is breathtaking. At the trade policy level, Communist China relies heavily on a wide range of mercantilist and protectionist tools to protect its own markets and unfairly exploit foreign markets. These instruments of Communist

Chinese trade aggression include high tariffs and nontariff barriers, currency manipulation, a heavy reliance on sweatshop labor and pollution havens, the dumping of unfairly subsidized exports, and widespread counterfeiting and piracy: Communist China is the world's largest source of counterfeit and pirated products. . . .

The clear lesson learned in both the Obama and Trump Administrations is that Communist China will never bargain in good faith with the U.S. to stop its aggression. An equally clear lesson learned by President Trump, which he was ready to implement in a second term, was that the better policy option was to decouple both economically and financially from Communist China as further negotiations would indeed be both fruitless and dangerous. . . .

The following policy options were on the drawing board or in discussion as preparations for a potential Trump second term were being made. . . . The next American President should strongly consider adopting all of them as a package:

- Strategically expand tariffs to all Chinese products and increase tariff rates to levels that will block out "Made in China" products, and execute this strategy in a manner and at a pace that will not expose the U.S. to lack of access to essential products like key pharmaceuticals.
- Provide significant financial and tax incentives to American companies that are seeking to onshore production from Communist China to U.S. soil. . . .
- Prohibit Communist Chinese state-owned enterprises from bidding on U.S. government procurement contracts (for example, contracts for subway and other transportation systems).
- Ban all Chinese social media apps such as TikTok and WeChat, which pose significant national security risks and expose American consumers to data and identity theft.
- Prohibit all Communist Chinese investment in high-technology industries.
- Prohibit U.S. pension funds from investing in Communist Chinese stocks. . . .
- Prohibit the use of Hong Kong clearinghouses as transit points for American capital investing in the Chinese mainland. . . .

Document 3. Chinese and US Public Opinion Polls (2024)

Tsinghua University asked Chinese about "US strategic policies toward China." Eighty-eight percent said that US policy is to "contain China's development." Forty-eight percent said US policy is "trying to conduct peaceful evolution in China," meaning regime change. Forty percent said the US wants to avoid war or military competition with China. Only six percent said the US "hopes to cooperate with China to advance shared prosperity."[31]

A poll conducted by the Chicago Council on Global Affairs found the lowest level of positive feelings toward China—only twenty-six out of 100 people—since this kind of poll was first conducted in 1978.[32] Other key findings:

- A majority of Americans (55 percent) say the United States should actively work to limit the growth of China's power, while four in 10 say the United States should undertake friendly cooperation and engagement with China.
- Americans' top goals for US-China relations: avoiding a military conflict (69 percent) and maintaining the US high-tech edge (60 percent).
- Nearly half of Americans (49 percent) view China as more influential than the United States in Asia (30 percent say equally influential, 21 percent say the US is more influential).
- A majority of Americans (56 percent) say US-China trade does more to weaken US national security than to strengthen it. 39 percent say the reverse.

Document 4. China Reacts to Trump's Election
(*Background:* The editorial collective Zhong Sheng published an editorial, "Stabilizing China-US Relations is in the National Interest of Both Countries," in the official *Renmin ribao* on November 8, 2024. The introductory paragraph below reiterates Xi Jinping's congratulatory message to Trump on his electoral victory.)

On November 7, Xi Jinping sent a congratulatory message to President-elect Trump that said: "A stable, healthy, sustainably developing China-US relationship fits with the common interests of the two countries and with the expectations of international society. I hope the two sides will keep to the principles of mutual respect, peaceful coexistence, and win-win cooperation, strengthen channels of dialogue, improve control over differences, expand mutually beneficial cooperation, and move down the road of correctly getting along in a new period, with prosperity for both countries and benefits to the world."

(China's America-watchers offered varying views of what Trump's election might mean for China.[33])

Document 5. Two Chinese Reactions to Trump's Tariff Threats
(*Background:* The first selection is an interview on November 16, 2024 of Zhang Yansheng, Chief Researcher at the China Center for International Economic Exchanges. He puts the tariff issue in the context of China's economic reforms and long-term strategy. Zhang has been involved in top-level economic planning for some time. *Source: South China Morning*

Post, https://www.scmp.com/economy/global-economy/article/3290720/economist-zhang-yansheng-how-china-can-survive-trump-threats-avoid-japans-mistakes). The second selection is from a Chinese readout of a meeting in Beijing between Premier Li Qiang and Senator Steve Daines (Republican from Montana) in March 2025. *Source*: Xinhua, https://english.news.cn/20250323/6d3f337c1488427e80827ae4d8294d7a/c.html).

Zhang Yansheng:

The importance of the domestic economic program. Expanding domestic demand comprehensively is also a priority, especially if external conditions worsen, such as potential tariffs or the removal of China's most favored nation trade status. Reducing dependency on external demand and bolstering domestic demand are key. Developing new productive forces through innovation and demand-driven strategies is critical. Increasing citizens" incomes and addressing their concerns will also be important for boosting the middle-income group's growth.

On Trump's 60 percent tariff on Chinese goods. Trump, in my view, has a great deal of contradictions. For example, he recently said that he would impose a 10 percent levy on China, 25 percent levy on Canada and Mexico, respectively. He blames Mexico and Canada for being irresponsible, [but] they don't control the drugs, they don't control the illegal immigrants. While for China, he said raw materials for drugs come from China. But what we don't know is whether such a statement is a negotiating move, or a threat of what he will actually do. This remains to be seen. . . .

Sixty percent is actually a big threat to China, and I would assume Trump would think the US is losing out as the trade deficit is too big. There is also the argument that China's most favored nation status should be revoked. How will this play out with his other threats? It doesn't make any sense. It's like a war.

There is a lot of ambiguity in Trump's threats, and he looks very random. Of course, judging from his previous run for the presidency, he has a trait called "talking the talk." He's a businessman, not a politician. So this is one aspect where we have to be on higher alert. There is also a theory that the tariff may be a bargaining process, but what will emerge at the end of the day? In my view, there's a consensus that we don't take countermeasures. As a famous Chinese saying goes, "A gentleman settles a dispute through communication instead of a fight." So we can take the moral high ground.

How to counter Trump's tariffs. Some studies show China may suffer a huge loss without countering. But no countering from China does not mean that China will not circumvent them. Countering is tit-for-tat action, while circumventing is what companies can do to avoid tariff barriers. . . . Will Mexico listen to you? You're going to put 100 percent tariffs on Mexico, and the Mexican president immediately said she's countering it. China's investment in Mexico can bring technology, tax revenue and jobs.

It's impossible for Mexico to hurt their own interests just for Trump. He thinks of himself as God. I think China will respond by saying free trade, free investment and free movement of labor and factors of production are good. China will tell the US, "If you are unkind to me, I won't fight you. You are doing wrong, why should I do wrong?"

The next step for China is we need to ensure the economy will be good. The most important card to play is further deepening reforms in a comprehensive manner and promoting modernization, with the most critical part being a high level of institutional opening up. We will also be open to the United States market because the US business sector wants to do business with us. We can distinguish between the vast American business and academic community from the few extremists in the government.

What is China's long-term goal? China must avoid the path of the Soviet Union or Japan. Instead, China should explore an open, inclusive and shared ecosystem for innovation, allowing the world to collaborate with us. . . . What did China do right in the past? First, reform and opening up. Second, seeking truth from facts. Third, focusing on development. No matter whom we face, if we stick to these three principles, we are unstoppable. Look at the US and its past competitors—none were defeated by the US; they all fell because of their own mistakes. If we lose to the US in the future, it will only be because we deviated from the right path.

Li Qiang Meets Steve Daines:

Li pointed out that economic and trade cooperation is an important foundation of China-U.S. relations. Over the past few decades, the fruitful economic and trade cooperation achieved between China and the United States is the result of joint efforts of both sides and should be cherished. The more difficulties bilateral relations face, the more important it is to safeguard and develop China-U.S. economic and trade cooperation, said the premier.

Li said that nobody gains from a trade war, and no country can achieve development and prosperity through imposing tariffs. He called on the two countries to solve problems, such as trade imbalance, by making the pie of cooperation bigger.

"China always welcomes companies from all over the world, including the United States, to share development opportunities in China, and will actively address their legitimate demands, treat domestic and foreign companies as equals, and continue to foster a sound business environment," Li said

Document 6. A Chinese Expert Addresses the Main Source of Future US-China Competition

(Background: Professor Yan Xuetong is a leading commentator on international relations and US foreign policy. He is head of the Tsinghua University Research Center on Strategy and Security. *Source:* This recap of

his talk on December 2, 2024, is at Weixin [in Chinese], https://mp.weixin.qq.com/s/_kHRuxhIOfoxMdZTlzMoTg.)

Yan Xuetong said that after Trump begins his second term, the economic conflict between China and the United States may become more serious. In addition, Trump's political isolationist policy will have the impact that the United States will reduce its exchanges with China, and the Trump administration will take measures to cancel the dialogue and communication channels established with China during the Biden administration.

Looking at the reality, the two conflicts between Russia and Ukraine and Palestine and Israel continue to stagnate, and the situation in the Taiwan Strait has become complicated. Young children are worried that there may be a war between China and the United States in the future. However, Yan Xuetong believes that although the competition between China and the United States may become more intense, there will be no "proxy" war. Because in the digital age, who can win the competition between China and the United States depends on who is more advanced in the technology war, and the "proxy war" cannot improve the technical capabilities of either party and reduce the technical dependence on the other party. Therefore, it is an ineffective means for both parties to compete through agents. In addition, Trump is different in one respect from all the leaders of the United States since the end of the Cold War in 1991. He is the only American president who has not been involved in a new war during his term in office. For Trump, the means of war are not conducive to consolidating and enhancing the United States' world hegemony.

Yan Xuetong believes that the competition between China and the United States has entered a new stage—efficiency competition. He mentioned the new appointment of . . . Elon Musk, the founder of Tesla and SpaceX, [as head of the] "Department of Government Efficiency" (DOGE). . . . Yan Xuetong believes that although Trump's DOGE will be difficult to realize its goal, it indicates that the United States will pay more attention to the impact of improving government efficiency on national competitiveness. "In the next four years, China and the United States will not only compete in diplomacy, but also in terms of domestic government reform." In Yan Xuetong's view, the effectiveness of government reforms in China and the United States will become a key factor affecting the power comparison between the two countries in the next four years. If China achieves significant results in government reform, it may narrow the gap with the United States.

What does Trump's victory show? Judging from the results of the 2024 US election, it is not that US leaders have changed, but that the type of leader has changed. This represents a profound change in the US political landscape. Trump won the election with a narrow advantage, a vote share only 1.6 percent ahead of his opponent. This is not a reflection of absolute consensus in society, but evidence of the serious division of US domestic politics. The conflict between liberal and populist values and political lines is intensifying. . . . This domestic political division directly affects US foreign policy, and Trump's return is likely to accelerate the process of deglobalization. His "America First" policy will first impact the United States, then affect allies, and eventually spread to the world. His reelection means a further strengthening of the trend of deglobalization, which will have a profound impact on international trade, tariffs and international order. What the outcome will be is still difficult to predict.

2

US-China Relations

The Strategic Competition

Introduction

Despite periodic high-level dialogue between Chinese and US leaders described in the previous chapter, China's economic rise led to growing suspicions in the United States about China's ambitions in and beyond East Asia. Starting roughly in the last few years of the Barack Obama administration, competition for influence and strategic advantage replaced hopes in Washington that economic development powered by trade and investment ties would be the bedrock of US-China relations. Their different strategic objectives dominated the agenda, often undermining diplomatic engagement and complicating trade and investment ties. US policy in Asia, at least until Donald Trump's ascension, was to deter China, clearly identified as the number-one national security threat, by bolstering defense of Taiwan and strengthening security ties with allies and friendly states around China's rim (**Selection 1 and Document 1**).

With his reelection, Donald Trump reset US relations with Russia and seemed to be thinking about using close ties with Moscow to disrupt its ties with China (**Selection 12**). His administration continued to regard China as the leading threat to the United States, yet endorsed budget cuts to programs, such as foreign aid, that were directed at reducing that threat (**Selection 13**).

The status of Taiwan is at the center of US-China strategic mistrust. US policy has been based on "strategic ambiguity" as to its defense of Taiwan, whereas China regards Taiwan as its internal affair, not subject to foreign interference. China's policy seeks to reunify with Taiwan and meanwhile prevent it from declaring independence (**Selection 2**). The Taiwan Relations Act (**Document 2**) expresses a US commitment to Taiwan's defense that is, however, not explicit. Thus, alternatives to strategic ambiguity have been offered (**Document 3**) as speculation has increased over the possibility of a Chinese attack on Taiwan. US war gaming of a Chinese attack on Taiwan has become a popular exercise for strategy experts as China's military capabilities in and near the Taiwan Strait have greatly expanded (**Selection 7**). Trump's commitment to Taiwan's defense is less clear than that of many of his Republican followers (**Selection 11**). For Taiwan's leaders, US support of their democracy and autonomy can no longer be taken for granted (**Selection 6**).

At the global level, the overall military balance favors the United States over China, in large part due to US overseas bases, security partnerships, and military spending (**Selection 3**). China has acquired at least one overseas military base, in Djibouti, East Africa, and possibly a naval base in Cambodia, but Beijing has no formal security alliances. Nor can China match the approximately 750 US military bases worldwide, many of which are positioned with an eye to deterring China. Still, China is rapidly increasing its air, naval, and nuclear-missile capabilities. China's declared position on the use of nuclear weapons has not changed over many years: no first use of a nuclear weapon, no use against a non-nuclear weapon state, and a minimum force for deterrence of a nuclear attack. But the Pentagon projects major increases in Chinese nuclear and missile forces—deploying 1,000 strategic nuclear weapons by 2030, for instance—as well as an operational naval reach beyond East Asia.

As China finds itself hemmed in by US security partnerships, tensions have risen between China and its neighbors, from Japan and South Korea in East Asia to the Philippines in Southeast Asia, India in South Asia, and some of the Pacific Island states (**Selections 8 and 10**). Most prominent among these partnerships are the Quadrilateral Security Dialogue group (the Quad for short: United States, Japan, Australia, India), and AUKUS (Australia, United Kingdom, United States). They supplement long-standing bilateral US security treaties in Asia with Japan, South Korea, the Philippines, and Australia.

Complicating the strategic picture are political and military incidents in recent years that have heightened US-China tensions and led to shutdowns in diplomacy. One was the visit of then-House Speaker Nancy Pelosi to Taiwan in August 2022, to which China responded with military exercises around Taiwan (**Selection 4**). Then followed the shooting down of a Chinese spy balloon in the United States early in 2023. These two incidents disrupted diplomatic contacts for months (**Selection 5**). Several close encounters have occurred between Chinese and US ships in the South China Sea, where China and the Philippines have competing territorial claims. Such events underscore the importance of US-China military-to-military meetings (**Selection 8**). Computer hacking further complicates the picture, with the

US and China periodically exchanging accusations of being the victim (**Selection 9**).

(1) The Threat Business: China Comes First

Dual Enemies, But Not the Same

For those in charge of US national security, the central challenge is identifying threats and determining how to counter them. The Biden administration, like the first Trump administration, cast China and Russia, in that order, as the major threats. China, said the Pentagon, was a "pacing challenger," whereas Russia was an "acute" challenger. Those rather odd designations mean, in plain English, that the administration considered China, once called a "peer competitor," an all-encompassing threat, not just military but also political, economic, and technological. Russia was downgraded from the Trump years. Whereas Russia was considered a military threat then, the Biden-Harris "National Security Strategy" paper (October 2022) considered China the greater threat because it "harbors the intention and, increasingly, the capacity to reshape the international order in favor of one that tilts the global playing field to its benefit, even as the United States remains committed to managing the competition between our countries responsibly." (The full text of the strategy paper's section on China is **Document 1**.)

At first glance, the Biden-Harris paper seemed to say that the Russian threat was actually far more serious than the threat from China. Russia, not China, was carrying out a war of aggression in Ukraine, condemned as such by the United Nations. China required managed competition, whereas Russia was a belligerent that "impacted stability everywhere" and posed a global nuclear threat. China, the paper said, sought to "become the world's leading power" and had both the intent and the capability to "reshape the international order." Russia was said to be pursuing "an imperialist foreign policy with the goal of overturning key elements of the international order." Was that a distinction without a difference?

At War with Russia

Despite all the contentious issues between the United States and China, they were not at war. To all intents and purposes, the United States *was* at war with Russia, which not only "has shattered peace in Europe" but has convinced US leaders that destroying Ukraine is just part of its mission to undermine the Western alliance. Those are the reasons the United States gave for being heavily invested in defending Ukraine: tens of billions of dollars in military aid and training, including advanced weapons capable of hitting targets in Russia; and sanctions on Russian officials and trade. In the Asia Pacific, by contrast, the US strategy did not rest on war-fighting scenarios so much as on deterrence of China, marked by strengthening security partnerships, particularly with Taiwan, Japan, and Australia. And whereas Washington worried that Russia might use a nuclear weapon in Ukraine, it showed no signs of worry that China would invade Taiwan, much less deploy a nuclear weapon.

In Congress, More Action to Counter China

In the US Congress, one found declining enthusiasm for supporting Ukraine, but plenty of enthusiasm for confronting China. Far-right Republicans in the House of Representatives were particularly anxious to reduce aid to Ukraine. Their line of argument closely followed Moscow's narrative on the war. But when it came to dealing with China, a Cold War-style consensus formed among House members across the political spectrum. Republicans organized a Select Committee on China and appealed for Democratic support. In the words of the committee's chair, Mike Gallagher of Wisconsin: "We want the Democrats to nominate serious, sober people to participate, because defending America from Chinese Communist Party aggression should not be a partisan thing."

Another hawkish congressional commission, comprised of twelve members drawn equally from both parties, warned that China-Russia cooperation put the United States at risk of a two-front war against both countries. "The new partnership between Russian and Chinese leaders poses qualitatively new threats of potential opportunistic aggression and/or the risk of future cooperative two-theater aggression," the Congressional Commission on the Strategic Posture of the United States said in a report published at the end of 2022. In contrast with then-current US policy, the report said: "The United States and its allies must be ready to deter and defeat both adversaries simultaneously. The US-led international order and the values it upholds are at risk from the Chinese and Russian authoritarian regimes." The Biden administration insisted the United States already has more than enough nuclear weapons to deter adversaries as well as a sizable lead in nuclear weapon reliability and global deployment. Yet the leaders of the commission insisted: "We must urgently consider additional adjustments to our own nuclear posture if we are to sustain deterrence against two nuclear peers." In the end, Biden increased budgeting for nuclear weapons.

The Commission used the old ploy of scare tactics, especially with respect to China. For instance, its report cited the Pentagon's figures that China had increased its strategic nuclear weapon inventory from about 350 to 500 and could have 1,000 by 2030. But that left China far behind the US inventory of roughly 5,500 strategic nuclear weapons, with hundreds on invulnerable nuclear submarines within easy range of Chinese targets. Furthermore, China, unlike the United States, subscribed to a no-first-use policy, meaning it pledged not to initiate use of a nuclear weapon in a conflict. At sea, the Pentagon highlighted China's growing naval strength, including work on a third aircraft carrier. But the United States had eleven aircraft carriers that were deployed all over the globe. And in the fall of 2024, the *New York Times* reported on a $1.7 trillion US nuclear modernization program, geared mainly to the China threat, that included construction of a dozen more nuclear-powered and -armed submarines. Those added to the eighteen nuclear-missile submarines already in the US arsenal.

Pentagon Capitalism

Let's not forget the bread and butter of the threat business: the weapons and money for the Pentagon and its military contractors. The *New York Times* reported in December 2022: "Military spending next year is on track to reach its highest level in inflation-adjusted terms since the peaks in the costs of the Iraq and Afghanistan wars between 2008 and 2011 . . . "[1] In a spirit of bipartisanship that national security always prompts, Congress voted for a record $858 billion in military spending. That's $45 billion *more* than the President requested. The war in Ukraine has been a boon to what Seymour Melman famously called the permanent war economy. One specialist found that US military contractors would receive about 40 percent of the latest round of military aid to Ukraine (about $47 billion).[2] Please note: All these spending decisions were made with virtually no debate. And an update: US military spending in 2025–26 will probably amount to around $1 trillion.

(2) US Policy on Taiwan, and China's Response

When Xi Jinping met President Biden in Bali, Indonesia in 2022, he described Taiwan as the "core of China's core interests." Like all leaders in the People's Republic before him, Xi considers "peaceful unification" with Taiwan to be China's destiny. US military aid and political support of Taiwan, in Beijing's view, amounts to outside interference. Yet ever since Nixon's visit, official US policy has been that Taiwan is "a part of China," and Washington has consistently discouraged Taiwan from moving toward independence. If Taiwan nevertheless were to declare independence, rather than continue functioning as an autonomous territory (and still recognized as the "Republic of China" by about a dozen countries), China has vowed to use force to make "one China" a reality. That would be the end of "strategic ambiguity." The United States would then have to make a momentous decision: whether to confront China and risk a major war.

In the meantime, tensions between China and Taiwan have risen in recent years, leading to several occasions in which Chinese air and naval forces have harassed Taiwan, intruding into its air defense zone and, more provocative still, crossing the median line between Taiwan and the mainland.

A Word of Caution from China

On May 19, 2023, one of China's most eminent America watchers, Professor Jia Qingguo of Beijing University, gave a talk in the United States that listed all the areas of Chinese government concern about US foreign policy. US interference (as the Chinese see it) in Taiwan occupied center stage. Jia pointed to three US pledges on Taiwan dating to the Nixon era that the United States had violated: to regard Taiwan as part of China, to terminate a mutual defense treaty with Taiwan, and to withdraw troops from Taiwan. His reference was to visits to Taiwan by senior US officials (such as former House Speaker Nancy Pelosi), which upgraded Taiwan's independent status; to recent statements by Biden promising defense of Taiwan if China attacked it, despite the defense treaty's abrogation; and to expanded US military aid to Taiwan that included training of Taiwanese forces. Jia mainly blamed the US Congress for these provocative moves. "So under these circumstances," Jia said, "China is rethinking its strategy of peaceful reunification."

US officials denied these Chinese charges. They insisted that the United States still upholds the One China principle, still adheres to "strategic ambiguity" when it comes to the question of defending Taiwan, and still provides only defensive aid to Taiwan. But Jia Qingguo's words were ominous, especially because they came from a longtime advocate of US-China engagement. He was suggesting that in the view of some influential Chinese, the US was drifting toward endorsement of Taiwanese independence. That would be crossing China's red line. China has never foresworn the use of force to take over Taiwan, but now, according to Jia, it was "rethinking" its policy of peaceful reunification.

Equally ominous was Jia's caution that China's nuclear policy, which has relied on a minimal force for retaliation in line with the doctrine of no-first-use of nuclear weapons, might change if US pressure on Taiwan continued. He pointed to "some Chinese" who were now advocating a policy change that would, among other things, support providing nuclear weapons or delivery systems to friendly countries, in the same way that the United States had promised to provide nuclear submarines to Australia.[3] A study by scholars at Harvard's Belfer Center supported Jia's observation. They concluded that China's nuclear weapons policy was becoming more offense-minded, in part out of concern about a shift in US policy that emphasized low-yield nuclear weapons. That shift, to the Chinese, made actual use of a nuclear weapon more likely than previously.[4]

These two potential Chinese policy changes—toward unification with Taiwan by force, and toward a more offensive nuclear posture—would dramatically increase tensions with the United States, putting us squarely in a new Cold War. As Professor Jia pointed out, the US emphasis on "strategic competition" with China omitted possibilities for cooperation. Among those possibilities is mutual nuclear weapons reductions, which have rarely been brought up in official meetings.

Strategic Ambiguity Remains Ambiguous

At a stopover in Tokyo during his Asia trip in mid-2023, President Biden was asked whether the United States would "defend Taiwan" if it were attacked. He said yes, because "that's the commitment we made." Actually, no formal "commitment," such as is contained in US security treaties with Japan and South Korea, has ever been made. Biden had made the same incorrect assertion twice before, and the State Department had to walk them back. But this time it was in the context of the war in Ukraine, suggesting— but by no means confirming—what defending Taiwan might actually mean. Biden did, however, provide just enough fuel to raise questions about his adherence to previous policy based on "strategic ambiguity."

Let's keep in mind that US presidents have supported Taiwan's defense for many years, not just by way of substantial military aid and active responses in crisis situations, such as in 1996 when China deployed missiles in an attempt to intimidate Taiwan during a presidential election. Presidents are also bound by the 1979 Taiwan Relations Act, which requires provision of defense assistance to Taiwan in the context of defining Taiwan as a US national security interest (**Document 2**).

From that perspective, Biden's comment was less consequential than it might seem. Chinese strategists would have to presume, as in the past, that attacking Taiwan would precipitate direct US intervention. Some specialists argue, unconvincingly, that China already outguns the United States in the Taiwan area and might overwhelm US naval forces seeking to defend Taiwan. These specialists even suggest that China would attack US bases in Japan, as though Beijing would risk World War III to get Taiwan back.[5] Such scenarios may be welcome in US military-industrial circles, but I think they vastly overstate Chinese capabilities and, most importantly, imply recklessness in their strategic planning.

The Enduring Value of Strategic Ambiguity

Those who persist in seeing a Chinese threat everywhere have been encouraged in that belief by Russia's Ukraine war, seeing parallels between Putin's view of Ukraine as a non-country and Xi Jinping's view of Taiwan as inevitably part of China. But aside from the differences in status between Ukraine and Taiwan—Ukraine is an independent country, whereas the United States and many of its allies have long recognized Taiwan as being part of "one China"—there are vastly different strategic considerations in Moscow and Beijing. While Putin refuses to recognize Ukraine as a legitimate country and is out to grab as much of its territory as possible, Xi has every reason to avoid launching a war on Taiwan. Though Xi would surely want to lay claim to being the Chinese leader who finally recovered Taiwan, he is rational enough to realize how militarily difficult and economically costly that would be—not least, probably destroying Taiwan's world-class semiconductor industries. Attacking Taiwan would also be contrary to the desires of its people, who overwhelmingly identify as Taiwanese, not Chinese. These considerations lay behind the assertion by one of China's leading Taiwan specialists, Professor Yan Anlin, that "the Beijing authorities do not have a specific timetable for reunification, but we do feel a sense of urgency," specifying that "full reunification" is "likely to take another five to ten years to achieve. . . . When I say it will take five to 10 years, I'm referring to peaceful reunification."[6]

"Strategic ambiguity" is not an ideal basis for policy on either side, for the simple reason that ambiguity can lead to miscalculations. But it has kept tense relations across the Taiwan Strait from leading to a blowup. US-China friction over Taiwan is bound to continue, but so long as Taiwan doesn't cross the red line on independence, and so long as Chinese leaders adhere to the policy of *peaceful* unification, friction need not lead to war. The United States needs to recalibrate its military and political relationship with Taiwan to avoid the appearance of supporting Taiwan's separation—in short, maintaining what some observers call a 1.5 China policy—and China needs to refrain from provocative military maneuvers near Taiwan. Both countries' leaders are sane enough to understand the costs of war, and for China especially, Ukraine demonstrates not an alluring precedent but a terrible price that attacking Taiwan would likely exact. Perhaps that is why, in 2025, senior Chinese officials are talking about building an "integrated development demonstration zone" between the mainland and Taiwan. The zone would seek to entice Taiwan to increase investments and exchanges, toward the end of "cross-Strait integration."[7]

(3) The US-China Military Balance

Any comparison of military forces should be treated with case, since many factors besides numbers of weapons and military budgets need to be taken into account. These other factors include weapons research and development

(R&D), military leadership, quality of strategic planning, force readiness and reliability, fighting experience, training, intelligence capabilities, and security allies and partners. (On this last factor, see **Selection 10** on US military capabilities in the Pacific.) Military spending is a particularly controversial issue. It has always been dogged by debate over methodology, such as how to factor in currency values and weapons pricing, and by China's reporting of its budget, which does not include spending on military R&D and the paramilitary police, among other security items.

One careful study by an Australian economist, Peter Robertson at the Centre for Economic Policy Research, uses purchasing power parity (PPP, a figure that reflects the prices in national currencies of the same good or service in different countries) to estimate China's military expenditure in 2024 at "$609 billion, or 67% of US actual spending of $916 billion." The figure for China far exceeds China's official military spending for 2023–2024 of $296 billion. In other elements of comparative military strength as

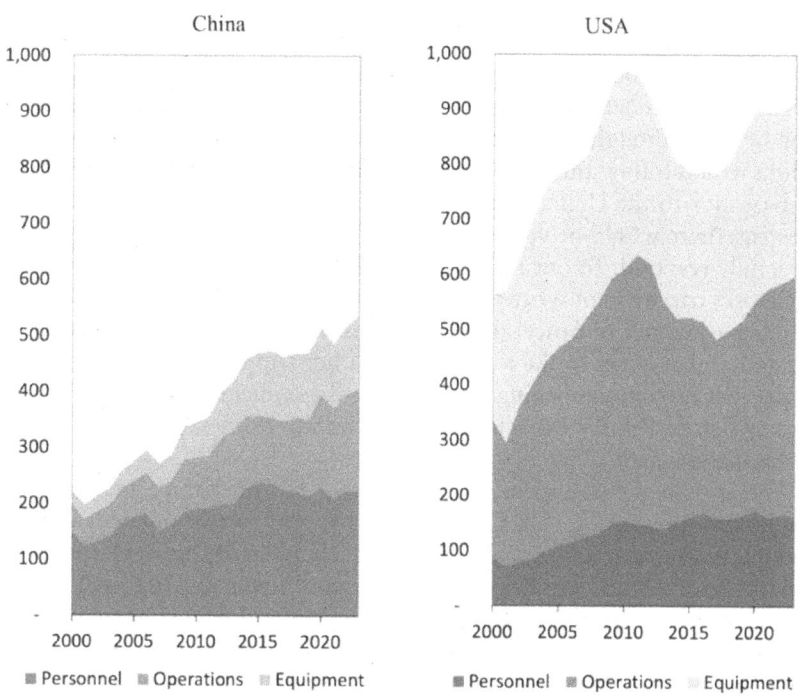

CHART 2.1 China and US Military Spending Since 2000 *(Source: VoxEU, Center for Economic Policy Research, https://cepr.org/voxeu/columns/chinas-military-rise-comparative-military-spending-china-and-us)*

of 2024, China leads the United States in active military personnel, while the United States leads in share of GDP devoted to the military (3.4 percent to 1.7 percent) and nuclear weapons (5,224 to 600). It is also worth pointing out that in recent years, China's weapons production has outpaced the US in jet fighters, hypersonic missiles, and other categories.[8] Some analysts warn that China might surpass the US, but Robertson says that "contrary to perceptions, the US has kept pace in recent years."[9]

Above is a side-by-side view of Chinese and US military spending since 2000, based on PPP.

(4) An Ill-advised Visit to Taiwan (2022)

House Speaker Nancy Pelosi was intent on visiting Taiwan to demonstrate unwavering support of Taiwan's democracy and (she wrote) confront China's imminent threat to Taiwan's security. She did so despite President Biden's misgivings and criticisms from many China experts. The *Washington Post* reported at the time that Xi Jinping personally asked President Biden to find a way to put off her trip.[10] According to the *Post*'s account, Biden explained to Xi that the independent role of Congress made it impossible for him to stop her, even though US intelligence officials were (correctly) convinced that China would follow through on its warnings of a forceful response. China's ambassador to the United States said: "We had warned that if Pelosi made the visit, there would be very serious consequences. China would firmly and forcefully respond. To our regret, the United States chose not to listen."

Pelosi's trip was not written in stone. She said she would not go to Taiwan if Biden asked her to cancel the trip. But as the *Post*'s account indicates, "In the end, Biden never spoke to Pelosi about her trip despite Xi's request that he prevent it from happening. In an offhand comment, Biden told reporters shortly before Pelosi's expected visit that military officials believed the trip was not a good idea."

The trip might not seem like a big deal to Americans, but given the heightened tensions in US-China relations, they were a big deal to US diplomats. As then-ambassador to China Nicholas Burns said years after the incident: "After Speaker Pelosi's visit to Taiwan in August 2022, the Chinese very unwisely and objectionably shut down eight channels of communication. We went for several months until November of 2022 with not a great ability to contact them."[11] The same disruption occurred, Burns said, after the spy balloon incident in February 2023, discussed in the next selection. Thus, a Taiwan trip by a senior person in the US government—in this case, the most senior in twenty-five years—was costly. Yet such visits by high-level US officials continue.

Here is why I think the timing and rationale for the trip were flawed.

A Needless Provocation

First, US-China tensions over Taiwan were running high. Both sides were responsible for that. President Biden did his part by consistently misstating the US commitment to Taiwan—there is no security treaty, Mr. President—and by authorizing increased military assistance to Taiwan. To the Chinese, these steps looked like a US effort to erode its official policy of "One China" and move closer to China's red line: Taiwanese independence. Meantime, China's air force patrols were regularly intruding into Taiwan's air defense zone, on occasion causing Taiwan's air force to scramble. A military incident that could have sparked serious fighting was becoming more likely with each passing week.

Second, Xi Jinping was expected to be given another term as party leader at a national congress later in the year. A high-level trip to Taiwan by a key US political figure in advance of that party congress could be seen as a personal provocation, particularly since Xi wanted to be seen as the leader who would complete China's national unification by "recovering" Taiwan. He may have felt compelled to react forcefully.

Third, China had already issued warnings of "severe consequences" if Pelosi went to Taiwan. Pelosi's trip should not have been the occasion for finding out. (As Pelosi was leaving Taiwan, China began live-fire drills very close to Taiwan's shores and inside Taiwan's territorial waters. China also imposed trade restrictions with Taiwan and hacked Taiwan government websites—all with promises of more to come.)

Fourth, one may question the purpose of Pelosi's trip. If she was going to Taiwan to show US support, or if she more specifically wanted to demonstrate that Democrats were as supportive of Taiwan as Republicans, she could have accomplished that at other times and in other ways.

In sum, Pelosi's trip was a needless provocation. It forced China's leaders to choose between a forceful response and a weak one. That kind of choice is the stuff of international crises—and really left Xi with no choice at all. A show of weakness on Taiwan would be deadly for any Chinese leader. For some time to come, US-China relations will be dogged by the same kind of dynamic that has occurred in three previous confrontations over Taiwan, each of which could have escalated to a violent level and one of which, in 1958, came close to involving US use of nuclear weapons. Pelosi did not do Taiwan a service; she made its security more precarious.

A Missed Opportunity?

It is fair to ask how President Biden might have handled the Pelosi trip differently. Consider this scenario: Biden, concerned about China's reaction to the visit, says to Xi:

I will do my best to persuade her, out of respect for China's sensitivity regarding Taiwan. But in return for her postponing her trip, I want your assurance that China's military will stop air and naval maneuvers that threaten Taiwan. And let's plan on holding high-level military-to-military and diplomatic discussions to promote mutual security in the Taiwan Strait area.

It was an engagement moment, prompted by the US national interest in competitive coexistence with China.

Would Biden have "looked weak" if he had succeeded in stopping the trip? He could have avoided such a charge by pointing out that Taiwan's security would not be undermined by the postponement, whereas Pelosi's trip would force China to make a show of strength. Biden could have pointed to the many ways his administration was supporting Taiwan: three recent military aid packages, public comments upholding strong ties with Taiwan, and the array of security arrangements, such as the Quad, that are focused on any Chinese threat in the Asia Pacific. A positive response to Xi was an opportunity to put US-China relations onto a more positive track at a time when those relations were rapidly deteriorating. At the least, Biden's proposal would have tested Xi's frequent assertions in support of improved relations.

(5) Evaluating the 2023 Spy Balloon Incident

The shooting down of a Chinese spy balloon in the United States that apparently went off course set back US-China relations for several months. Everything from the balloon's launch to its destruction was mismanaged by both governments, providing lessons that may or may not have been learned.

The first lesson stems from the question of whether or not deploying the balloon over the United States, near a military base in Montana, was a Chinese leadership decision. It almost certainly wasn't, but at the time it was treated in Washington as though the balloon was the brainchild of Xi Jinping himself. Afterward, the Biden administration reversed course, starting with the President's own assertion that Xi probably did not know about the balloon's mission. Xi "got very upset" over it, Biden said in the same off-camera remarks in which he called Xi a dictator. The Biden administration "wants to bury [the incident] because they know that Xi Jinping really didn't have anything to do with it, that it wasn't some sort of effort against the United States and that no one intended it to be over Montana," said Dennis Wilder, former National Security Council director for China. US officials confirmed two weeks after the shoot-down that winds had blown the balloon off course.

The lesson here applies to government decision-making everywhere: What might initially appear to be a calculated, high-level move by an adversary may turn out to be the ordinary miscues of a bureaucracy—in this case, the division of the Chinese military responsible for spy balloons. But domestic politics in the United States intruded: Conservatives in Congress argued that the Biden administration's decision-making during the balloon incident, which included postponing a trip by Secretary of State Antony Blinken to Beijing, was influenced by a desire to placate China. To which the administration retorted: "If we had been pulling our punches, we would have gone ahead with the trip." I disagree: If keeping up the momentum from the Biden-Xi summit in Bali was policy, the Blinken trip *should* have gone ahead. That would have been sound strategic thinking, not accommodation of China. Instead, the administration probably acted in some part out of fear of the far right's accusations of being soft on China.

Lesson 2 is to ask questions before shooting. The incident set off crisis-level charges—from Washington, that the balloon was a strategic threat, hence needed to be shot down, and from Beijing that the United States was acting hysterically, since the balloon was purely for weather forecasting. Neither charge was correct: It *was* a spy balloon, but hardly of the sort that needed to be treated as an imminent threat and shot down.

Lesson 3 is to get your story straight. What exactly did the balloon carry? Then-Joint Chiefs of Staff Chair Mark Milley said "there was no intelligence collected by that balloon." The Pentagon backed that claim, saying the balloon "did not collect any intelligence while it transited the United States and that it did not transmit any intelligence back to China." But the Pentagon, which had promised to publicly release all information on the balloon's capability and its data, never did so, fueling right-wing and other theories about the China threat and a Pentagon cover-up in deference to getting along with China.

A fourth lesson: Apologies are important. One of the scantily reported upshots of the balloon incident is that China apologized. "The Chinese side regrets the unintended entry of the airship into U.S. airspace," China's foreign ministry said. An apology from Beijing is a rarity, yet the Biden administration did not acknowledge the apology. Granted, the apology fell short of saying that the balloon was on a spy mission. Nevertheless, the administration could have accepted the apology, recognized that the balloon was not the result of a top-level Chinese decision, and moved on with Blinken's trip.

The spy balloon incident will take its place beside other dicey incidents in US-China relations, such as the accidental US bombing of the Chinese embassy during the war in the former Yugoslavia, the downing of a Chinese jet near Hainan in 2001, and Chinese missile tests near Taiwan during its 1996 presidential elections. All these incidents involved crisis management that avoided a more serious confrontation. That's the fifth lesson.

(6) Taiwan's Autonomy: A Provocative Issue for China

Taiwan's 2024 Presidential Election

Does Taiwan "belong" to mainland China, as Beijing claims, or is it autonomous and deserving of independent status? In China's view, Taiwan should be reunited with the People's Republic after a long separation at the end of the Second World War, followed by US interference in China's civil war that culminated in the retreat to Taiwan of the US-supported Guomindang government. But Taiwan to all intents and purposes is a fully autonomous state, with a democratic political system, a vibrant, world-class economy, and a population that overwhelmingly considers itself Taiwanese, not Chinese. Every election in Taiwan is testimony to its resilience in the face of pressure from the mainland. But in Beijing, every Taiwan election is a provocation, all the more so since Taiwan has strong US support.

In normal times, a presidential election in Taiwan is mainly about domestic issues, not relations with China. But the January 13, 2024, election put unusual focus on those relations, pumped up by dire warnings from Beijing and baseless predictions from some politicians and military officers in the United States that China was preparing to invade Taiwan by 2030 if not earlier.

The presidential candidates were: from the ruling Democratic Progressive Party (DPP), the country's vice president since 2020, Lai Ching-te; from the Kuomintang (KMT), Hou Yu-ih, the mayor of New Taipei City; and former Taipei Mayor Ko Wen-je of the Taiwan People's Party (TPP). Beijing paid very close attention to this election, since the DPP emphasizes Taiwan's autonomy but resists speaking of Taiwan's independence, and the KMT favors closer relations with the mainland. The TPP shied away from the China issue and talked more about economic and social issues.

The results: victory for the DPP and Lai Ching-te. He won 40 percent of the vote, a plurality sufficient to win in the Taiwan system, though not nearly as strong a win as outgoing President Tsai Ing-wen of the DPP had scored twice, with around 50 percent of the popular vote each time. Lai had to deal with opposition control of the Legislative Yuan, though indications are that at least on national security issues, he has majority support for protecting Taiwan's independent spirit.

Beijing's Reaction

Predictably, Beijing reacted to the election by reaffirming that nothing had changed: Taiwan belongs to China. Chinese officials referred to President

Biden's statements reaffirming opposition to Taiwan's independence and support for unification with the mainland so long as it was accomplished peacefully and by decision of the Taiwanese. Left unsaid was continued Chinese military harassment of Taiwan and continued US military aid and diplomatic support for Taiwan.

The new Taiwanese president's remarks on taking office, in which he emphasized Taiwan's sovereignty, ensured that nothing would change: China would continue displaying force. Although Tsai Ing-wen had also insisted that Taiwan be treated as a separate entity, she did not officially embrace the idea of Taiwan's sovereignty. She understood, as does the current president, that Beijing's red line for direct intervention is a Taiwan declaration of independence. President Lai did not speak of *declaring* independence, but he did say: "According to international law, we are already a sovereign and independent country." Lai has also noted that Taiwan celebrated a 113th birthday, which showed that it could not consider the People's Republic of China the "motherland." After all, said Lai, the PRC had only celebrated its seventy-fifth birthday. Therefore, said Lai, Taiwan "may actually be the motherland of the people over 75 years old in the People's Republic of China." But in any case, Lai said, the two peoples are not brethren.

Such statements were enough to make Lai a target of official Chinese attacks and, more importantly, an escalation of harassing air and naval maneuvers near the island. China's military drills around Taiwan intensified in 2024. In May, China carried out a two-day exercise dubbed *Joint Sword* that included army, navy, air force, and rocket forces. It was the first time that China had simulated a full-scale attack, Taiwanese military experts said, rather than an economic blockade. Then, in October, a Chinese military drill involved the most air and naval craft ever: 153 military aircraft and twenty-six ships. The drill put Chinese forces all around the island, conveying the idea that China is capable of blockading Taiwan. Of particular interest to military experts was China's increasing deployment of heavily armed coast guard vessels along with naval craft. The day after that drill, the harassment dropped to the more usual number: around twenty-two ships. But Beijing announced it would conduct more live-fire drills in the Taiwan Strait in the future. And it did: In April 2025,

> Beijing started another series of joint military and coastguard drills around Taiwan . . ., which included the *Shandong* aircraft carrier . . . According to the PLA's Eastern Theatre Command, the patrols and exercises included simulated air and land strikes, as well as control of key passages to test the joint combat readiness of its troops.[12]

These Chinese exercises are not merely provocative; they can lead to disastrous miscalculations on all sides. What they are doing in the United States is encouraging war games focused on Chinese attacks on Taiwan, even though there is no sign that China's exercises are preparatory to an attempted takeover of Taiwan by force. Still, the question is worth asking: What might China do in Taiwan if Beijing did take it over? Here's what China's ambassador to France, Lu Shaye, speaking on French television, said: "reeducate" the population. "Why do I say 'reeducate?' Because the Taiwan authorities have imposed a 'de-Sinicization' education on the population, which is effectively indoctrination and intoxication. Reeducation is necessary to eliminate separatist thought and secessionist theory." Does this view represent official Chinese policy? Beijing didn't rebuke the ambassador, but neither did it say anything about a post-"liberation" policy.[13]

(7) War Games and False Alarms

Sounding the Alarm

Ever since Vladimir Putin and Xi Jinping met in Beijing early in 2022 and issued a joint statement of solidarity, pundits left and right, and some US military officials, have sounded the alarm over Taiwan. They have incorrectly concluded from that statement that it is only a matter of time before China, emboldened by Russia's attack on Ukraine, attacks Taiwan. The only questions in the minds of these analysts are when the attacks will occur, and how.

Here's one example: Retired Admiral Mike Studeman, former head of the Office of Naval Analysis, predicted a Chinese invasion of Taiwan "most likely in the back half of the 2020s or front half of the 2030s." Rather than seeing China as too preoccupied with domestic problems to conduct a war or deterred by US military power, Studeman contended that "China's trajectory signals deepening danger and a hardening of Xi's intent to execute an act of aggression similar to Russia's invasion of Ukraine." (There's that analogy to Ukraine again.) Among other factors in support of his thesis, he cited Xi's ambitions, China's conventional and nuclear weapon modernization, and recent military deployments. He interpreted every move by Xi as a sign of China's imminent hostility—for example, that Xi's emphasis on economic self-reliance demonstrated a priority to "security over the economy." Even the exceptional costs to China of a war with the US over Taiwan would, in Studeman's view, be bearable: "In the coming years, [Xi] may conclude he has everything to gain and nothing to lose by waiting any longer."

A Reality Check

Allow me to deconstruct this analysis, which (again) is very similar to others that have come from members of Congress, military leaders (usually based in the Pacific), and a few right-wing China specialists. First, the admiral avoided any discussion of US policy on Taiwan. His analysis never considered provocative diplomatic and military moves by the United States during the last two administrations, discussed earlier in this chapter, that raised Chinese concerns about US support for Taiwan's independence.

Second, the admiral and other analysts did not take seriously statements from both Biden and Xi, as well as other top officials, that lowered tensions in the Taiwan Strait. Biden several times assured China that the United States supported the One China principle and not Taiwan's independence. For his part, Xi consistently said that China stood by its traditional policy of peaceful unification between China and Taiwan—so long as Taiwan did not declare independence. China also called for talks with the United States on adopting a common policy of "no-first-use" of nuclear weapons, with conflict over Taiwan evidently a concern.

Third, these doomsayers misconstrued what was happening in China's economy and military. It was not a matter of "security over the economy" as Studeman says, but the reverse. Economic development is the highest form of security, as we will see in Chinese statements in Chapter 7. And one reason for saying so is that US export controls on advanced technology have, in the Chinese view, forced China to pursue self-reliance in advanced technology. In a word, *China was not on a wartime footing*, as these analyses would have us believe, but rather was hunkering down for long-term economic competition with the United States.

Fourth, we should be aware that participants in these games—all well versed in war strategy and in devising scenarios designed to test tactical maneuvering, comparative weapons systems, and decision-making processes on both sides—do not include Chinese players, only Americans who think they know the Chinese mindset. Maybe they do and maybe they don't. But where are the conflict resolution experts? Their absence can have dangerous implications. First, war game theorists focus mainly on violent conflict; they don't give conflict management and diplomatic alternatives to fighting an equal opportunity to resolve it. Second, the games present worst-case situations in US-China relations. You don't hear about gaming global warming prevention strategies or exercises for overcoming trade barriers. Third, publicizing the games skews public and Congressional opinion, promoting anticipation of an eventual war with China and giving a boost to funding of the military budget. When, for example, an admiral says the Navy is planning for war with China by 2027, rest assured his supporters in Congress will use that prediction to push for another aircraft carrier in the Pacific. Or, as another example, when a war game finds the US lagging in response to a hypothetical Chinese attack on Taiwan's communications and energy systems, the conclusion is the need for bolstering US military space options. Those defense "needs" invariably push aside consideration of US options for reducing tensions with China and thereby negating the need for more weapons.

Here's the bottom line: The Taiwan Strait is a potential flash point and has been one for decades. But it need not be. Chinese party and military leaders are not so reckless as to believe there is "nothing to lose" by attacking Taiwan. US and Chinese diplomacy has largely been successful at maintaining the status quo and avoiding violent confrontations. Thus, false alarms can help create a crisis where none exists.

(8) Close Encounters: The Dangers of the Asia Pacific Strategic Competition

Countries friendly to the United States, or at least concerned about a threat from China, have been investing more in their security, with US encouragement and in some cases with substantial US funds. The Chinese response has, almost needless to say, been highly critical. But China has also stepped up its diplomatic and economic engagement with US allies in Asia, reflected especially in becoming the top trading partner of nearly all of them.

Philippines-China Confrontations

In mid-2024, US Secretary of State Antony Blinken and Secretary of Defense Lloyd Austin met with Philippines President Ferdinand Marcos Jr. They announced new US military funding of $500 million to boost the Philippines' external defense and help establish a military intelligence-sharing pact between the two nations. Confrontations were occurring quite regularly between heavily armed Chinese coast guard vessels and Philippine ships in a part of the South China Sea (SCS) that belongs to the Philippines but which China has claimed in recent years.[14] Each side accuses the other of reckless actions. The Chinese have amassed an armada of heavily armed coast guard vessels and other ships to block Filipino ships from supplying a sunken vessel on one shoal that symbolizes their claim. Two minor collisions have occurred. Close encounters in the air are also occurring—in March 2025, between an Australian surveillance jet and a Chinese jet, and between a Philippine patrol plane and a Chinese military aircraft. Both incidents drew angry exchanges between those governments and Beijing's foreign ministry.

The United States has no territorial claim in the SCS area, but it is a security partner of the Philippines, its former colony, and is engaged in joint air and sea patrols there. Warships from Japan and Europe began to participate in those exercises in 2025. The United States has indicated a number of times that it will come to the aid of the Philippines if it or its forces are attacked—for example, when President Biden, on October 25, 2024, invoked the 1951 security treaty with the Philippines and said the US commitment to its defense was "ironclad."[15] A Chinese foreign ministry spokesperson said the United States "no right to get involved in a problem between China and the Philippines."

A war of words has added to the tension. In November 2023, the Philippines withdrew from involvement in China's Belt and Road Initiative, citing funding delays on rail projects but clearly responding to armed incidents in the SCS.[16] By 2025, the Philippines leader was calling China a bully. Its defense secretary was denouncing China as "the greatest external threat" to his country, and warning China not to declare an air defense identification zone in the SCS.[17] Comments like that show how far relations with China have fallen.

US-Japan Security Cooperation

US-Japan strategic integration has been especially intense during the Biden years (see also Chapter 5). The US ambassador to Japan, Rahm Emanuel, said following talks between President Biden and then-Prime Minister Kishida Fumio that a stronger US partnership with Japan as well as with the Philippines intended to "isolate" China. "Isolate" here really means "contain." The characterization fit with a little noticed official Japanese statement that pinpointed China as a *hypothetical enemy* in US-Japan military exercises. As one scholar observed: "After the defeat in World War 2, the practice of labeling other countries as hypothetical enemies became a powerful taboo in Japan."[18] That is because Japan had previously applied that label to the United States, signaling the inevitability of war. The Japanese defense establishment's revival of the label demonstrated (according to this scholar) "the weakening of the hypothetical enemy taboo and the growing threat perceptions vis-à-vis China in the minds of Japanese defense planners. This development does not bode well for Sino-Japanese relations." Indeed it didn't, though high-level China-Japan diplomacy resumed in 2024 nevertheless.

Vietnam, the Indian Ocean, and the Pacific Islands

Vietnam has also been active in response to adverse developments with China, notwithstanding all the years of Chinese support of Vietnam during its war with the US in the 1960s and 1970s. Vietnam's war with China in 1979 and their dispute over territorial claims in the SCS changed all that. Vietnam moved to normalize relations with the United States even as it maintained ties with China. A Vietnamese coast guard vessel visited the Philippines for a joint exercise in 2024. And Vietnam did what China has been doing: expanding island outposts in the SCS that it controls by adding land, clearly in response to tensions between China and the Philippines.[19] But Vietnam's movement in the US direction may change after Trump's imposition of a 46-percent tariff on Vietnamese imports in 2025—a rate that, if implemented, would take a considerable bite out of Vietnam's GDP, which depends heavily on exports.

In 2024 and 2025, the US Navy was reportedly investigating sites in the Indian Ocean for base construction. The potential locations include Australia's Cocos Islands, Timor Leste, and Papua New Guinea for anticipated construction projects under the Pacific Deterrence Initiative. And the United States revived a diplomatic offensive in the Pacific islands as China stepped up the competition (see **Selection 9**). Washington opened embassies in the Solomons and other previously neglected Pacific Island states, promising them development and environmental assistance. None of this US activity would have occurred without a "China threat" to counter, as Denghua Zhang writes.[20]

China Defends Its Security Interests

Looking at US policy from China's perspective, it had to seem disturbingly inconsistent with Washington's professed intentions. On April 2, 2024, just prior to the summits with Japan and the Philippines, Biden had a telephone conversation with Xi Jinping that broke no new ground but did embrace an overall positive appraisal of the relationship. According to the Chinese readout of the conversation, Xi said relations had "stabilized"— the new watchword Chinese officials were using to characterize China-US relations— though important negative developments needed attention. Strategically, the "bottom line" should be "no conflict, no confrontation," he said.[21]

Did Beijing regard the latest US-Japan security arrangement as confrontational or stabilizing? The answer came from a number of high-level Chinese sources, all of which said that the United States and its allies were ganging up on China. Its foreign ministry issued a statement that said in part: "US-Japan relations should not target other countries, harm their interests or undermine regional peace and stability. China firmly opposes the Cold War mentality and small group politics. China firmly rejects anything that creates and drives up tensions and may undermine other countries' strategic security and interests." When Antony Blinken visited Beijing in late April, Foreign Minister Wang Yi told him: The US should not establish "exclusive small groupings, refrain from pressuring regional countries to take sides, stop deploying land-based intermediate-range missiles, stop undermining China's strategic security interests and stop undermining the hard-won peace and stability in the region."[22] Xi said the same thing: "China is committed to non-alliance, and the U.S. should not create small blocs. While each side can have its friends and partners, it should not target, oppose or harm the other."

The reference to "exclusive small groupings" is important. To Beijing, US-organized security coalitions that target China are more threatening than bilateral US security relationships such as the US-Japan alliance. The Quad group tops the list. When it met in fall 2024, US officials assured one and all that the Quad was not directed at China. But at a press briefing on September 23, 2024, China's foreign ministry spokesperson said:

> The Quad is identified as the premier regional grouping that plays a leading role in the US's Indo-Pacific strategy. It is a tool the US uses to contain China and perpetuate US hegemony. . . . Though the US claims that it does not target China, the first topic of the [Quad] summit is about China and China was made an issue throughout the event. . . . The US needs to get rid of its obsession with perpetuating its supremacy and containing China, stop using regional countries as its tool, stop glossing over the strategic intention behind all kinds of exclusive groupings, and act on its word that the revitalization of its alliances is not targeted at China . . . .[23]

Trilateral Diplomacy Resumes

The diplomatic side of China's reaction to US alliance politics has been mainly with Japan and South Korea. A leadership-level meeting took place on May 27, 2024 between Kishida, Chinese Premier Li Qiang, and South Korean President Yoon Suk-yeol. It was the first gathering of the three leaders since 2019. They agreed to regularize communications, seek a free-trade agreement, and address supply chain problems. These were aspirations, however; on key issues that divide Japan and South Korea from China—defense of Taiwan, the war in Ukraine, North Korea's missile tests—no agreements were reached.

The three countries' foreign ministers met on March 22, 2025, with substantially the same agenda—and outcome. There were pledges of cooperation, deeper ties, and support for the denuclearization of the Korean peninsula. Japan's foreign minister said, "it has become more important than ever to make efforts to overcome division and confrontation through dialogue and cooperation." The South Korean minister urged attention to the "shared responsibility" for Korea's stability, while China's foreign minister reminded everyone of the need to "sincerely reflect on history." Left unsaid, at least in public, was a common concern: the Trump administration's high tariffs on all three countries.[24]

Yet this meeting did have benefits for each party beyond face-to-face dialogue: for China, cutting into the US alliance system and helping prevent a decoupling of economies; for Japan, easing tensions with China and improving the trade environment; and for South Korea, getting Beijing's attention on the nuclear and missile issue with North Korea.

Will diplomatic engagement be consistent and effective enough to deflect security tensions brought about by territorial disputes and US security coalitions directed at China? Nicholas Burns, the former US Ambassador to China, wondered about the effectiveness of crisis management: "Can we [the US and China] have the kind of higher level connectivity so that if 24-year-olds collide in ships [they pilot] in the Spratlys or the Paracels or the Senkakus [or Diaoyudao, in the East China Sea], senior people can intervene and diffuse the crisis?"[25] The answer remains beyond reach.

(9) Cyber Hacking: Who's Doing it to Whom?

The *Washington Post* acquired a trove of leaked documents which, it said, showed the Chinese government "attempting large-scale, systematic cyber intrusions against foreign governments, companies and infrastructure—with hackers of one company [in Shanghai] claiming to be able to target users of Microsoft, Apple and Google." Chinese cyber hacking is by now not news, nor is it news that Chinese hacking operations are active in several countries besides the United States, including the United Kingdom, Taiwan, and Thailand. What is news is the role of private hacking-for-sale Chinese companies that compete with one another for government and state corporation contracts.[26] The leaked documents indicate that the Shanghai company probably had ties to China's intelligence services—a departure from the past, when hacking was mainly the responsibility of a unit of the People's Liberation Army.

Christopher A. Wray, the FBI director under Biden, said that Chinese hacking operations were now directed against the United States at "a scale greater than we'd seen before," larger than that of "every major nation combined." "In fact, if you took every single one of the FBI's cyberagents and intelligence analysts and focused them exclusively on the China threat, China's hackers would still outnumber FBI cyber personnel by at least 50 to one," he said. How he knows the number of Chinese hackers is beyond me. What we also do not know is the actual value of all the Chinese hacking, which in the past had mainly taken the form of economic espionage. In 2024, nine US telecommunications companies were hit with a cyberattack believed to have originated in China. But more recent attacks were on US government agencies. As 2025 began, Chinese cyberespionage was declared responsible for security breaches in the US Treasury Department's office in charge of international sanctions, many of which are directed at Chinese entities.

We also don't know about the hacking operations the United States and other governments are conducting against China, and how they compare in size and effectiveness with China's cyber operations. It's fair to assume the US and its partners are conducting them. The Chinese have reported US-backed hacking incidents on occasion. For example, in 2024 a national computer emergency response center in China claimed that in two incidents, US cyber attacks had led to the theft of "a large amount of trade secrets." The targets were said to be an advanced materials design and research unit and a large-scale high-tech company focused on intelligent energy and digital information. And in 2025, China's foreign ministry claimed: "At the ninth Asian Winter Games, the U.S. government conducted cyberattacks on the information systems of the Games and the critical information infrastructure in Heilongjiang [Province]."[27] China identified three hackers who had worked for the US National Security Agency.

(10) Chinese Opportunism and Western Reactiveness in the Pacific Islands

"Partner of Choice"

When we think of the South Pacific, pristine beaches, starry nights, and maybe the 1949 musical hit come first to mind. Now, something very different is going on: great-power competition, starkly revealed in the aftermath of three days of rioting in November 2021 in the capital city of the Solomon Islands, located about 1,000 miles from Australia's east coast. Two issues were apparently involved: a protest of the Solomons government's decision to switch diplomatic recognition from Taiwan to China, and anger over government corruption and neglect by people from the most densely populated and poorest of the several hundred islands that make up the Solomons. The demonstrations, which destroyed a good deal of property, much of it owned by ethnic Chinese, were put down, but in their wake, a secret document was leaked in 2022 that showed the Solomons government had agreed to China's takeover of police training that once was provided by Australia. The Solomons Prime Minister Manasseh Sogavare called China the "security partner of choice" (CNN, August 1, 2022). Chinese police could be used in case of further political unrest in the islands. China might also be able to use the Solomons as a stopover for military operations.

Revelation of the secret agreement rang alarm bells in Australia, New Zealand, Japan, and the United States, where officials worried about a Chinese base in the heart of the South Pacific. The Solomons prime minister said speculation about a Chinese base was an insult. The Solomons prime minister basically wanted to preserve his job from people protesting corruption and the decision to switch diplomatic recognition from Taiwan to China. Still, the prime minister was correct to insist that his country had the right to choose its partners, just as other Pacific Island states (PIs) such as Micronesia and Fiji have chosen to rely on the US and Australia for security.

Meeting the Needs of Pacific Islanders

The central issues for PIs are climate change, poverty, health care, and education. China has been forthcoming with development aid to Kiribati and Tonga, among others, but its capacity to meet the primary needs of the PIs remains to be seen. The eighteen members of the Pacific Islands Forum, a group that coordinates cooperation (see box below)—want to avoid alignment and reap whatever advantages may come from working with both the United States and China. Worries about aligning with China emerged in 2022 when Foreign Minister Wang Yi proposed a regional security pact, called the China-Pacific Island Countries Common Development Vision. It stated that China and the PIs will "strengthen exchanges and cooperation in the fields of traditional and non-traditional security," including "intermediate and high-level police training for Pacific Island countries through bilateral and multilateral means." The pact would also have granted China access to natural resources and marine mapping rights.[28] Ten Forum members rejected the idea, fearing undue Chinese influence.[29]

> ### MEMBERS OF PACIFIC ISLANDS FORUM
>
> Solomon Islands, Papua New Guinea, Federated States of Micronesia, Palau, Republic of Marshall Islands, Samoa, Nauru, Tuvalu, Vanuatu, Fiji, Kiribati, Tonga, Australia, New Zealand, New Caledonia, French Polynesia, Niue, Cook Islands

This rebuff to China by states that it sought to win over should be familiar to anyone who follows US foreign policy. A great power that uses aid to win political and military allegiance in rivalry with another great power doesn't always succeed, as weak states may effectively play both sides or decide not to play the game at all. For most PI states, granting too much access by China risks bringing the Cold War directly into the region. Pacific Islanders would rather have China and the United States, as well as Australia and Taiwan, address their real development needs than "work through their affiliated Pacific nations, which in turn creates tensions among those Pacific nations." Sione Tekiteki, a former official at the Pacific Islands Forum secretariat, made that comment and specifically said of the China-Taiwan rivalry: "It's only a big issue for us because everyone else talks about it and pulls in Pacific nations."[30]

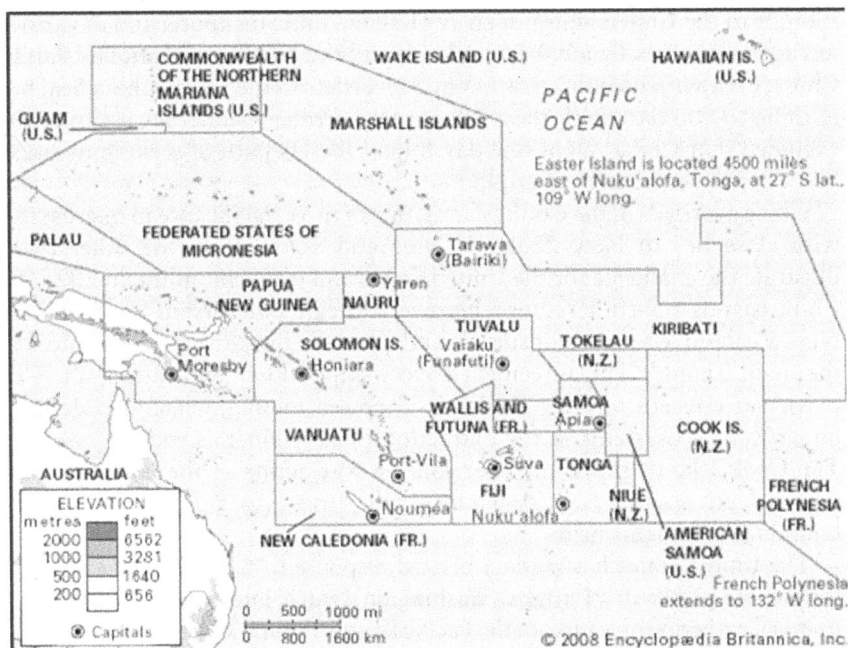

CHART 2.2 Members of the Pacific Islands Forum. *Source: Brittanica, "Pacific Islands," https://www.britannica.com/place/Pacific-islands.*

The US-China Competition

The primary US concern in the South and Western Pacific is strategic—that China might obtain bases or other access privileges that endanger long-standing US military primacy in the region. But so far, China has not acquired basing or deployment rights and may not actually be seeking them for fear of sparking a very negative response from most governments there, not to mention from Australia and New Zealand. China's interest in the region seems to be mainly economic (resources) and political (diplomatic recognition), in short.[31] We also must keep in mind the great distance of these islands from China, and the fact that the US military has long been deeply entrenched in what is now called the Indo-Pacific region, which stretches from Hawaii to India. A 2023 Congressional Research Service report noted that "the United States maintains and uses at least 66 significant defense sites" in the region.[32] Those sites, which range from bases to places for rotational deployments, are in countries that have security treaties with the United States, such as Japan, the Philippines, and South Korea; in security coalition countries, such as Australia; in states that are in "free association" with the US (Micronesia, the Marshall Islands, and Palau); in countries friendly to the United States, such as Thailand and Singapore; and in various territories, such as Guam, Wake Island, and the Northern Mariana Islands. China, even with its militarization of a few islets in the South China Sea, has nothing to compare with these US security arrangements. But it cannot be excluded that China might one day follow the US path of seeking overseas bases in the Pacific Islands group.

China's inroads in the Cook Islands, one of three Pacific Ocean microstates with close ties to New Zealand (Niue and Tokelau are the other two), illustrate the challenge for the United States and its Pacific allies. In 2025 the Cook Islands signed a "comprehensive strategic partnership" with China. New Zealand was not consulted, and protests broke out on Rarotonga, the main island.[33] The agreement covers shipbuilding, education, and—of particular concern to New Zealand—deep sea mining, which can damage underwater ecosystems in the extraction of key minerals such as cobalt.[34] The Cook Islands prime minister said he was acting in the country's best interests, but assured New Zealand that the "free association" that has long bound them remains firm.

The United States has made a belated response to China's emergence as a formidable player in PI affairs. Washington swung into action in 2022 at a triennial gathering of leaders of the Pacific Islands Forum. Vice President Kamala Harris offered economic assistance (on fisheries), announced the opening of a US Agency for International Development office, and said the Peace Corps would be returning to the region. Would US involvement last, and would it lead to a meaningful contribution to human development in the island states or to a knee-jerk military response focused on the supposed "China threat?" Good questions, since the Trump administration essentially ended USAID programs everywhere. A Solomon Islands journalist, Dorothy Wickham, offered some thoughtful advice to Americans. What the United States should learn from China's initiatives in the South Pacific, she wrote, is this: "You have got to show up. And the United States has not." Unless it does, "China will pick us off one by one with its promises of business projects and development aid."[35]

Australian and Taiwan Interests

Australia is very much part of the US-China competition. Historically, it has been the largest donor to the PIs by far (China now ranks second). Australia shares the US concern about China's strategic moves in the Pacific. Late in 2024, Australian Prime Minister Anthony Albanese announced agreements with the Solomon Islands, Nauru, and Papua New Guinea that put Australia back in the game. The agreement with the Solomons to assist its police forces is particularly important even though it does not match the level of the Solomons-China security cooperation agreement. Under Australia's treaty with Nauru, Nauru pledged not to enter into any security agreements without consulting Canberra. In exchange, Australia pledged $90 million in financial support and announced that Commonwealth Bank of Australia would offer its services in Nauru after another Australian bank departed. Nevertheless, Nauru shortly thereafter announced that it would switch diplomatic recognition from Taiwan to China. As for Papua New Guinea, Australia announced that it would fund the establishment of a National Rugby League team.[36]

Taiwan is courting the Marshall Islands, Tuvalu, and Palau, three PIs that recognize Taiwan as the Republic of China. The three are all members of the UN, unlike Taiwan. Lai Ching-te, Taiwan's president, visited those countries at the end of 2024. Taiwan is a "development partner" in the Pacific Islands Forum, giving it a voice (over China's objections) in that gathering.

(11) Trump on Taiwan

Too Far Away to Defend

Carefully managing the Taiwan issue may prove very difficult in the second Trump administration. As he has demonstrated in the past, financial gain and vindictiveness are hallmarks of Trump's approach to international relations, whether with friends or adversaries. When Trump first entered office in 2017, he bellowed that both Japan and China had ripped off the US in trade relations, setting the stage for the imposition of high tariffs on their exports. So when he was asked in an interview with *Bloomberg News* in June 2025 what his Taiwan policy would be, his thoughts were not about defending the island, which Republicans in Congress consider a high priority, but this: "They did take about 100% of our chip business. I think, Taiwan should pay us for defense. You know, we're no different than an insurance company. Taiwan doesn't give us anything. Taiwan is 9,500 miles away. It's 68 miles away from China." Taiwan's advanced semiconductor industry is the great prize for China, Trump said—"the apple of Xi's eye," Trump kept saying, therefore something the Chinese want to acquire without bombing. The main point is that Taiwan is too far away to defend, Trump seemed to say. He then repeated his upset:

> They took almost 100% of our chip industry, I give them credit. That's because stupid people were running the country. We should have never let that happen. Now we're giving them billions of dollars to build new chips in our country, and then they're going to take that too, in other words, they'll build it but then they'll bring it back to their country.[37]

Will Trump abandon Taiwan? He would face heavy Republican pressure to adhere at least to strategic ambiguity, which was US policy in his first administration. But that was then. Taiwan officials recall that when Russia invaded Ukraine, they effectively argued that, like Europe, their country was on the front line in the fight to preserve democracy. Ukraine's defeat, it was said in Taiwan—and in the US Congress too—would embolden China to attack Taiwan, no matter what Xi Jinping said. In 2025, with Trump abandoning Biden's strong support of Ukraine, Taiwan officials think the island's security is again tenuous. If the United States can so easily toss aside its commitments to Ukraine, it can do the same to Taiwan—or so the thinking goes. And if Trump can treat Ukraine as nothing more than a resource provider in a big minerals deal with Russia, so might Taiwan be treated as part of a major business transaction with China. Defense of democracy, Taiwan leaders now believe, is no longer a high US priority.

The Art of the Deal

Perhaps Trump was merely following his usual practice of indirectly threatening a partner in order to get a better deal. Taiwan got the message: It must again demonstrate its value to the United States—which it did by promising higher defense spending (i.e., more orders for US arms) and getting TSMC's agreement, in spite of Trump's pessimism, to invest in a huge semiconductor chip-making facility in the United States.[38] Even so, US officials have not sounded encouraging. Taiwan is "very important" to the United States, but it is not an "existential interest," said Elbridge Colby, Trump's nominee for undersecretary of defense for policy in the Pentagon, told a Senate confirmation hearing in March 2025. He also said Taiwan's defense spending "should be more like 10 percent" of gross domestic product. That figure is quadruple the 2.45 percent Taiwan currently allocates. And in April 2025, Taiwan was hit with a 32-percent tariff by Trump, based on its trade surplus with the US of around $70 billion. Taiwan's legislature decried the tariffs as "deeply unreasonable" and "highly regrettable." Taiwan said it would try to negotiate lower tariffs; in the meantime it would commit substantial funds to help businesses hurt by the tariffs.

Hearing such lukewarm support from Washington, the Lai Ching-te administration in Taiwan might want to avoid doing anything to provoke China, such as with references to Taiwan's sovereignty. In an "America First" administration, US reliability on security matters is far from certain.

(12) Trump's Reverse-Nixon Strategy

The Trump administration's extraordinary U-turn on policy toward Russia in the third year of Russia's war on Ukraine may have had China in mind as much as Europe. The strategy Trump and Secretary of State Marco Rubio seemed to be pursuing was a reverse of President Richard Nixon's in 1970–1971: align with Russia to confront China. Trump intimated as much when he made an offhand comment on Fox News that "as a student of history—which I am, and I've watched it all—the first thing you learn is you don't want Russia and China to get together." Rubio had earlier said the administration hoped that "peeling them [the Russians] off of a relationship with the Chinese" might be possible. "I also don't think having China and Russia at each other's neck is good for global stability because they're both nuclear powers, but I do think we're in a situation now where the Russians have become increasingly dependent on the Chinese and that's not a good outcome either if you think about it."[39]

Strengthening Russia would surely be at the expense of Ukraine's and Europe's security. That conclusion was affirmed when a secret Pentagon strategic guidance memo was leaked in March 2025 that said preparing for a Chinese invasion of Taiwan would be the primary US concern. "China is the Department's sole pacing threat, and denial of a Chinese *fait accompli* seizure of Taiwan—while simultaneously defending the U.S. homeland is the Department's sole pacing scenario," the memo said.[40] As for the rest of the world, the memo said the US will "assume risk in other theaters," meaning the Middle East, Europe, and elsewhere in Asia. What makes this strategic planning so questionable is that at no time since Russia's invasion of Ukraine in 2022 has China shown any preparation for invading Taiwan, though it has conducted harassing maneuvers around the island to counter any move toward independence by Taiwan.

In light of the numerous expressions of unbreakable strategic partnership exchanged between Vladimir Putin and Xi Jinping since 2022, as discussed in Chapter 3, the notion that Russia could be weaned away from China seemed far-fetched and with high risks if the strategy failed.

(13) Trump's Budget Cuts: A Glaring Contradiction

If you're a Chinese analyst tuned in to the Trump administration's budget cuts demanded by Elon Musk's Department of Government Efficiency, you have to be pretty happy. Among the many cuts are those to programs that compete with Chinese activities or investigate Chinese projects directed at the US: the US Agency for International Development, the Office of Net Assessment in the Pentagon (which evaluates future threats), Radio Free Asia (which calls attention to human rights violations), and the Cyber Safety Review Board (which investigates foreign penetration of US agencies). The contradiction is glaring, one observer noted, between the administration's focus on the China threat and its undermining of key programs designed to reduce the threat. Michael J. Green, chief executive of the United States Study Center at the University of Sydney in Australia, said: "When we reveal human rights abuses or Chinese misinformation, it's another form of competition with China. And getting rid of it only creates a vacuum that Beijing is going to try to fill. And we are already seeing that happening." A former career CIA officer said the cuts were self-defeating: "We affirm Chinese beliefs that they are ascendant, and that our decline is accelerating."[41]

Documents

Document 1. The Biden-Harris National Security Strategy Paper (2022) on China
(*Source:* The White House, *National Security Strategy*, October 2022, https://bidenwhitehouse.archives.gov/wp-content/uploads/2022/10/Biden-Harris-Administrations-National-Security-Strategy-10.2022.pdf)

The PRC [People's Republic of China] is the only competitor with both the intent to reshape the international order and, increasingly, the economic, diplomatic, military, and technological power to do it. Beijing has ambitions to create an enhanced sphere of influence in the Indo-Pacific and to become the world's leading power. It is using its technological capacity and increasing influence over international institutions to create more permissive conditions for its own authoritarian model, and to mold global technology use and norms to privilege its interests and values. Beijing frequently uses its economic power to coerce countries. It benefits from the openness of the international economy while limiting access to its domestic market, and it seeks to make the world more dependent on the PRC while reducing its own dependence on the world. The PRC is also investing in a military that is rapidly modernizing, increasingly capable in the Indo-Pacific, and growing in strength and reach globally—all while seeking to erode U.S. alliances in the region and around the world.

At the same time, the PRC is also central to the global economy and has a significant impact on shared challenges, particularly climate change and global public health. It is possible for the United States and the PRC to coexist peacefully, and share in and contribute to human progress together.

Our strategy toward the PRC is threefold: 1) to invest in the foundations of our strength at home –our competitiveness, our innovation, our resilience, our democracy, 2) to align our efforts with our network of allies and partners, acting with common purpose and in common cause, and 3) compete responsibly with the PRC to defend our interests and build our vision for the future. The first two elements—invest and align—are described in the previous section and are essential to out-competing the PRC in the technological, economic, political, military, intelligence, and global governance domains.

Competition with the PRC is most pronounced in the Indo-Pacific, but it is also increasingly global. Around the world, the contest to write the rules of the road and shape the relationships that govern global affairs is playing out in every region and across economics, technology, diplomacy, development, security, and global governance. In the competition with the PRC, as in other arenas, it is clear that the next ten years will be the decisive decade. We stand now at the inflection point, where the choices we make and the priorities we pursue today will set us on a course that determines our competitive position long into the future. . . .

We will hold Beijing accountable for abuses—genocide and crimes against humanity in Xinjiang, human rights violations in Tibet, and the dismantling of Hong Kong's autonomy and freedoms—even as it seeks to pressure countries and communities into silence. We will continue prioritizing investments in a combat credible military that deters aggression against our allies and partners in the region, and can help those allies and partners defend themselves.

We have an abiding interest in maintaining peace and stability across the Taiwan Strait, which is critical to regional and global security and prosperity and a matter of international concern and attention. We oppose any unilateral changes to the status quo from either side, and do not support Taiwan independence. We remain committed to our one China policy, which is guided by the Taiwan Relations Act, the Three Joint communiques, and the Six Assurances. And we will uphold our commitments under the Taiwan Relations Act to support Taiwan's self-defense and to maintain our capacity to resist any resort to force or coercion against Taiwan. . . .

While we compete vigorously, we will manage the competition responsibly. We will seek greater strategic stability through measures that reduce the risk of unintended military escalation, enhance crisis communications, build mutual transparency, and ultimately engage Beijing on more formal arms control efforts. We will always be willing to work with the PRC where our interests align. We can't let the disagreements that divide us stop us from moving forward on the priorities that demand that we work together, for the good of our people and for the good of the world. That includes on climate, pandemic threats, nonproliferation, countering illicit and illegal narcotics, the global food crisis, and macroeconomic issues. In short, we'll engage constructively with the PRC wherever we can, not as a favor to us or anyone else, and never in exchange for walking away from our principles, but because working together to solve great challenges is what the world expects from great powers, and because it's directly in our interest. No country should withhold progress on existential transnational issues like the climate crisis because of bilateral differences.

Document 2. The 1979 Taiwan Relations Act
Declares that peace and stability in the [Taiwan] area are in the political, security, and economic interests of the United States, and are matters of international concern. States that the United States decision to establish diplomatic relations with the People's Republic of China rests upon the expectation that the future of Taiwan will be determined by peaceful means and that any effort to determine the future of Taiwan by other than peaceful means, including by boycotts or embargoes is considered a threat to the peace and security of the Western Pacific area and of grave concern to the United States.

Document 3. Three Views of How US Policy on Taiwan Should Change
(*Background*: The Quincy Institute is a think tank whose website describes it as promoting "ideas that move U.S. foreign policy away from endless war, toward military restraint and diplomacy in the pursuit of international peace." Ryan Hass is a foreign policy analyst and director of the China center at the Brookings Institution in Washington, DC. Jude Blanchette is a China specialist at the RAND Corporation in Santa Monica, California. Matt Pottinger is a visiting fellow at the Hoover Institution and a former US deputy national security advisor. Mike Gallagher is a former four-term Republican Congressman from Wisconsin.)

Quincy Institute for Responsible Statecraft: Credible Assurances

"Acknowledging the high stakes involved, both Washington and Beijing have repeatedly stated their desire to prevent the relationship from veering into a severe crisis or conflict, and to add more stability to their interactions. One major way of doing this is for each side to offer credible assurances that it will not deliberately or inadvertently threaten the most vital interests of the other. The key words here are "credible," meaning believable and durable, and "most vital," meaning those interests that directly affect the security and well-being of the nation and its governing system.

Achieving this requires each nation to match its formal statements clearly and reliably with its actual behavior—in other words, to avoid hypocrisy—with regard to what each side regards as its vital interests, and to do so consistently over time. This in turn requires both sides reaching a mutual understanding of what their vital interests are, the meaningful assurances regarding them that each desires, and what would constitute violations of those assurances and, hence, threats to the concerned party's vital interests."[42]

Ryan Hass and Jude Blanchette: Multipart Deterrence

"Deterrence requires an extensive toolkit, including diplomatic patience, nuance, surprise, brinkmanship, and also reassurance and credibility. It is this holistic view of deterrence that is needed in Washington today. Key features of a more effective strategy include a measured U.S. approach to diplomacy that avoids provocative political stunts and a renewed effort to build a deeper, wider, and stronger coalition of countries to support Taiwan's continued security and prosperity. To preserve the peace in Asia, Washington must adopt a more comprehensive vision of deterrence that not only prevents an outright invasion or blockade, but also ensures that Taiwan's economy, democracy, and people can flourish.... The purpose of Washington's strategy in the Taiwan Strait is to incentivize behavior that serves U.S. interests while disincentivizing actions that threaten them. Hard power is a critical element of the United States' efforts to uphold peace and stability in the Taiwan Strait. It is a variable in the equation, however, and not the solution. To protect its interests, U.S. leaders must become more adept at combining efforts to bolster military capabilities with clarity in their strategic objectives, strength in their coalitions, solid coordination with Taiwan, and a sharper comprehension of the psychology of decision-makers in Beijing. The United States has protected its interest in peace and stability in the Taiwan Strait for nearly 45 years. It has to up its game to continue doing so for the next 45."[43]

Matt Pottinger and Mike Gallagher: Invest More in Taiwan's Defense

"Xi [Jinping] is preparing his country for a war over Taiwan. On its current trajectory, the United States risks failing to deter that war, one that could kill tens of thousands of U.S. service members, inflict trillions of dollars in economic damage, and bring about the end of the global order as we know it. The only path to avoid this future is for Washington to immediately build and surge enough hard power to deny Xi a successful invasion of Taiwan.... Instead of spending about three percent of GDP on defense, Washington should spend four or even five percent, a level that would still be at the low end of Cold War spending. For near-term deterrence in the Taiwan Strait, it should spend an additional $20 billion per year for the next five years, the rough amount needed to surge and disperse sufficient combat power in Asia. Ideally, this money would be held in a dedicated "deterrence fund" overseen by the secretary of defense, who would award resources to projects that best align with the defense of Taiwan."[44]

3

China's Relations with Russia and Europe

Introduction

China is the European Union's (EU) second-most important trade partner after the United States, with a total trade in 2024 valued at around $830 billion. The EU's trade deficit with China was about $346 billion. (Total EU-US trade in 2024 was over $976 billion, with an EU trade surplus of $235 billion.) In recent years, the twenty-seven members of the EU have debated one critical issue concerning relations with China: how to navigate between a China policy that is independent of the United States and takes into account the desire for strong trade and investment ties with China, on one hand, and on the other, deep concern about China's commercial practices, repression of human rights, and support of Russia in the Ukraine war. Finding common ground has been difficult, since Europeans are divided about how much to sacrifice on "European values" for the sake of doing business with China. The Chinese have used Europe's dependence on China and different views among EU members to avoid being penalized for policies that offend some members of the EU (**Selections 3 and 4**). Xi Jinping typically appeals to Europe for partnership by emphasizing economic globalization and "multipolarity," meaning European independence of the United States (**Document 2**). That appeal became even stronger in April 2025 when President Trump imposed high tariffs on the EU as well as on China, possibly providing an incentive for them to resolve their differences (**Selection 8**).

China's relations with Russia are said to rest on non-alliance, strategic coordination, and consensus on international affairs, most importantly on the war in Ukraine and policies to deal with the United States. Beijing has not altered its stance in favor of Russian policy in the war despite asserting support for Ukraine's independence (**Selection 1**). There are, however, important differences in their foreign policy perspectives, such as the meaning of "no limits" to their partnership (**Selections 1 and 2; Document 1**). There are limits, but the United States did not seek to take advantage of them until Donald Trump's return to the White House in 2025. His reset of relations with Russia, partly in order to focus on China, only seemed to strengthen Sino-Russian declarations of "strategic partnership." The reset also reinvigorated China's diplomacy in Europe around the ideas of "multipolarity" and opposition to (US) "unilateralism" (**Selection 7**). So far, as **Selections 5 and 6** indicate, China's navigation between Russia and Europe has largely succeeded with Russia and only partly with the EU. But changing global trade conditions brought on by Trump's tariff war could change China-EU relations very quickly.

(1) China-Russia Relations on the Eve of War in Ukraine

"No Limits" Has Limits

In the war in Ukraine, the China-Russia relationship is a wildcard. The notion persists, going back to the Putin-Xi meeting in Beijing just before Putin launched his war on Ukraine in February 2022, that (as they declared) their "strategic cooperation partnership" has "no limits." In fact, China is Russia's most important partner, but within certain limits. On one hand, China is a major purchaser of Russian oil and is one of Russia's key trade partners overall, though China had a staggering trade surplus of nearly $1 trillion in 2024. Russia and China continue to conduct joint military exercises to demonstrate their solidarity as strategic partners. Xi Jinping and other top Chinese officials have unfailingly supported Russia's argument that NATO is responsible for the war in Ukraine. They say nothing about Putin's war crimes. Chinese leaders may believe that a Russian defeat would leave China alone against Western pressure, whereas a Russian victory of some sort would strengthen Beijing's diplomacy, especially among developing countries. Some observers also speculate that China's ambition to reunify with Taiwan would be fed by a Russian victory, though I dispute that (see **Selection 5**).

On the other hand, the limits to the partnership are significant, though we should not go so far as China's ambassador to the European Union, Fu Cong, who stated (in 2023, and with a European audience evidently in mind) that "'No limit' is nothing but rhetoric."[1] One limit is that China has never condoned Russian territorial seizures from Ukraine, and to the contrary has more than once indirectly criticized Russia by condemning attacks on independent countries. Although China supported Russia's interventions in Kazakhstan and Belarus to quell potential regime changes, it did not support Russia's seizure of Crimea from Ukraine in 2014. Second, major Chinese technology firms and banks have been reluctant to challenge US sanctions on Russia for fear of being sanctioned themselves. Thus, Russia's apparent inability to get a loan from China. "Negotiations with Chinese partners have been going on for a long time. So far there is no decision," said Russia's finance minister. The key stumbling block apparently is the risk factor. Chinese banks don't want to get caught up in Western sanctions if they advance loans to Russia. Third, China claims it has never supplied Russia with finished weapons, though various reports indicate that China has sent Russia drones, so-called nonlethal military assistance such as spare parts and equipment, and semiconductor chips that could have military applications.

Behind the scenes, we know that China's alignment with Russia in the war was debated, at least outside the circle of top leaders. A large segment of Chinese public and scholarly opinion was critical of the government's support of Russia's invasion. As the historian Cheng Yawen described it, "Many Chinese people believed that China had failed to 'stand on the side of justice' and against 'the mainstream of human civilization' by not opposing Russia." But Cheng was among those arguing that such an alignment would have been calamitous for China. It would have risked turning both the US and Russia against China. Strategic self-interest, in short, was more important to China than the principle of supporting an independent country under attack.[2]

A Marriage of Convenience

In around forty meetings between Xi and Putin, the China-Russia relationship has consistently been described in the most exalted terms. They're "dear friends," their relations are "the best in history," they are "a model of interstate cooperation in the 21st century." Aside from their trade, which has risen substantially every year, joint military maneuvers have become a regular event. They are aligned with one another in viewing the United States as their principal opponent and chief obstacle to the achievement of their respective aims in Asia and Europe. But theirs is a marriage of convenience, not a security alliance.

China and Russia are divided on many issues, including a history of conflicting national interests and ideological differences, unresolved territorial claims, and the large (and growing) gap between them in economy and technology. While US analyses typically lump China and Russia together as threats to US national security, they are actually far apart in their international economic relations. Unlike Russia, China has taken full advantage of globalization—in everything from contributions to UN peacekeeping and tourism to scholarly and scientific exchanges and overseas investments, notably with the United States, the EU, and the Global South. Thomas Christensen reports on

> a former Chinese diplomat stationed in Russia, Shi Ze, who summed up the difference between Moscow and Beijing this way: "China and Russia have different attitudes. Russia wants to break the current international order....Russia thinks it is the victim of the current international system, in which its economy and its society do not develop. But China benefits from the current international system. We want to improve and modify it, not to break it."[3]

While Russia relies heavily on military power to impose its will in its near abroad, China mainly projects its influence through soft power: the Belt-and-Road Initiative, Confucius Institutes, sporting events, radio and television programming, and money-backed public diplomacy.

(2) China Between Russia and the US in the Ukraine War

US Concerns and China's Response

Chinese military aid to Russia became a matter of US concern soon after the Russian invasion of Ukraine began. In February 2022, Secretary of State Antony J. Blinken indicated that he had evidence that Beijing was "considering providing lethal support to Russia in its aggression against Ukraine." Blinken said he warned Wang Yi, China's top foreign policy official, that there would be serious consequences were that to occur. It now appears that Blinken's warning was based on US intelligence intercepts of *Russian* communications in which the *expectation* was raised about receiving Chinese weapons in covert shipments.[4] Other US officials (unnamed) disputed that report: "We have not seen evidence," said one, "that China has transferred weapons or provided lethal assistance to Russia. But we remain concerned and are continuing to monitor closely." And President Biden himself was unconvinced, saying on March 24, 2023: "I've been hearing now for the past three months about China's going to provide significant weapons to Russia. They haven't yet—doesn't mean they won't—but they haven't yet."

The Chinese response to these warnings has been unequivocal: "It's the U.S., and not China, that has been incessantly supplying weapons to the battlefield, and the U.S. is not qualified to issue any orders to China," the foreign ministry spokesman said in late February 2023.[5] Chinese military aid to Russia has never been mentioned in any of the final statements following meetings between Russian and Chinese leaders. Indeed, "no limits" was not repeated when Putin and Xi met in March 2023. Their final statement was chock-full of laudatory statements about Sino-Russian peace, friendship, and mutual support. But Ukraine was barely mentioned.

Russia gave its support to China's initial peace plan for the war, which heavily favored Russian security interests. The Chinese foreign ministry's text of the March 2023 statement said: "Resolving the Ukraine crisis requires respecting every country's just security concerns and preventing [its] becoming a confrontation between camps and throwing fire on oil. Both sides emphasized that responsible dialogue is the best path to steadily resolving problems." But again, nothing was said about upgrading their military cooperation, much less suggesting that China and Russia were now in a security alliance.

The evident US strategy was to use warnings to China as a means of deterring weapons shipments. But China's restraint may have been due less to US warnings than to self-interest: Why become party to a war in which China has no direct security interests, and which would risk coming under US trade sanctions and other pressures from US allies? In a word, relations with the United States and allies such as Japan, Australia, and NATO are already very bad; there's no compelling reason to worsen them. Still, relations *were* worsening. Nor were US pressures the only issue. Britain told Chinese diplomats that good relations depended on China stopping its military aid to Russia. The European Union just then was considering imposing sanctions on Chinese companies that were supplying Russia with dual-use goods, such as microchips for missile guidance systems. China's response contained the usual implicit threat, this from a foreign ministry spokesman: "If the report you cited is true, the EU move will erode mutual trust and cooperation with China and sharpen division and confrontation in the world, which is extremely dangerous. We call on the EU not to take that wrong course. Otherwise, China will take resolute measures to safeguard our legitimate and lawful rights and interests."

(3) The Evolution of Europe's View of China (2022–2023)

In the short space of a few decades, Europe in Chinese eyes has gone from being a "pole" in a multipolar world to being a major target of China's attention. Some of the same issues that plague the relationship remain from the early 2000s, such as China's human rights policies and a European arms embargo. But now China's economic diplomacy is at the center of Beijing's approach to Europe.

Watching China Watching Europe

David Shambaugh, writing in 2007 in one of the first major works on China-Europe relations, noted that

> China's Europe Watchers are almost uniformly upbeat and optimistic. They praise EU policy as being enlightened and farsighted . . . and they take great satisfaction in the China–EU "comprehensive strategic partnership" (proclaimed in 2003). Nonetheless . . . Chinese analysts are constantly looking for fault lines across the Atlantic, which can possibly be exploited by China. . . . Some see the US and EU trying to collectively manipulate or pressure China—for example, on questions of human rights, trade policy, political liberalization, and civil society development.[6]

Shift to more recent years and we find that China's often clumsy and abrasive diplomacy, carried out by "wolf warrior" diplomats; the Xinjiang genocide; and Beijing's support of Putin's war on Ukraine have to some extent poisoned the well. EU governments have become wary of China's economic power. They finally abandoned the strategy of "change through trade"—that is, viewing trade as an instrument for liberalizing China's politics and mellowing its diplomacy. The EU rejected Huawei's 5G technology on security grounds, sharply criticized China's human rights policies, and decided not to ratify a Comprehensive Agreement on Investment that had been concluded in December 2020. US pressure on the EU certainly played a part. Chinese efforts to punish European intellectuals and academic institutions that criticized Beijing's repression backfired as the EU sanctioned Chinese officials in Xinjiang. Chinese Europe-watchers decried the way "European values" had taken precedence over business interests, notably in Germany. They cited, for example, German concerns that its technology, including technology acquired through Chinese takeovers of German firms, might be used in weapons development.

Money Talks, But Autos Take Center Stage

But all that was in the Angela Merkel era that ran from 2005 to 2021. Once she stepped down as chancellor, money began talking loudly again. Chinese investors bought up thirty-five German firms; and European companies continued to invest heavily in China. European political leaders again flocked to China in the post-Covid period in search of deals. Neither China's human rights practices nor its backing of Russia in Ukraine were allowed to damage trade and investment ties—a development contrary to the view of some observers that the EU would significantly toughen its China policy.[7]

But a new problem entered the picture: Chinese auto competition and the possibility of a trade war between China and the European Union. The overarching challenge for European multinationals doing business with China was this: How to deal with Chinese-subsidized imports, especially electric vehicles (EVs), that were outcompeting European products as China surged to the lead in European and world markets, not just in EVs but also solar panels. China's EVs, which accounted for about 11 percent of the EV market in Europe in 2024, are priced far too low, say Europeans, threatening their industry and many of the nearly 14 million people it employs. Some European countries have again embedded their tariff policy in political concerns about China. France has argued that China's human rights record—specifically, its repression of the Uyghurs—should be taken into account, and Denmark's prime minister has said: "We cannot continue a situation where China helps Russia in a war . . . in Europe, without consequences. They have to be held responsible for their activities."

Germany's View

Germany is the biggest player in this drama, and it opposes the tariffs—as do the major German car manufacturers. In their view, higher tariffs will only hurt the industry more, since China would retaliate with high tariffs on imports of Volkswagens and other autos. Those sales accounted for about a third of total European car sales in China. Volkswagen alone produced 3.2 million vehicles in China in 2022. Thus, VW, Mercedes, BMW, and Porsche are caught in a bind: Either put their robust sales in China in jeopardy or (as VW has said) consider shutting down some of its factories in Germany.

Behind the German view is an unwillingness to directly confront China on either human rights or trade. In 2023, when an EU-China "dialogue" on human rights was set to resume—much to the displeasure of human rights groups—Chancellor Olaf Scholz led the way in softening the EU's approach. He rejected human rights sanctions on China even as he said that Germany rejects "hegemonic Chinese dominance." On trade, Scholz vowed to reduce "risky [trade] dependencies" with China and "insist on reciprocity" when it comes to intellectual property rights and market access. But he made clear that Germany would not decouple its economy from China or embrace trade protectionism as the Americans seemed to be doing.[8]

(4) EU-China Trade Politics

The Tariff Debate Ends

After months of debate and an investigation within the EU, the vote to raise tariffs on Chinese autos passed in October 2024. The new tariffs, which come on top of existing import duties of 10 percent, vary based on the amount of subsidies each foreign automaker in China received, starting at 7.8 percent for Tesla and going up to 35.3 percent for SAIC Motor of Shanghai. (The US and Canada have imposed 100 percent tariffs on Chinese EVs.) The tariffs are in effect for five years. Reflecting disagreement about how to confront China's competition, but also a consensus that China unfairly subsidizes its auto exports, ten countries voted for the higher tariffs (including France and Italy), five voted against (led by Germany), and twelve abstained. One observer commented that the vote sent "a signal that there's an emerging consensus in Europe that stronger pushback against China on the economic front is needed." Both Beijing and the EU agreed to continue negotiations, reflecting a common desire not to damage their huge commercial relationship more than necessary.

It remains to be seen whether China will retaliate with tariffs on EU imports, which include autos. One Chinese official vowed that China would "take all measures to firmly safeguard the interests of Chinese companies." When the EU investigated Chinese marketing practices, China's commerce minister warned that China might have to rethink its investments, specifically in Italy, in hopes that Italy would vote against continuing the tariffs. Beijing rejected the argument that it was subsidizing EV exports, saying its pricing reflected a tight global supply chain and the help EVs were giving to Europe's green economy. In November 2024, China brought a formal complaint before the World Trade Organization's dispute settlement mechanism, contending that the EU tariffs constituted trade protectionism.

The US Takes a Different Position

The United States is also involved in a running dispute over Chinese autos, but in the US case, the chief concern is said to be national security. The Commerce Department published a proposed rule in September 2024 to ban imports of Chinese and Russian vehicles, as well as key hardware and software components, that assertedly could be used to spy on Americans or potentially even take control of their cars. "Cars today have cameras, microphones, GPS tracking, and other technologies connected to the internet," Secretary of Commerce Gina Raimondo said. "It doesn't take much imagination to understand how a foreign adversary with access to this information could pose a serious risk to both our national security and the privacy of U.S. citizens." The Chinese vigorously protested this "generalization of the concept of national security." One wonders if "national security" was a pretext for simply reducing Chinese auto imports.

There is a minority view within the foreign policy establishment. The former US treasury secretary, Henry M. Paulsen, Jr., warned that US efforts to isolate China would backfire:

> Although many countries share Washington's antipathy to China's policies, practices, and conduct, no country is emulating Washington's

playbook for addressing these concerns. It is true that nearly every major U.S. partner is tightening up its export controls on sensitive technologies, scrutinizing and often blocking Chinese investments, and calling out Beijing's coercive economic policies and military pressure. But even Washington's closest strategic partners are not prepared to confront, attempt to contain, or economically de-integrate China as broadly as the United States is.[9]

Trump's Election Changes the Landscape

The second Trump administration's dramatic alignment with Russia on the Ukraine war, and its imposition of high tariffs on around ninety countries, alienated traditional allies in Europe and Asia. Trump made his distrust of Europe very plain, saying at his first cabinet meeting: "The EU was formed in order to screw the US, that's the purpose of it. And they've done a good job of it. But now I'm president." He dismissed the idea that the EU could retaliate against his tariffs. Trump's cabinet was equally if not more disdainful. In late March 2025, the editor-in-chief of *The Atlantic* was inadvertently included in a top-secret chat about Middle East war plans on the app Signal. In the conversation, Vice President JD Vance said: "I just hate bailing out the Europeans again." "I fully share your loathing of European freeloading," said Pete Hegseth, the secretary of defense. "It's PATHETIC." More than a security breach, the conversation showed how purely transactional US policy on Europe had become and how unappreciative US officials were of European contributions to defense, trade, and democratic values.[10]

US hostility toward the EU could bring Europe's understanding of multipolarity closer to China's, where the emphasis is on fighting "hegemony," acting independently, and working toward a new and more equal world order—all translating to distancing Europe from the United States. At the least, Europe may be more open than ever to improved relations with China, itself subject to Trump's tariff increases. For example, China and the EU may seek to revive the idea of a comprehensive investment agreement.[11] Beijing's support of Trump's one-sided plan for a settlement of the Ukraine war, rejected by Ukraine and widely criticized within the NATO membership as an imposed peace, may not pose as much of an obstacle to EU-China relations as it previously did.

(5) China's Wartime Balancing Act in 2024

Putin the Supplicant

Xi Jinping's balancing act with Russia and the West took on a new challenge with Vladimir Putin's arrival in Beijing on May 16, 2024. Once again Xi had to demonstrate loyalty to Russia in its war in Ukraine while also showing sensitivity to European commercial interests and US pressure on China to limit its military support of Putin's war. At least on the surface, Xi came through for Putin: He promised to expand all manner of China-Russia ties—fully supporting the "comprehensive strategic partnership," increasing "strategic coordination," and supporting Russia's "special military operation" (not *war*) in Ukraine. The joint statement condemned US "dual containment" of China and Russia. It gave no indication of differences on either global strategy or specific issues. Once again there was no mention of "no limits" to the partnership.

Too much attention has been paid to "no limits" and not enough to the upper hand Xi has maintained with Putin. In a word, Russia needs China far more than the reverse. The Chinese determine how much and what kind of assistance to provide to Russia, whether as a customer or an exporter. So far, China has stepped up, though not to the extent of challenging US and European sanctions. Alexander Gabuev at the Carnegie Russia Eurasia Center underscored the extent of Russian dependence on China:

> China has emerged as Russia's single most important partner, providing a lifeline not only for Mr. Putin's war machine but also for the entire embattled economy.... Before the war, Russia's trade with the European Union was double that with China; now it's less than half. The Chinese yuan, not the dollar or the euro, is now the main currency used for trade between the two countries, making it the most traded currency on the Moscow stock exchange and the go-to instrument for savings.[12]

As for military aid to Russia, China is again the key provider. As the *New York Times* reported: "Last year [2023], some 89 percent of the 'high-priority' imports necessary for Russian weapons production came from China, according to a customs data analysis by Nathaniel Sher, a researcher at the Carnegie Endowment for International Peace. Those include everything from machine tools used to build military equipment to optical devices, electronic sensors and telecommunications gear, the analysis found." US and European Union (EU) efforts to get Beijing to cut back on dual-use items that support Russia's military industry have gone nowhere. There is no evidence that these Chinese dual-use exports have abated since that report.

Likewise on getting Xi to persuade Putin to end the war in Ukraine. Xi has been able to use the EU's dependence on Chinese trade and investment to nod yes on peace and do nothing to promote it. China's line on the war has not changed since the war's start: calls for a peace settlement, defense of the principle of respect for territorial integrity (a nod to Ukraine), support of a country's legitimate security interests (a nod to Russia), and willingness to take part in a peace conference when both sides agree. These are evasions, not positive interventions, as China's leadership clearly believes the Ukraine war has more benefits than costs.

China Presents a Peace Plan with Brazil

China's Foreign Minister Wang Yi, speaking at a meeting of the BRICS foreign ministers late in 2024, said: "On the Ukraine issue, we must insist on preventing the spillover of conflict, avoiding the escalation of warfare, and preventing any party from fueling the fire. The crisis should be resolved through dialogue and negotiation. Brazil and China jointly issued the 'Six-Point Consensus,' which has received positive responses from more than 100 countries to varying degrees."[13] The Ukraine delegation at the UN circulated its strong disapproval of China's latest peace plan. "China wants to work behind the scenes at the United Nations to enlist international support for an agreement to end the war in Ukraine on terms favorable to Russia," according to a Ukrainian government document. Ukrainian officials were alarmed by a proposal that again amounted to legitimizing Russian "security interests."

(6) France Charts Its Own Course on China, But the EU Commissioner Disagrees

Not Followers

French President Emmanuel Macron and European Commission President Ursula von der Leyen visited China in the spring of 2023. You can bet Joe Biden and his national security team gnashed their teeth over Macron's Gaullist diplomacy. So did many Europeans. It wasn't just the predictably fruitless attempt to persuade the Chinese to help negotiate an end to the war in Ukraine. It was also Macron's touting of French strategic autonomy, in tune with Xi Jinping's long-standing aim to drive a wedge between Europe and the United States. Macron allowed Xi to get away with saying nothing consequential on Ukraine—no criticism of Russia, no commitment to a peace process, not even a promise to make a phone call to Ukraine's President Volodymyr Zelensky—all while simply repeating the mantra about how awful the use of nuclear weapons would be in the Ukraine war (as Putin then appeared to be threatening) and how essential humanitarian aid is to war victims.

"Strategic autonomy" bears directly on France's China policy. As France's finance minister Bruno Le Maire stated at the World Economic Forum in Davos, Switzerland, in 2023: "China cannot be out, China must be in. This is the difference of view we have between the U.S. and Europe." "We don't want to oppose China, we want to engage with China, we want China to obey by the same rules."[14]

Washington must be particularly chagrined that Macron would give Beijing the gift of promising to stay out of the tensions over Taiwan. Macron had the audacity, moreover, to speak for Europe when he said "the great risk" Europe faces is that it "gets caught up in crises that are not ours, which prevents it from building its strategic autonomy." In an interview, he was quite specific: "The question Europeans need to answer . . . is it in our interest to accelerate [a crisis] on Taiwan? No. The worst thing would be to think that we Europeans must become followers on this topic and take our cue from the U.S. agenda and a Chinese overreaction."[15] That unqualified support of the One China principle was surely music to Xi's ears.

EU's Leader Begs to Differ

Von der Leyen was not on the same page as Macron—not on world order, not on Taiwan and Ukraine, not on human rights. Prior to the trip, she issued a blunt statement about China's efforts to establish a "new world order." As reported by the *Wall Street Journal*: "Citing China's backing for Russia in the Ukraine war, its Belt and Road global infrastructure initiative and its assertiveness in multilateral bodies, Ms. von der Leyen said the Chinese Communist Party's 'clear goal is a systemic change of the international order with China at its center.'"[16] And in that new order, "individual rights are subordinated to national sovereignty. Where security and economy take prominence over political and civil rights." She no doubt had in mind Xi Jinping's "Global Security Initiative," announced several months earlier. Xi proposed a development model in which regime security, internal controls, and divorce from Western commercial and financial institutions are central to a country's stability and prosperity. The model seemed to be China's answer to Joe Biden's democracy-vs.-autocracy framework, which Xi explicitly rejected when they held their summit meeting the previous November.

On Taiwan, von der Leyen again departed from Macron's hands-off statement. She told Xi: "The threat of, or the use of, force to change the status quo is unacceptable, and it is important that the tensions that might occur should be resolved through dialogue." Neither her declaration nor Macron's stance kept China from carrying out a three-day military exercise near Taiwan, evidently in retaliation for US House of Representatives Speaker Kevin McCarthy's hosting of Taiwan's president.

As for the war in Ukraine, von der Leyen took a much tougher and more principled stance than Macron. In the same speech mentioned above, she was critical of China's peace plan, saying that any proposal "which would in effect consolidate Russian annexations" of Ukrainian territory—and that is precisely what China's proposal did—"is simply not a viable plan." "How China continues to interact with Putin's war will be a determining factor for EU-China relations," she added. That was quite the opposite of Macron's message to Xi, probably because he and the many business executives who accompanied him were more concerned about trade and the EU's trade deficit with China (then over $400 billion) than about human rights. Reportedly, Macron said nothing about repression in Xinjiang or Hong Kong.

(7) Trump's Reset with Russia: Pluses and Minuses for China

A New Strategic Triangle

In what is being called the "reverse Nixon" effect, the Trump administration seemed to adopt a view of Russia-China relations reminiscent of the Nixon-Kissinger strategic triangle policy in the 1970s, only this time getting closer to Russia in order to deal more forcefully with China. The strategy probably caused some head scratching in Beijing. China had to worry that Trump would largely abandon the traditional US policy of support for European defense against Russia in order to devote more military and economic resources to containing China. With the United States free of its Ukraine "problem," Chinese strategists might be thinking, the Americans might become even more troublesome—for example, on Taiwan, the South China Sea, and trade. If Trump didn't get his way on trade and tariffs, would he become more supportive of Taiwan independence or of the Philippines and Vietnam in their South China Sea territorial dispute? The American shift on Russia validated China's choice to back Russia on the Ukraine war. According to the historian Cheng Yawen (see **Selection 1**), "if China had chosen to 'side with the Americans.' today it might find itself facing a Russo-American alliance working to cut China down to size."

A Renewed Opportunity for China?

On the other hand, Trump's devaluation of NATO and legitimation of Putin's war might be an opportunity for China. These policy shifts caused alarm in Europe. Following parliamentary elections in February 2025, Germany's new chancellor went so far as to say that the US was "indifferent to the fate of Europe" and that NATO members might need to consider creating "an independent European defense capability."[17] Comments like that fit perfectly with China's pitch to Europe to embrace multipolarity and oppose US unilateralism in its foreign policy. And not only to Europe: At a G-20 meeting in South Africa, which the US secretary of state refused to attend, Foreign Minister Wang Yi emphasized multipolarity, mutual gain, and equal rights as he met with ministers from countries on friendly terms with the United States, including Australia, Turkey, and Saudi Arabia as well as from the EU. Quite possibly, therefore, the evident US attempt to convert its dual-adversary (Russia+China) strategic situation in the Biden years into a single-adversary (China) situation will fail. China-Russia relations may become stronger than ever, and Trump's pressure tactics may not work with Beijing.

To ensure that result, China-Russia diplomacy intensified in 2025. Xi Jinping and Vladimir Putin exchanged calls in February to reaffirm their countries' strong ties. "History and reality show us that China and Russia are good neighbors who won't move away, and true friends who have been through thick and thin together, support each other and develop together," Xi told Putin. To which Putin responded: "The leaders emphasized that the Russian-Chinese foreign policy link is the most important stabilizing factor in world affairs," and said the relationship was "not subject to external influence."[18] Following that call, Xi met with Sergei Shoigu, secretary of the Russian Federation Security Council in March. Xi referred to "promoting the spiritual core of China-Russia relations in the new era characterized by permanent good-neighborliness, comprehensive strategic coordination, and mutually beneficial win-win cooperation, and unceasingly deepen strategic coordination and practical cooperation . . . ." Wang Yi went further, describing the relationship as a "new type of major power relationship," the same language once used to characterize China-US relations. And in May, Xi traveled to Moscow, closing a number of economic and cultural deals, but also issuing common declarations that extolled the two countries' commitment to the UN Charter and global order.[19]

(8) Trump's Tariffs Rattle Europe (2025)

When the United States imposed a 20-percent tariff on European Union imports in April 2025, it joined with China as the only countries that vowed retaliation. The French reaction was typical, with President Emmanuel Macron saying the tariff hike should mean "not to invest in America for some time until we have clarified things." Those EU countries most exposed actually were not France, Spain, or Italy but Ireland, Belgium, and Germany. But the EU economy makes up 22 percent of global GDP and so is in a position—which the EU Commission strongly supports—to fight back, with the US services sector and agriculture the most lucrative targets. Still, the EU faced problems if it decided to retaliate, especially in the energy sector, because of its reliance on US natural gas. Reports suggested that while the

EU would discuss imposing some tariff hikes, it would stop short of a trade war and seek talks with Trump. After all, its trade surplus with the US was around $235 billion in 2024, second only to China's surplus with the US. The EU did not appear to want to antagonize Trump further, but neither was it prepared to surrender to Trump's trade demands.

China might emerge the winner in the EU-US tariff controversy. Critics of China in the EU seemed to be turning soft. The "widespread disruption" caused by Trump's tariffs, said Ursula von der Leyen, the EU Commission head, prompted her to propose "a negotiated resolution" of their trade issues to China. It was, she said, "the responsibility of Europe and China, as two of world's largest markets, to support a strong reformed trading system, free, fair and founded on a level playing field."[20] Like von der Leyen, Germany's new chancellor, Friedrich Merz, also had a well-documented mistrust of China. Before Trump's tariff hikes, Merz had spoken of the risks of investing in China. After Trump's decision, many in Merz's circle were calling for a strong reaction against it—and that would have to mean either closer trade ties with China or a search for other markets. But Germany's bargaining position is weak: Its GDP is heavily dependent on trade—over 80 percent—and it has twice as many imports as exports in trade with China.

By June 2025, EU leaders had resumed their criticisms of China. Von der Leyen went so far as to say that "Donald [Trump] is right—there is a serious problem" with China. The "problem" is that China was restricting raw materials exports to Europe, just as it was to the United States, subsidizing its industries, and "weaponizing" its controlling interest in other key commodities. The alternative: back to the drawing board with Trump in search of common ground on tariffs.[21]

Documents

Document 1. Xi Jinping and Vladimir Putin Exchange New Year's Greetings (2024)
(*Source*: Xinhua, December 31, 2024, https://english.news.cn/20241231/3e1febc64b544ee08aef7e501b5c2751/c.html)

BEIJING, Dec. 31 (Xinhua) -- Chinese President Xi Jinping on Tuesday exchanged New Year greetings with his Russian counterpart, Vladimir Putin.

On behalf of the Chinese government and people, Xi extended sincere congratulations and best wishes to Putin and the Russian people.

Xi said that 2024 marks the 75th anniversary of the establishment of China-Russia diplomatic relations, a new significant milestone in the bilateral relationship.

In the extraordinary journey over the past 75 years, China-Russia relations have grown more mature and stable, he said.

In face of the accelerated transformation unseen in a century and a volatile international landscape, China and Russia always move forward hand in hand along the right path of non-alliance, non-confrontation, and not targeting any third party, Xi said.

Over the past year, the two heads of state held three meetings in Beijing, Astana, and Kazan, and maintained communication through phone calls, exchanges of letters, and other means, Xi said, adding that they had candid exchanges of views and reached broad consensus on bilateral relations and major international and regional issues of common concern.

The political mutual trust and strategic coordination between the two sides have been advancing toward higher levels under the strategic guidance of the two leaders, he added.

Practical cooperation in various fields has yielded tangible outcomes, such as the completion of the China-Russia east-route natural gas pipeline, and the successful launch of the China-Russia Years of Culture has fostered a closer bond connecting the two peoples through generations, Xi said.

China and Russia also support each other as chairs of the BRICS [Brazil-Russia-India-China-South Africa] mechanism and the Shanghai Cooperation Organization (SCO), contributing significantly to solidarity and cooperation among the Global South, he added. . . .

The Chinese president voiced readiness to maintain close exchanges with Putin and keep China-Russia cooperation on the right course so as to continue consolidating and deepening China-Russia ties featuring permanent good-neighborly friendship, comprehensive strategic coordination and mutually beneficial cooperation, injecting strong momentum into the development and modernization of the two countries, and contributing to the well-being of the two peoples and safeguarding international fairness and justice. . . .

Recalling his three successful meetings with Xi in 2024, Putin said that they have advanced the Russia-China comprehensive strategic partnership of coordination for a new era to new heights.

The mutually beneficial cooperation between the two countries in such areas as economy, trade, energy, transportation, science, and technology is progressing in an orderly manner, and the successful launch of the Russia-China Years of Culture has created more opportunities to expand people-to-people exchanges, he said. . . .

Document 2. "Xi Calls China-EU Partnership One of Mutual Achievement," a conversation with European Council President Antonio Costa, January 14, 2025 (*Source:* Xinhua, January 14, 2025, https://english.news.cn/20250114/1fb61ee5fb0849b5ad4a8b6db68661eb/c.html).

The history of China-EU relations demonstrates that as long as both sides uphold mutual respect, treat each other as equals, and engage in candid dialogue, they can advance cooperation and make significant achievements, Xi said.

Xi said that like-mindedness makes for partnership, and seeking common ground while respecting differences also defines partnership.

The key lies in respecting each other's choice of social systems and development paths, as well as each other's core interests and major concerns, Xi said, adding that China has always regarded Europe as an important pole in a multipolar world, firmly supported European integration, and backed the EU's pursuit of strategic autonomy.

Both sides should summarize the experiences of China-EU relations, draw important lessons, jointly safeguard the political foundation of their relations, and advance their relationship, so as to bring greater benefits to the peoples of China and Europe and contribute more stability and certainty to an increasingly turbulent international landscape.

Over the past 50 years, China-EU relations have not only contributed to their respective development but also made significant contributions to global peace and prosperity, Xi said, adding that the more severe and complex the international situation becomes, the more China and Europe should adhere to the original aspirations of their diplomatic ties. . . .

The economic and trade cooperation between China and the EU is mutually complementary and beneficial, with both sides serving as defenders of the multilateral trading system, Xi said, adding that the two sides have already formed a strong economic symbiotic relationship. . . .

Both sides should also ensure the success of activities celebrating the 50th anniversary of diplomatic ties, enhance cultural exchanges and people-to-people interactions, encourage mutual visits between their people, and support local exchanges and educational cooperation, so as to strengthen the foundation of public goodwill in China-EU relations, Xi added.

For his part, Costa said that 2025 marks an important year for EU-China relations. The EU side is willing to work with China to celebrate the 50th anniversary of the diplomatic relations, enhance dialogue and communication, deepen strategic mutual trust, strengthen the partnership, and open up a brighter future for EU-China relations, he added.

The EU is ready to properly address economic and trade differences with China through dialogue and consultation, Costa said.

Both the EU and China respect the principles of the UN Charter, uphold multilateralism, safeguard free trade, and oppose bloc confrontation, and they should cooperate rather than compete, he said.

In this era full of challenges, the world needs closer EU-China cooperation to tackle global challenges such as climate change, and to contribute to world peace, stability and development, Costa said.

The two sides also exchanged views on issues such as Ukraine, with Xi elaborating on China's principled position of promoting peace talks.

4

China and the Global South

Introduction

"Global South" (*quan qiu nan fang*) is China's preferred term for all the developing countries, including China itself. This vast region—which China called the "intermediate zone" during the Cold War, and the Third World thereafter—has always been at the center of China's foreign policy. "South-South cooperation" is critical to China's identity as a developing country, to its championing of common political causes (independence, nationalism, resistance to great-power interference), and most recently to China's economy—its export markets and its minerals and other resource needs. **Selection 3** provides a case study.

With the advent of China's economic rise, Beijing has taken on leadership roles in Global South groups that are meant to rival the major Western-dominated global financial institutions—the World Bank and the International Monetary Fund (IMF). The most prominent of these rival groups are the BRICS (Brazil-Russia-India-China-South Africa), which is steadily adding members to the original five in 2015 as well as to its New Development Bank (**Selection 5 and Document 1**); the Shanghai Cooperation Organization, which includes Russia and the former Soviet-era republics in Central Asia; the Asian Infrastructure Investment Bank, another multilateral development bank headquartered in Beijing; the Regional Comprehensive Economic Partnership, with fourteen Asian countries; and the China-ASEAN (Association of Southeast Asian Nations) Free Trade Area, which links China with the ten member-states of ASEAN.

Central to China's international outreach is development projects under the Belt and Road Initiative (BRI). China claims that over 150 countries and thirty international organizations have signed on to the BRI. BRI low-interest development loans are granted without "conditionality"—

requirements of the recipient usually imposed by the World Bank and the International Monetary Fund, such as protection of human rights and the environment, and openness to foreign investment. Developing countries with highly centralized governance, low income, and weak protections for workers and the environment find the BRI especially attractive. Many of those same governments are also the main customers of China's Global Security Initiative, under which China exports key tools of its own security practices: surveillance equipment and police training. And "security" has also come to mean an expanding mission for China's People's Liberation Army (**Selection 7**).

Like any other country's foreign aid, BRI loans and grants serve political as well as economic purposes. One is enhancing China's reputation: For some Global South countries, particularly in Africa, China is by far the leading donor (**Selection 1**). Another goal is winning support for Chinese policies, such as for the One China policy and noninterference in China's internal affairs (meaning human rights and its claim to Taiwan), for multilateralism rather than unilateralism as a central feature of international relations, and for the virtues of an independent foreign policy. China's diplomacy with the Global South also seeks to promote China as a peacemaker in regional conflicts and as a "model for human advancement" (**Selection 8 and Document 7**). Especially ambitious is a set of three global initiatives in development, security, and civilization (**Documents 2, 4, and 6**) that incorporate a model for economic growth and world order distinctive from Western models.

On the economic side, the BRI has been heralded by some recipient countries as meeting their development objectives. Peru and Brazil, for example, have credited Chinese aid for making significant contributions to their economies and societies, such as in public health and transportation (**Document 2**). BRI renewable energy projects abroad have begun rising in global importance (**Selection 2**). Trade with BRI countries is a major portion of China's total trade: 47 percent in 2024, with Chinese exports much higher than imports as China seeks markets for its manufactured products. As **Selection 6** shows, Chinese money can be quite persuasive in diplomacy, though money doesn't always win friends. Money can also prove to be irrelevant, as witness China's brokering of Saudi Arabia-Iran normalization of relations. It was a diplomatic success, but of short duration as the Middle East descended into warfare and Iran faced another nuclear weapon controversy with the United States (**Document 8**).

BRI loans have become quite controversial, even within China where the program has raised questions about economically inadvisable lending and poor return on investment (**Document 3**). Some developing countries have charged China with "neo-colonialism" for using BRI agreements to bring in Chinese workers and extract mineral resources at the expense of local labor, the environment, and earnings by the host government and companies.

Occasional reports from Africa cite labor rights violations by Chinese-owned mines and factories (**Selection 3**). The United States and others charge China with creating "debt traps"—plying developing countries with large loans that cannot be repaid, making them dependent on Beijing and thus subject to political pressure (**Document 5**). Among the few European countries that have joined the BRI, Italy withdrew in 2024 and Greece's grant of port rights to China in Petraeus is controversial. The second Trump administration has, in a way, given China's BRI new life by dismantling USAID, leaving Chinese and other countries' economic development and humanitarian programs with opportunities to step in (**Selection 4**).

(1) China in Africa: Winning the Competition with the West

Mineral Resources: A Common Pursuit

China pays a great deal of attention to Africa, far more than does the United States. Xi Jinping has visited Africa five times, and Beijing has organized many China-Africa dialogue groups in addition to the Forum on China-Africa Cooperation (FOCAC) discussed below. China's BRI is active in fifty-four African nations, and China has been Africa's largest trading partner for the last fifteen years. Total trade with Africa was $167.8 billion in the first half of 2024, according to Chinese state media. All that attention, and consequent diplomatic and commercial interaction, has to be weighed alongside the debt-trap argument and the competition for control of Africa's mineral resources.

One critical mineral resource is antimony. Christina Lu reports that China is going to make it more difficult for the US and European allies to purchase antimony, which is vital in the defense industry for nuclear weapons, infrared missiles, and night-vision equipment. "No country," she writes, "maintains as dominant a grip on the metal's global trade as China, which accounts for nearly half of all production and more than 60 percent of U.S. imports. Beginning September 15, 2024, Beijing will require exporters to apply for a license for certain antimony products as well as require permission for related smelting and separation technology exports."[1] Although the United States and Europe will be seeking alternative sources of antimony, that will take considerable time. China is imposing export controls on vital minerals such as antimony, gallium and germanium in retaliation for export controls on semiconductors imposed by the United States and its allies in Europe and Asia.

Minerals are only a part of the China-in-Africa story. China likes to boast about its contributions to grassroots development in Africa. And indeed, the figures do point to important contributions. According to the official *People's Daily*: "By the end of 2023, over a ten-year period, China had established twenty-four agricultural technology demonstration centers in Africa, promoting more than 300 advanced agricultural techniques. These efforts have led to an average increase of 30 percent to 60 percent in local crop yields, benefiting over 1 million small-scale African farmers." That report also mentions a substantial number of green energy projects and digital payments platforms China has established for farmers.

BRI in Africa

At the FOCAC meeting in October 2024, China announced a $50-billion financial aid package for Africa and $30 billion in credit lines. Beijing's loans to African nations in 2023 were its highest in five years. Top borrowers were Angola, Ethiopia, Egypt, Nigeria, and Kenya. Putting loans and grants together, Johns Hopkins University's China Africa Research Initiative reported that China's foreign aid rose from $631 million in 2003 to $3.14 billion in 2015. After a drop in foreign aid expenditures to $2.37 billion in 2016, they rebounded to $3.01 billion in 2023. Nearly half of all Chinese aid has gone to Africa.[2]

AidData calculates that China provided $1.34 trillion in loans and grants to nearly 18,000 overseas development projects between 2000 and 2021, averaging about $61 billion a year. But repayment of many of the loans is due in 2025, and the total developing-country debt to China comes to over $1 trillion.[3]

(2) BRI: The Energy Side

Although outside observers tend to fixate on the BRI's loans for extractive projects, its renewable energy assistance is noteworthy. Solar power has taken off, with wind power rapidly growing. In 2024, China installed 24 gigawatts of power under the BRI, of which a third was solar power. These were records for the BRI. Alex Whitworth, head of Asia Pacific power and renewables research at Wood Mackenzie, says: "Chinese companies are heavily prioritizing greener technologies overseas and these make up over two-thirds of the project pipeline. As Chinese manufacturers drive down the costs of renewable power technology, Chinese companies are leading its deployment in many developing markets that could not previously afford it." Growth in solar and wind power projects is expected to be substantial, with Saudi Arabia, Indonesia, Vietnam, and Malaysia the major BRI markets.[4]

(3) The Battle Over Cobalt

In recent years, intense international competition has centered on copper, uranium, rare earth metals, and so-called "blood diamonds"—diamond mining that helped fund civil wars in Africa. We can add lithium in Bolivia to the list as Chinese, American, and other countries' firms are seeking to gain the upper hand on a mineral that is vital in electrical products. The latest battle is over cobalt, another essential mineral in cell phones but especially in electric car batteries—a link between mining and the climate crisis.

China and the United States are the principal combatants, and the battlefield is the Democratic Republic of Congo (DRC) in central Africa. The DRC holds most of the world's cobalt mines. That means sudden riches for the mining companies and some government officials, but it also means terrible working conditions for miners, exploitation of child labor, and destruction of the environment to make way for the mines. In fact, the DRC was just one of several African countries in which Chinese mines and factories were charged with violations of labor rights.[5]

Thanks to investigations by the *New Yorker* and the *New York Times*, we have a well-rounded understanding of how cobalt mining has jumped to the top of the international environmental and trade agendas. It's not a pretty picture.

The Back Story

In 2016, the American multinational Freeport McMoRan sold one of the main cobalt mines in the DRC to China Molybdenum, a Chinese state bank-supported company. US officials in Washington, preoccupied with other world problems, evidently disregarded warnings of the sale and took no steps to support a US stake in the mines. Additional mine sales followed. China Molybdenum now either owns or finances fifteen of nineteen DRC cobalt mines, leaving US officials wondering how to get back in the game and US automakers worrying about supply sources and substitutes for cobalt.

Here, then, is a case study of how the climate crisis intersects with the US-China competition for strategic metals. China's dominant position in cobalt mining reflects its interest in taking the lead in the EV market, just as Joe Biden's green economy program sought to transition Americans away from gas-guzzling autos. His goal was to have electric cars account for half of US auto sales by 2030, but that seems far out of reach. *The Guardian* reported that "electric cars will make up just 4% of American sales in 2021, compared with 9% in China and 14% of new sales in Europe." And Chinese annual EV sales are rising nearly twice as fast as US sales.[6] The only way the US could have come close to Biden's goal is if it had done what China has done: provide government incentives to consumers and the industry to buy and manufacture electric cars, such as tax credits on purchases and incentives to manufacturers. The first Trump presidency ended those programs.

Dirty Hands

One factor that might favor the United States when it comes to the cobalt competition: the Chinese firm's conduct in the DRC, which includes charges of cheating and failing to deliver on contracts, safety and environmental violations, and corrupt practices with Congolese officials. The Congolese government announced that the head of its mining company, often accused of corruption in his dealings with foreign companies, had been removed and replaced by the country's president. His predecessor, Joseph Kabila, and the Kabila family are suspected of having taken huge bribes from a Chinese consortium, using their bank as an intermediary. It was Kabila who first opened the DRC to foreign mining interests. As graft took hold, Western companies departed, leaving the field to Chinese firms with money to burn.[7]

US-based companies such as Tesla and Apple don't have clean hands either, however. As part of the supply chain, they are caught up in child labor abuse suits being brought by various NGOs. Mining of cobalt is difficult and dangerous, made worse by inexperienced workers who dig pits independently of company employees. Hence, both US and Chinese companies, as well as the DRC government and mine workers, would benefit from a cooperative and more regulated approach to cobalt mining. Secretary of State Antony Blinken proposed cooperation with China on aid to Africa, but he got nowhere.[8]

(4) The Withering of US Aid Competition

USAID is Gone

Donald Trump's decision at the start of 2025 to recall nearly all US Agency for International Development (USAID) workers and basically shut down the entire organization, justified as a budget-saving move, was not only a blow to countries that had depended on AID for humanitarian and other assistance. The shutdown was also the kind of gift to China that Beijing could never have imagined, since it removed a major aid competitor. By April 2025, USAID was reduced to a skeleton staff from 6,000 workers once on active duty. Over 5,000 programs were terminated.[9] Programs focused on poverty alleviation, health care, and other humanitarian assistance amounted to about $72 billion in fiscal year 2023. The United States was "the single-largest aid donor in the world, according to the United Nations, accounting for more than 40% of all humanitarian aid the UN tracked in 2024."[10] Yet US aid was a minuscule part of the total government budget—usually around 1 percent. (China's foreign aid figures are difficult to compare with US aid, since the BRI is mainly loans and therefore not "official development assistance" as defined by the Organisation for Economic Cooperation and Development.)

There are many examples of how closures of USAID programs affected developing countries and the international roles of both the United States and China. In Vietnam, for example, USAID was important for cleaning up Agent Orange defoliation attacks, an important project in US-Vietnam reconciliation. And in Myanmar, dwindling international assistance during its civil war led to more reliance than usual on US aid to groups advocating for human rights and medical assistance. Then came a devastating earthquake in 2025 that killed nearly 4,000 people. USAID would normally have been able to respond with medicine and transportation. Instead, it sent $2 million in aid. Beijing pledged over $13 million and sent relief workers.[11] USAID also had an important presence in Africa until the shutdown, plowing over $6 billion into African humanitarian and development projects. Also gone is US aid to NGOs that conducted research on China, such as on the condition of ethnic minorities and environmental protection. It was an astounding abandonment of a long tradition of US aid.

Potential Opportunities for China

Michael Schiffer, the assistant administrator of USAID's Asia bureau from 2022 to January 20, 2025, pointed out how Trump's "destruction of USAID" undermined US policy in Asia and helped China's BRI make further gains. He claimed that US development cooperation is "a vital tool for reinforcing shared values, strengthening civil society, enhancing economic resilience, underwriting regional stability and security, and providing a compelling alternative to China's increasingly assertive regional ambitions." The Trump administration, on the other hand, "threatens to undermine this strategic advantage.... These reductions have not only undercut development outcomes for vulnerable populations but have also damaged the broader diplomatic and security framework that sustains U.S. alliances in the Indo-Pacific."[12]

(5) The Significance of the BRICS for China (2024)

Politics Rules

Using its newfound wealth, China's diplomacy aims at aligning Global South countries with China's political objectives, often under the heading of a "comprehensive and strategic partnership" with China. Partnership follows a uniform script that reflects China's "soft power": official visits by senior Chinese officials (far more than by Western leaders); exports of labor; people-to-people exchanges; and cooperative undertakings in science and technology. In return, China expects the partner's support of the One China principle on Taiwan; adherence to the "five principles of peaceful coexistence" (which include mutual noninterference and nonaggression)—principles that have been standards of China's foreign policy since the 1950s; and support of, or at least no objection to, Chinese policy on controversial issues such as human rights and wars in the Middle East and Ukraine.

When the BRICS first formed in 2009, it was dismissed in Western circles as nothing more than a talking shop of the discontented. But as Keith Johnson wrote in 2024, "it is hard to appreciate just how much resentment there is of Western hypocrisy and hegemony, all mortar helping to bond the loose membership of BRICS."[13] The Chinese certainly take the organization seriously, since it provides another wedge for China's development model, trade, and investments. Foreign Minister Wang Yi has referred to the BRICS as "the first echelon of the Global South." He has pointed to the critical role of economic development financing in supporting poverty reduction, energy and food security, and industrial transformation. "We have invested and mobilized nearly $20 billion in various development funds," Wang claims, "established more than thirty cooperation platforms in eight key areas, established a Global Development Promotion Center, and are actively preparing to build a 'Global South' Research Center. The initiative mobilizes development resources and incubates cooperation platforms to help the Global South get on the fast track of development."

(**Document 1**, Xi Jinping's speech to the BRICS summit meeting in October 2024, adds to the discussion of China's hopes for the group.)

China's Diplomacy at the 2024 BRICS Summit

Development financing and resentment of the West took center stage when the BRICS leaders held their summit meeting in the Russian city of Kazan in 2024. The five BRICS core membership expanded to include Egypt, Ethiopia, Iran, and the United Arab Emirates. Indonesia, Malaysia, and Thailand were scheduled to be added in 2025. In all, thirty-two countries attended the Kazan meeting. The BRICS now has a New Development Bank with headquarters in Shanghai and regional offices in the five BRICS nations. The NDB is meant to one day rival the World Bank and International Monetary Fund. Development financing has become the key bonding mechanism.

During the summit, China's high-profile diplomacy was on center stage. Xi Jinping met with Iran's newly elected President Masoud Pezeshkian, who said: "China is Iran's most important partner for cooperation." He added that "Iran is also ready to work with China to continue firmly supporting each other on issues concerning their respective core interests and opposing hegemony and bullying." Xi Jinping said:

> The Chinese side supports Iran in safeguarding national sovereignty, security and national dignity, steadily advancing its own economic and social development, and improving and deepening good-neighborly and friendly relations with neighboring countries. The Chinese side stands ready to work with Iran to firmly support each other, uphold the basic norms governing international relations such as non-interference in internal affairs, and safeguard the legitimate rights and interests of the two countries, adding that his country is also willing to strengthen exchanges and cooperation with Iran in various fields . . .

Also important was a speech by India's Prime Minister Narendra Modi. He called for reform of the major international security and financial institutions:

> We must move forward in a time bound manner on reforms in global institutions such as the UN Security Council, Multilateral development banks, and the World Trade Organization. As we take our efforts forward in BRICS, we must be careful to ensure that this organization does not acquire the image of one that is trying to replace global institutions, instead of being perceived as one that wishes to reform them.

Modi also urged greater financial integration among the BRICS members, using local currencies, presumably instead of the US dollar. What he avoided mentioning is that India and Brazil, key members of the BRICS, have refused to join China's Belt and Road Initiative.

The New Development Bank's head, Dilma Rousseff, an economist who was Brazil's president from 2011 to 2016, spoke about moving away from the dollar in development financing, saying:

> The New Development Bank envisages and wants to focus on financing in national currencies. This is very important for us to increase our capacity for financing. This is our strategy. The target for 2022–2026 was to implement 30 percent of financing in national currencies. Today, we have reached 28.3 percent, so we are almost reaching our target of 30 percent.

While the new bank is making headway, two key US economic development programs are on the verge of expiring by September 2025 for lack of continuing Congressional authorization: the International Development Finance Corporation and the African Growth and Opportunity Act.

Donald Trump, as President-elect, threatened to raise tariffs on BRICS imports by 100 percent unless BRICS made a "commitment" to abandon its de-dollarization plan. Yet China and its partners in BRICS have a long way to go to outclass the dollar in international transactions. The dollar is actually rising in usage: In early 2025, according to Bloomberg, it accounted for just over 50 percent of all currencies used in Swift, the global financial messaging service that facilitates transactions between banks and financial institutions. The next largest currency, the euro, constitutes some 23 percent on average, followed by the British pound with 7.1 percent.[14]

(6) How Money Talks

The power of China's economic diplomacy is on display in several ways. Here are three examples. In the first one, countries with Muslim-dominant populations pretend not to notice China's repression of the Uyghurs and other Muslim minorities. Those countries see the payoff for their silence in development loans and/or political support. In the second case, we see China's reach into Latin America, once the US backyard, with big-time spending to secure deep-water access in Peru for expanded trade. (**Document 2** is Xi Jinping's article in a Peruvian media outlet extolling the port project.) The third example connects BRI loans with support of China's position on Taiwan. Nevertheless, China has not always gotten its way, as the concluding part of this section shows.

Abandoning Human Rights

You would think that countries that once were colonies, as well as Muslim organizations and countries with large Muslim populations, would support the Uyghurs if not the Tibetans in response to Chinese repression. But money and politics frequently talk louder than defense of human rights in international affairs. Delegations of the World Muslim Communities Council, for example, have visited Xinjiang and voiced support for the province's economic development and China's fight against terrorism.[15] Seventy Muslim-dominant countries, led by Pakistan and joined by Palestine, voted in the UN in 2024 to support China's repressive policies by agreeing with Beijing that what goes on in Xinjiang stays in Xinjiang. Most of the pro-China vote was predictable. The Palestinian vote is easily explained by China's position on the war in the Middle East. Foreign Minister Wang Yi said: "On the Palestinian issue, China stands firmly with Arab countries. We must promote a comprehensive and lasting ceasefire in Gaza as soon as possible, support Palestine to become a formal member of the United

Nations, implement the 'two-state solution,' and achieve lasting peace in the Middle East." Other countries that supported China, such as Russia, North Korea, Laos, Sri Lanka, Gabon, and Solomon Islands, are all trade and aid partners. The central African states, such as Niger and Burkina Faso, had recently experienced pro-Russian coups that toppled governments friendly to the West. Overall, the list of China supporters shows that the BRI has had important payoffs in Africa, South Asia, and the Pacific Island states.

China's Peruvian Venture

Chinese leader Xi Jinping traveled to Peru in November 2024 to officially open a deep-water port in Chancay, which is about fifty miles north of the capital city, Lima. The port is estimated to cost $3 billion when completed, but it is expected to pay for itself in short order, since it will create a direct route across the Pacific Ocean that will prove attractive to other investors. China's state shipping company, Cosco, invested $1.3 billion in the project in 2019 and will be the exclusive operator of the port. US military officials are concerned that the port could one day accommodate warships, though the Chinese assert their interest is purely commercial.

The commercial advantages of the port for both countries are substantial. For China, the port's fifteen docks will be the first place in South America able to host carrier ships too big to fit through the Panama Canal. Chinese researchers have said the route will cut costs by significantly shortening sailing times. In the big picture, the port venture continues China's overseas reach into regions once dominated by US official and private interests. The project points to how China is challenging the United States in infrastructure building. For Peru, President Dina Boluarte, the project will be a high-tech "nerve center" joining the continent to Asia, one that could create 8,000 jobs and $4.5 billion in economic activity annually.[16]

Winning Support on the Taiwan Issue

One study finds widespread support among BRI loan recipients for China's position on unification with Taiwan. 117 UN member-states (out of 193) accept China's sovereignty over Taiwan in principle, and most of them do not distinguish between a peaceful and a forceful Chinese takeover.[17] The majority of those 117 countries receive BRI loans.

Case in point: China's BRI projects in several Caribbean countries, including Guyana and Suriname, which have major oil and gas deposits. Winning over countries that still have diplomatic relations with Taiwan is also on China's agenda, since five of the twelve countries that still recognize the Republic of China on Taiwan are in the Caribbean. The US interest under Trump has been limited to security concerns such as drug trafficking, not to development aid. And some Caribbean nations, such as Guyana, were hit with high tariffs by Trump in 2025.

When Money Isn't Enough

One example of when money *doesn't* talk came at the start of 2025, when President Trump threatened to take over the Panama Canal. He charged, with little merit, that the canal was under Chinese control. Ownership of port assets was in the hands of Li Ka-shing, a Hong Kong billionaire, and his conglomerate, CK Hutchison. Trump's threat worked, up to a point. Panama dropped out of the Belt and Road Initiative, and though it didn't agree to sell the canal to the United States, or end fees paid by US military vessels to use the canal, it did bend to the US insistence that the Canal Zone port assets—two ports on the Atlantic and Pacific ends of the canal—be sold off. The US investment firm BlackRock bought the ports, though the giant Danish shipping firm Maersk then bought a railway line that parallels the canal and links the ports. Trump couldn't have been happy about that.

The matter didn't end there. Beijing, probably fearing that US control of the canal would hinder China's trade, accused Li Ka-shing of everything from profit seeking to treachery for selling to the American firm. Once again, we see Beijing overseeing and intervening in Hong Kong's affairs (see Chapter 8). An official Chinese statement called the sale to BlackRock "spineless groveling" and a "betrayal" of the Chinese people.[18] China charged the US with "coercion" and with running a smear campaign against the BRI.[19] But businesses in Hong Kong resented Beijing's intervention, fearing it would scare off investors in the territory.[20]

Money also isn't enough when China's own actions undermine the BRI's appeal. Take the Southeast Asian neighbors that rely on the Mekong River for fishing. Chinese dams are taking a large bite out of their fishing industry, arousing anger. Mongolia, long economically dependent on China, in 2024 reached out to the United States for trade and struck a major deal with Google for computer assistance. Vietnam's Communist Party-led government agreed with the United States in 2023 to a strategic partnership, and to a presidential visit by Joe Biden. (All that backfired in 2025, however, when Trump imposed high tariffs on Vietnam's exports to the US, forcing the Vietnamese to propose eliminating their 9 percent tariff rate on US goods in exchange for Trump's dropping of his 46 percent tariff on Vietnam.) The Philippines, which under President Rodrigo Duterte had accommodated China and been a BRI participant, under President Ferdinand Marcos Jr. reverted to a strategic partnership with the US in 2024 in response to Chinese pressure in the South China Sea.

(7) Exporting for Security: China's Surveillance Equipment and Military Abroad

Internal Security is a Selling Point

One of the least noted aspects of China's growing international presence is its police forces and surveillance equipment that are deployed to numerous countries. The International Institute of Strategic Studies (IISS) reported in 2024 that China exports its surveillance equipment to fifty countries, has bilateral policing agreements with at least ten countries, and has joint patrol arrangements with five countries. By far, most of these arrangements are with Global South countries that have economic and other ties to Beijing. Its security support is part of China's Global Security Initiative, launched in 2022 and designed to promote security cooperation with China in "areas such as counter-terrorism, cybersecurity, biosecurity, emerging technologies, and international policing."[21]

That last element incorporates the police and surveillance equipment. Policing is supposed to protect Chinese businesses and individuals abroad, while donating surveillance equipment helps track police targets. But the purposes of these programs, according to the IISS, go further: to "popularise Chinese policing and security norms and standards abroad (thus normalising them internationally)." "The export of technology and the integration of Chinese technicians and equipment into the security agencies of foreign countries" provide China with intelligence opportunities, says the IISS. Recipients of these services get a taste of Chinese methods used at home—methods often criticized for being part of a ubiquitous suppression of ethnic minorities and dissidents.

The overarching purpose of these agreements is to gain acceptance of the Chinese idea that enhanced internal security measures are a better security alternative than engaging in agreements with the West, especially the United States, such as hosting military bases. Toward that end, China has committed significant funds to African security projects. At a meeting with Nigeria's foreign minister on January 9, 2025, Foreign Minister Wang Yi said:

> China will establish and carry out a Global Security Initiative partnership with Africa, create an initiative cooperative demonstration zone, . . . supply Africa with RMB 1 billion in grants in military assistance to Africa to help African countries train 6,000 military personnel and 1,000 police law enforcement personnel. China will continue to sustain support for African standby forces and rapid response forces, and support African nations in developing peacekeeping and counter-terrorism operations.[22]

(Worth mentioning is that rapid response forces can become instruments of mass violence. The paramilitary Rapid Response Force in Sudan is an example. The US State Department accused it of genocide in January 2025.)

The PLA Has a New Mission

China's own force projections to Africa undermine the claim of supporting strictly all-African security operations. At one time, China's involvement was limited to United Nations peacekeeping and anti-piracy operations. Now, as China's businesses, personnel, and property holdings expand worldwide, China has had to prioritize defense of sea lanes, evacuation of Chinese nationals in emergencies, and protection of hard investments such as mines and energy facilities. Africa is a case in point. As one writer observes, "Today, the PLA's [People's Liberation Army] largest overseas deployment is in Africa. It maintains continuous naval flotillas, has more troops in United Nations missions than any other permanent UN Security Council member and, besides France, trains more African students. It also instructs more African civilian, military, and law enforcement professionals." The PLA's mission now entails long-distance deployment of troops to Africa—in 2024, to Tanzania and Mozambique—for joint air and sea exercises. While these Chinese forces then only numbered about 1,000, the trend clearly is to expand their size as well as their capabilities and their partnerships with African countries.[23]

Nothing unusual here; after all, the United States and other major powers have all conducted military operations far beyond the homeland once their economic interests needed protection. Those operations have had deadly consequences, such as deep involvement in Middle East politics and military interventions to defend oil interests. As Chinese interests abroad multiply, it may one day face fateful decisions about intervening to protect them, perhaps against the wishes of local governments.

(8) A Big Deal but Not Enough: China's Middle East Diplomacy, 2023-2025

Brokering Normalization of Relations

By any stretch of the imagination, the March 10, 2023 announcement of China's brokering of a Saudi Arabia-Iran agreement to resume diplomatic relations and exchange security assurances was a big deal. As one observer put it, "China's prestigious accomplishment vaults it into a new league diplomatically and outshines anything the U.S. has been able to achieve in the region since Biden came to office."[24] Washington reacted as though not much had happened. But that was a false front. Fact is, the United States and Israel were suddenly put on the sidelines, watching as two powerful autocracies were being brought together by a third.

The strange thing about this announcement is that it came just a day after reports that the Saudis were hoping for another big deal, with the United States, one that would have established diplomatic relations with Israel in return for security guarantees, increased Saudi access to US weapons, and secured Israeli help with Saudi Arabia's nuclear energy ambitions.[25] Israel might have welcomed such a deal, but for the United States it may have been a few steps too far. First, the reported deal required trust that the Saudis wouldn't seek a nuclear *weapon* once having gained access to nuclear technology. Second, it called for the United States to promise protection for an authoritarian regime that has a horrendous record on human rights, including the murder of the dissident journalist Jamal Khashoggi. Third, any such deal required US trust in Crown Prince Mohammed bin Salman (MBS), who had proven unreliable when the Biden administration wanted him to increase Saudi Arabia's oil output and when MBS, in December 2022, signed numerous economic development and trade agreements with China. The two countries declared a "comprehensive strategic partnership"—an "epoch-making milestone in the history of China-Arab relations," according to China's foreign ministry spokesperson.[26]

Implications for Middle East International Relations

In the immediate aftermath of the Saudi-Iranian engagement, it appeared that major changes in the Middle East political landscape were put in motion. First, the deal was clearly a win for all three parties. For China, the deal showed the virtues of opportunistic over aggressive "wolf warrior" diplomacy. Having made its first foray into a major regional dispute, China gained increased recognition as a great power. Xi Jinping said China should "actively participate in the reform and construction of the global governance system" and promote "global security initiatives." That's China's wish list, but secure access to Saudi and Iranian oil supplies may be of more immediate interest to Beijing.

For Saudi Arabia, restoring relations with Iran while still being closely tied to the United States was a victory for MBS' so-called flexible foreign policy. Improved relations with Iran might not only moderate long-standing competition in Lebanon and Syria; it might also bring the costly civil war in Yemen to a close, since under the agreement, Tehran and Riyadh were supposed to stop supporting their proxy forces. Iran also cemented close economic ties with China, possibly opened economic opportunities with alienated neighboring countries, and gave the Ayatollah Ali Khomeini regime a boost in prestige as it tried to end antigovernment protests at home.

The Saudi-Iranian deal also diminished US influence in the Middle East. Washington's unsteady relations with the Saudis and its enmity with Iran left it unable to match China's feat. As two observers commented, China stepped into "the diplomatic vacuum left by a [US] foreign policy that led with the military and made diplomacy all too often an afterthought."[27] As for Israel, it became even more isolated in the Middle East and more reliant than ever on the US. This was a time of domestic upheaval in Israel. Prime Minister Benjamin Netanyahu's government relied on the support of far-right politicians who were pushing for "judicial reform," which meant limits on the power of courts. Netanyahu needed improved relations with the Biden administration as well as normalization of relations with Saudi Arabia.

Questions and Options

Now, a reality check.

Two years after the Saudi-Iranian announcement, no Middle East realignment or reconciliation took place, mainly due to events that followed the October 7, 2023 Hamas attack on Israel: Israel's genocidal assault on Gaza and its Palestinian population; expansion of Israel's war with Hamas to include attacks on Hezbollah in Southern Lebanon; the collapse of Bashar al-Assad's rule in Syria, followed by Israeli air strikes on Syria's military arsenals; exchanges of fire between Iran and Israel, and the revival of talk of an Israeli strike on Iran's nuclear facilities; and in Yemen, attacks by the Houthis on Western shipping. The Biden administration contributed directly to Israel's war policies with military aid that flatly contradicted its own restrictions on the use of US weapons in ways that undermined human rights. Biden left office in January 2025 with Israel's far-right leadership firmly in control and determined not just to eliminate Hamas and Hezbollah as capable resistance forces, but also to reoccupy Gaza, forcibly remove the Palestinian population from the territory, and expand Israeli-occupied territory in the West Bank and Southern Lebanon. Those developments ensured that normalization of Israeli-Saudi relations would not happen. China's diplomatic coup was at best put on hold.

The incoming Trump administration showed no interest in halting Israel's military actions in Gaza or anywhere else. It also decided in May 2025 not to link Saudi recognition of Israel to US help with a Saudi nuclear energy program. (The latter would be pursued separately.) Trump said he wanted to strike a nuclear deal with Iran, but simultaneously signed off on a presidential memorandum that promised "maximum pressure" on Iran if it did not stop further enrichment of uranium to bomb-making level. The possibility of a US attack on Iran, or an Israeli attack with US support, reportedly caused concern in Beijing, since its expanding economic interests in Iran include a sizable stake in Iran's oil exports. Moreover, as a party to the 2015 nuclear deal with Iran that President Obama spearheaded, Beijing's diplomatic prestige was also on the line. Those considerations paved the way for a high-level three-way meeting of Iranian, Russian, and Chinese officials in mid-March 2025 that culminated in a five-point Chinese statement on how to settle the Iran nuclear issue (**Document 8**).

The statement proved irrelevant when Israel carried out ten days of air attacks on Iran in June 2025 that decimated Iran's nuclear enrichment facilities and killed key figures in its military leadership. President Trump sided with Israel and warned Iran to negotiate a new nuclear deal or face obliteration. When Iran insisted on the right to enrich uranium for energy purposes, Trump ordered US strikes on Iran's hardest-to-reach nuclear sites, then called for an Israel-Iran ceasefire. Whether or not the ceasefire holds and Iran still has the capability to weaponize its nuclear program are large uncertainties. As for China, it could only be a bystander in the war. Xi Jinping said the "international community, especially major powers that have a special influence on the parties to the conflict, should make efforts to promote the cooling of the situation, rather than the opposite." That weak statement spoke volumes about the limits of Chinese diplomacy in the Middle East.

Documents

Document 1: Xi Jinping Addresses the BRICS Summit in Russia, October 24, 2024
(*Source*: Xinhua, October 24, 2024, https://english.www.gov.cn/news/202410/24/content_WS67196533c6d0868f4e8ec3b9.html.)

As the world enters a new period defined by turbulence and transformation, we are confronted with pivotal choices that will shape our future. Should we allow the world to descend into the abyss of disorder and chaos, or should we strive to steer it back on the path of peace and development? This reminds me of a novel by Nikolay Chernyshevsky entitled *What Is to Be Done?* The protagonist's unwavering determination and passionate drive are exactly the kind of willpower we need today. The more tumultuous our times become, the more we must stand firm at the forefront, exhibiting tenacity, demonstrating the audacity to pioneer and displaying the wisdom to adapt. We must work together to build BRICS into a primary channel for strengthening solidarity and cooperation among Global South nations and a vanguard for advancing global governance reform.

—We should build a BRICS committed to peace, and we must all act as defenders of common security. We humans are an indivisible community of security. Only by embracing the vision of common, comprehensive, cooperative and sustainable security can we pave the way for universal security. The Ukraine crisis still persists. China and Brazil, in collaboration with other countries from the Global South, initiated a group of Friends for Peace to address the crisis. The aim is to gather more voices advocating peace. We must uphold the three key principles: no expansion of the battlefields, no escalation of hostilities, and no fanning flames, and strive for swift de-escalation of the situation. While the humanitarian situation in Gaza continues to deteriorate, the flames of war have once again been rekindled in Lebanon, and conflicts are escalating among the parties. We must promote an immediate ceasefire and an end to the killing. We must make unremitting efforts toward a comprehensive, just and lasting resolution of the Palestinian question.

—We should build a BRICS committed to innovation, and we must all act as pioneers of high-quality development. As the latest round of technological revolution and industrial transformation is advancing at an accelerated speed, we must keep pace with the times and foster new quality productive forces. China has recently launched a China-BRICS Artificial Intelligence Development and Cooperation Center. We are ready to deepen cooperation on innovation with all BRICS countries to unleash the dividends of AI development. China will establish a BRICS Deep-Sea Resources International Research Center, a China Center for Cooperation on Development of Special Economic Zones in BRICS Countries, a China Center for BRICS Industrial Competencies, and a BRICS Digital Ecosystem Cooperation Network. We welcome active participation from all interested parties to promote the high-quality upgrading of BRICS cooperation.

—We should build a BRICS committed to green development, and we must all act as promoters of sustainable development. Green is the defining color of our times. It is important that all BRICS countries proactively embrace the global trend of green and low-carbon transformation. China's high-quality production capacity, as exemplified by its manufacturing of electric vehicles, lithium batteries and photovoltaic products, provides a significant boost to global green development. China is willing to leverage its strengths to expand cooperation with BRICS countries in green industries, clean energy and green mining, and promote green development through the entire industrial chain, so as to increase the "green quotient" of our cooperation and upgrade the quality of our development.

—We should build a BRICS committed to justice, and we must all act as forerunners in reforming global governance. The international power dynamics is undergoing profound changes, but global governance reform has lagged behind for a long time. We should champion true multilateralism and adhere to the vision of global governance characterized by extensive consultation, joint contribution, and shared benefits. We must ensure that global governance reform is guided by the principles of fairness, justice, openness and inclusiveness. In light of the rise of the Global South, we should respond favorably to the calls from various countries to join BRICS.

We should advance the process of expanding BRICS membership and establishing a partner country mechanism, and enhance the representation and voice of developing nations in global governance.

The current developments make the reform of the international financial architecture all the more pressing. BRICS countries should play a leading role in the reform. We should deepen fiscal and financial cooperation, promote the connectivity of our financial infrastructure, and apply high standards of financial security. The New Development Bank should be expanded and strengthened. We must ensure that the international financial system more effectively reflects the changes in the global economic landscape.

—We should build a BRICS committed to closer people-to-people exchanges, and we must all act as advocates for harmonious coexistence among all civilizations. BRICS countries boast a profound and illustrious historical and cultural heritage. It is important that we promote the spirit of inclusiveness and harmonious coexistence among civilizations. We should enhance the exchange of governance experiences among BRICS countries, and fully harness the untapped potential for cooperation in areas such as education, sports, and the arts so that our diverse cultures can inspire one another and illuminate the path forward for BRICS. Last year, I proposed an initiative for BRICS digital education cooperation, and I am delighted to see that it has become a reality. China will implement a capacity-building program for BRICS digital education. We will open 10 learning centers in BRICS countries in the next five years, and provide training opportunities for 1,000 local education administrators, teachers and students. This will be a tangible step to deepen and strengthen people-to-people exchanges among BRICS countries.

Colleagues, China is willing to work with all BRICS countries to open a new horizon in the high-quality development of greater BRICS cooperation, and join hands with Global South countries in building a community with a shared future for mankind.

Document 2. Xi Jinping Touts China's Development Assistance ("China-Peru Friendship: Setting Sail Toward an Even Brighter Future" (*Source*: Xinhua, November 14, 2024, https://english.news.cn/20241114/4f59d3a ef3594a3198aae38eb5ee40aa/c.html)

This is my second visit to Peru, a "neighbor" of China across the Pacific Ocean, since I took office as President of the People's Republic of China. Peru is home to ancient civilizations such as Caral, Chavín, Chimú, and Inca. Peruvians endearingly refer to the Chinese people as paisano. Peru's Congress has recently declared every February 1 as the Peru-China Fraternity Day. Chinese restaurants in Peru are called *chifa*, which is similar to the Chinese word *chifan*, meaning dining. Every time I came here, I was overwhelmed by the friendly sentiments of the Peruvian people toward the Chinese people.

This bond of friendship and affection is rooted in the wisdom of our ancient civilizations. The Chinese civilization is the only one in the world that has continued uninterrupted for more than 5,000 years. The maritime civilization represented by Caral and the continental civilization represented by Inca are a testament to the time-honored history, profound richness, and tremendous diversity of the Peruvian civilization. It is widely believed in the archeology communities of China and other countries that the Chinese civilization and the civilizations of the Americas were in fact created by descendants of the same ancestors at different periods and different locations. . . .

The bond of our friendship and affection has become stronger through China-Peru win-win cooperation. Peru is one of the first Latin American countries to establish diplomatic relations with the People's Republic of China. For over 50 years, our bilateral relations have been progressing steadily. Especially since the elevation of our relationship to a comprehensive strategic partnership in 2013, our ties have grown stronger and our practical cooperation fruitful, bringing tangible benefits to our peoples. In fighting the COVID-19 pandemic, China sent a medical expert team to Peru. We also provided vaccines and other medical supplies to the best of our ability. We have proven through concrete actions that China is a trustworthy friend that Peru can rely on in crucial moments. Peru is the first Latin American country to sign a package FTA [Free Trade Agreement] with China. It is also among the first in Latin America to participate in cooperation under the Belt and Road Initiative. China has been Peru's largest trading partner and largest export market for 10 consecutive years. Last year, Peru's exports to China accounted for 36 percent of its total exports. Chinese businesses have an investment stock of about US$ 30 billion in Peru. The Las Bambas copper mine, a project with investment from Chinese enterprises, contributes to about 1 percent of Peru's GDP, creating tens of thousands of job opportunities. The Saúl Garrido Rosillo Hospital in Tumbes, a project undertaken by a Chinese enterprise, will serve over 100,000 local residents. The water project in the three districts of Lima will enable more than 400,000 people to access clean water and sanitation services. . . .

During my upcoming visit, President Boluarte and I will attend via video the inauguration ceremony of Chancay Port. This is not only an important project under Belt and Road cooperation, but also the first smart port in South America. The first phase of the project, when completed, will reduce the sea shipping time from Peru to China to 23 days, thus cutting logistics costs by at least 20 percent. It is expected to generate US$4.5 billion in yearly revenues for Peru and create over 8,000 direct jobs. The completion of Chancay Port will enable Peru to put in place a multi-dimensional, diverse and efficient network of connectivity spanning from coast to inland, from Peru to Latin America and further on to the Caribbean. It will also help build an Inca Trail of the New Era with Chancay Port as its starting point, thus boosting the overall development and integration of the region. . . .

Document 3. Xi Jinping Addresses Problems and Opportunities with the BRI (*Background*: Xi's speech, at a BRI Work Conference, was entitled "Maintain Strategic Certainty, Dare to Overcome All Kinds of Difficulties and Challenges." The speech was carried by *Renmin ribao* on December 5, 2024. *Source*: trackingpeoplesdaily@substack.com, December 4, 2024, translated by Manoj Kewalramani.)

Xi has said that "in the current severe and complex international environment, advancing the high-quality development of the Belt and Road Initiative presents both opportunities and challenges, but overall, opportunities outweigh challenges. . . . Correctly handling the relationship between enhancing the sense of gain of partner countries and adhering to what is beneficial to us is an inherent requirement for promoting the high-quality development of BRI, and it is also an important principle and direction that must be firmly grasped at all times. It is necessary to persist in doing our best and acting within our capabilities, find the points of cooperation and the intersection of interests, coordinate the construction of major landmark projects and "small but beautiful" livelihood projects—helping to jointly build national economic and social development of partner countries and improving people's livelihood—and continuously enhance the sense of participation, gain, and happiness of the people of partner countries. It is necessary to persist in what is beneficial to us, mutual benefit and win-win, do what should be done and not doing what should not be done, do not issue any bad checks [i.e., empty promises] and do not raise appetites [i.e., don't create unrealistic expectations], balance the political, strategic, overall, long-term, and economic accounts, and effectively safeguard China's strategic interests."

Document 4. Xi Jinping on "China's Story"
(*Background*: This is Xi's speech, "Building a Just World of Common Development," at the G20 Summit Meeting in Rio de Janeiro, November 18, 2024. *Source*: Xinhua, November 19, 2024, https://english.news.cn/20241119/7596373a694a4074b81ee6ca11098c5c/c.html)

I pointed out at this forum that prosperity and stability would not be possible in a world where the rich become richer while the poor are made poorer, and countries should make global development more inclusive, beneficial to all, and more resilient. At the Hangzhou Summit, China placed development at the center of the G20's macroeconomic policy coordination for the first time, and the Summit adopted the G20 Action Plan on the 2030 Agenda for Sustainable Development and the G20 Initiative on Supporting Industrialization in Africa and Least Developed Countries. The Rio Summit this year has chosen the theme "Building a Just World and a Sustainable Planet." It places fighting hunger and poverty at the top of the agenda, and decides to establish a Global Alliance Against Hunger and Poverty. From Hangzhou to Rio, we have been working for one and the same goal, that is, to build a just world of common development.

China's development is an important part of the common development of the world. We have lifted 800 million people out of poverty, and met the poverty reduction target of the UN's 2030 Agenda for Sustainable Development ahead of schedule.

This achievement did not just fall into our laps. It is the fruit of the strenuous, unified efforts of the Chinese government and people. Everything China does, it always places the people front and center, and it solemnly declares that "not a single poor region or person should be left behind." To tackle poverty, we make targeted policies tailored to each village, each household and each person; we facilitate growth by vigorously channeling talent, funds and technologies to underdeveloped regions; we help localities generate growth by fostering industries with distinctive features and upgrading infrastructure, all in light of their own conditions; and we promote common prosperity by pairing up well-off regions with less developed ones. I have worked from village to county, city, provincial and central levels. Poverty alleviation has always been a priority and a major task I am determined to deliver.

China's story is proof that developing countries can eliminate poverty, and that a weaker bird can start early and fly high, when there is the endurance, perseverance, and striving spirit that enables water drops to penetrate rocks over time and turns blueprints into reality. If China can make it, other developing countries can make it too. This is what China's battle against poverty says to the world.

Colleagues,

China will always be a member of the Global South, a reliable long-term partner of fellow developing countries, and a doer and go-getter working for the cause of global development. A single flower does not make spring. China wants to see a hundred flowers in full blossom and will go hand in hand with fellow developing countries toward modernization. Today, I wish to outline China's eight actions for global development.

First, pursuing high-quality Belt and Road cooperation. On top of RMB700 billion yuan added financing windows and an additional RMB80 billion yuan injection into the Silk Road Fund, China is moving ahead with the development of the multidimensional Belt and Road connectivity network, one that is led by the building of a green Silk Road and will empower a digital Silk Road.

Second, implementing the Global Development Initiative. On the basis of over 1,100 development projects already in operation, we will make sure the Global South research center that is being built is fit for purpose, and the 20 billion U.S. dollars of development funds will continue to be put to good use to support developing countries and deepen practical cooperation in areas such as poverty reduction, food security and the digital economy.

Third, supporting development in Africa. At the Summit of the Forum on China-Africa Cooperation held in September this year, I unveiled ten partnership actions on joining hands with Africa to advance modernization over the next three years and, in this connection, a commitment of RMB360 billion yuan in financial support.

Fourth, supporting international cooperation on poverty reduction and food security. China has decided to join the Global Alliance Against Hunger and Poverty. We support the G20 in continuing to convene the Development Ministerial Meeting, and will stay a committed host of the International Conference on Food Loss and Waste.

Fifth, China, alongside Brazil, South Africa and the African Union, is proposing an Initiative on International Cooperation in Open Science to help the Global South gain better access to global advances in science, technology and innovation.

Sixth, supporting the G20 in carrying out practical cooperation for the benefit of the Global South and using such outcomes as the Roadmap to Increase Investment in Clean Energy in Developing Countries and the High-Level Principles on Bioeconomy to good effect. China supports the work of the Entrepreneurship Research Center on G20 Economies based in Beijing, and supports cooperation on digital education and the digitization of museums and ancient archives.

Seventh, implementing the G20 Anti-Corruption Action Plan. We are strengthening cooperation with fellow developing countries in fugitive repatriation and asset recovery, denial of safe haven, and anti-corruption capacity building.

Eighth, China is pursuing high-standard opening up, and unilaterally opening our doors wider to the least developed countries (LDCs). We have announced the decision to give all LDCs having diplomatic relations with China zero-tariff treatment for 100 percent tariff lines. From now to 2030, China's imports from other developing countries are likely to top 8 trillion dollars.

Colleagues,

The Chinese often say, "A journey of a thousand miles begins with the first step." China is ready to take steps together with all parties to build a just world of common development, leave poverty in the past, and turn our vision into reality.

Document 5. Sri Lanka's Indebtedness to China
(*Source*: *Nikkei Asia*, "Sri Lanka Meltdown Exposes China Loan Policy," May 13, 2022, www.nikkeiasia.com)

Here are five things you need to know about China's economic interests in Sri Lanka.

What is China's role in Sri Lanka's $81 billion economy?
Sri Lanka's tilt toward a pro-Beijing foreign policy during [Prime Minister] Mahinda Rajapaksa's second term as president, from 2010 to 2015, paved the way for China's rise as the island's leading banker and builder. Over $5 billion in Chinese loans fueled an infrastructure boom after a nearly 30-year civil war ended on Mahinda's watch. Some of the new landmarks were in Southern Sri Lanka, the Rajapaksa clan's traditional bailiwick, ranging from a new port to an airport and broad highways that cut across the rural hinterland.

China had been a key weapons supplier to Colombo as the final years of the war intensified under Mahinda, with Chinese arms sales rising to $1.8 billion.

Beijing's financial tap, with few conditions on transparency and accountability as Rajapaksa confidants have admitted, enabled China to edge out Japan, for decades Sri Lanka's leading development partner, and India.

China has also invested $1.4 billion in Belt and Road money in what is to be a modern business hub on reclaimed land off Colombo's coast. Like the currency swap, this has given Beijing sway over its strategic Indian Ocean asset. The business development is to complement China's multimillion-dollar stake in the nearby Colombo port, the country's busiest harbor.

How do Chinese loans compare with others?
By 2020, Sri Lanka's inability to honor maturing external debts was looming. The International Monetary Fund put the island's foreign debt at $38.6 billion, or 47.6% of the central government's total debt. China's slice was 10%, as was Japan's, placing the leading bilateral lenders after the main foreign creditors, international sovereign bondholders and the Asian Development Bank.

But the cost of borrowing from China set that debt apart. Numbers crunched by Verite Research, a Colombo-based think tank, show that the interest rates on Chinese loans averaged 3.3%, versus 0.7% for Japan's. And the maturity period averaged 18 years for Chinese debt, shorter than India's 24 years and Japan's 34 years.

None of this hindered the Rajapaksas' appetite for Chinese credit, opening the door for the Asian powerhouse to fund over a third of 313 debt-funded projects in post-conflict Sri Lanka.

How did China become Sri Lanka's go-to bank?
China's deep pockets enabled it to come to Sri Lanka's rescue when Colombo needed to raise commercial loans, pushing aside the IMF as the traditional

lender of last resort. By 2018, the Chinese cash flow was even tapped by the pro-Western coalition government that succeeded Mahinda's second term as president, with Wickremesinghe as premier. The China Development Bank offered a $1 billion syndicated loan on terms that Colombo found more attractive than competing bids from Western-leaning international banks: an eight-year maturity period, with a three-year grace period, at 5.25% interest.

Thereafter, China wanted to tip the scales further with an offer to buy an entire $1 billion sovereign bond issue. But the Sri Lankan government declined, preferring to go to the international capital markets "in the interest of diversity" to limit the country's exposure to Chinese creditors, a commercial banking source revealed to Nikkei Asia.

Yet the impact of COVID-19 in 2020 saw the Rajapaksas, back in power, turn to Chinese creditors for more syndicated loans. In April 2021, the China Development Bank approved a $500 million loan, the second tranche of a $1 billion bailout that Colombo had sought from Beijing in early 2020, as the economic pain from the pandemic spread.

The second tranche came with a maturity period of 10 years and a grace period of three.

How has Beijing responded to Sri Lanka's crisis?
Earlier this year, with Sri Lanka having to pay off foreign debt of $6.9 billion, President Gotabaya and Prime Minister Mahinda sought financial relief from Beijing, asking that the debt payments maturing in 2022 be restructured. The amounts owed to Chinese creditors included $119 million to the China Development Bank Corporation, $232 million to the China Development Bank and $232 million to the Export-Import Bank of China, according to estimates by the Advocata Institute, another Colombo-based think tank.

But Beijing responded with a dose of tough love to its pro-China Sri Lankan allies. In April, after Sri Lanka decided to default on its foreign payments—a first for the country—and seek an IMF bailout, Beijing grumbled. "China has done its best to help Sri Lanka not to default but sadly they went to the IMF and decided to default," Qi Zhenhong, the Chinese ambassador in Sri Lanka, told reporters.

Later, China appeared lukewarm to Colombo's plans to restructure its debts with all its creditors, suggesting it would offer Sri Lanka a new loan to settle existing debt. The two countries have been in talks for months on a $1.5 billion credit line and $1 billion syndicated loan. China's position threatens to scupper plans by Sri Lanka's central bank to treat all creditors equally about an inevitable haircut during its debt restructuring negotiations at the IMF.

What are the implications for other countries indebted to China?
Beijing's detractors in the West and in India have scrutinized the Chinese lending that has underwritten Sri Lanka's post-conflict growth. The China-funded Hambantota Port in the South has been painted as the poster child of Beijing's "debt-trap diplomacy."

Now, in capitals across small Southeast and South Asian nations where Chinese loans have also poured in, officials are following how China handles Sri Lanka's economic woes. Beijing's debt map spans Cambodia, Laos and Myanmar to the Maldives and Nepal. As one senior Southeast Asian government official put it, "All eyes will be on the Chinese haircut or if Beijing will balk and worsen the situation for Sri Lanka."

Document 6. The Chinese Model for Humanity

(*Background:* This report by a Chinese Community Party think tank was presented at an international forum in Brazil. Its authors laud the achievements of China's economy and society under the party's leadership: "rapid economic surge and maintaining long-term social stability —both remarkable miracles rarely created throughout the world." The report then claims that China "has developed its distinct path to modernization, and thereby created a new model for human advancement,which provides effective solutions to the problems facing the entire humanity and China's own answers to the three questions raised by the world." What follows is an excerpt from the report that notes three global initiatives under Xi Jinping in development, security, and civilization. *Source:* "A New Model for Human Advancement and Its Global Significance," Institute of Party History and Literature of the Chinese Communist Party Central Committee and New China Research, November 2024.)

GDI for World Economic Prosperity
In response to the serious challenges in global economic and social development, Chinese President Xi Jinping proposed the Global Development Initiative (GDI) in Beijing on September 21, 2021 during an important speech via video at the General Debate of the 76th Session of the United Nations General Assembly. The GDI advocates for staying committed to development as a priority, a people- centered approach, benefits for all, innovation-driven development, harmony between man and nature, and results-oriented actions. It calls upon the international community to tackle challenges together and pushes for international efforts to consolidate and expand consensus on development.

China has taken active steps to transform the GDI from a proposal into an international consensus and from a cooperative vision into collective action, and injected Chinese strength into the implementation of the United Nations' 2030 Agenda for Sustainable Development. Since the GDI's introduction,

China has established over 30 cooperative platforms and initiated more than 1,100 projects in eight key areas including poverty alleviation, food security, COVID-19 response and vaccines, development financing, climate change and green development, industrialization, digital economy, and digital-age connectivity, which cover all 17 Sustainable Development Goals (SDGs) of the Agenda. So far, China has invested and mobilized a range of development funds totaling nearly USD 20 billion and launched more than 600 projects from the GDI project database. From technological cooperation to capacity building, from poverty allevia- tion education to digital economy, and from high-yield rice cultivation to Juncao technology, China's pragmatic actions have yielded substantial results, helping accelerate the Global South's development and injecting into the stagnant global growth positive energy.

The GDI has received a positive response from over 100 countries and international organizations, particularly the global South countries, exerting a significant and far-reaching international influence. As a "recommitment" to the Agenda, the GDI calls on the international community to accelerate the Agenda's implementation, pursue more robust, greener, and more balanced global development, and build a global community of development of shared future. In doing so, it outlines a blueprint for the development of all countries and for international development cooperation, and provides a clear direction for advancing global development. . . .

GSI for World Peace and Stability
Confronted with emerging challenges and difficulties, the world seeks new solutions,
and the global security calls for new international public goods. Chinese President Xi Jinping put forward the Global Security Initiative (GSI) when delivering a keynote address via video at the opening ceremony of the Boao Forum for Asia Annual Conference on April 21, 2022. The GSI is underpinned by "six commitments", specifically, staying committed to the vision of common, comprehensive, cooperative, and sustainable security; staying committed to respecting the sovereignty and territorial integrity of all countries; staying committed to abiding by the purposes and principles of the Charter of the United Nations; staying committed to taking the legitimate security concerns of all countries seriously; staying committed to peacefully resolving differences and disputes between countries through dialogue and consultation; and staying committed to maintaining security in both traditional and non- traditional domains, with a
view to jointly promoting a global community of security for all. It addresses such questions of the times as what security concept the world needs and how countries can achieve common security.

China has forged ahead through crises and challenges and translated the GSI into concrete actions . . . China has issued position papers on the Ukraine crisis, the Palestinian-Israeli conflict, and the Afghan Issue, and spared no efforts to promote talks for peace, rekindling hope for political settlement of hot-spot issues; China has deepened cooperation with various countries in such areas as international peacekeeping, counterterrorism, climate change, disaster prevention and reduction, and combating transnational crime, thus strengthening collaborative international security governance; China has continuously established platforms for exchanges and dialogue on international security such as the Boao Forum for Asia Annual Conference and the Beijing Xiangshan Forum and actively led and participated in security-related exchanges and cooperation under the frameworks of the Shanghai Cooperation Organization (SCO), the Conference on Interaction and Confidence Building Measures in Asia, and the East Asian Cooperation Mechanism, thereby creating a robust foundation for promoting international security collaboration. In a world marked by upheaval, China has steadily advanced global security cooperation, achieving continuous progress and fostering global consensus on international and regional security challenges, thereby injecting greater stability into an unsettled world. . . .

GCI for Exchanges and Mutual Learning among Civilizations
Equal exchanges and mutual learning among civilizations will provide crucial momentum.

and a fundamental basis for humanity in addressing the pressing challenges of our time and achieving common development. On March 15, 2023, Chinese President Xi Jinping introduced the Global Civilization Initiative (GCI) during his keynote speech at the CPC in Dialogue with World Political Parties High-Level Meeting. The GCI presents "four joint advocacies" of respecting the diversity of civilizations and upholding the principles of equality, mutual learning, dialogue, and inclusiveness among civilizations; of humanity's shared values of peace, development, fairness, justice, democracy, and freedom; of attaching importance to the inheritance and innovation of civilizations and fully harnessing the relevance of histories and cultures to the present times; and of enhancing international people-to-people exchanges and cooperation and exploring the building of a global network for inter-civilization dialogue and cooperation. . . .

Following its introduction, the GCI has gradually gained broad understanding and recognition from the international community. On June 7, 2024, the 78th Session of the UN General Assembly unanimously adopted a China-proposed resolution to designate June 10 as the International Day for Dialogue among Civilizations and to invite all member states and UN agencies to commemorate the day. The UN's resolution on establishing this International Day, which centers around the GCI's core tenets of "four advocacies", states that all civilizational achievements are the collective heritage of humankind, advocates respecting the diversity of civilizations, emphasizes the crucial role of dialogue among civilizations in maintaining world peace, promoting common development, enhancing human well-being, and achieving collective progress, and calls for equal dialogue and mutual respect among different civilizations. . . .

Document 7. China's Position on the Israel-Palestine Conflict (2024)

(*Background:* China and Israel established diplomatic relations in 1992. For many years, Israel supplied military and other technology to China, sometimes incurring US objections. Trade flourished despite political differences over the Palestinian issue, which included China's early support of Hamas as the legitimate governing authority in Gaza. But the war that began with the Hamas attack on Israel on October 7, 2023 strained Israel-China relations, including trade, as Beijing condemned Israel's response to the attack and reiterated its support for Palestinian statehood. *Source*: Xinhua, November 27, 2024, "Xi Extends Congratulations on International Day of Solidarity with Palestinian People," https://english.news.cn/20241127/bc9 aeaee299e45978a4f31bade3f4fee/c.html)

[Xi Jinping] said the pressing task is to comprehensively and effectively implement the relevant UN Security Council resolutions to end the war as soon as possible and ease the regional situation. The fundamental way out is to implement the two-State solution and promote the political settlement of the question of Palestine, establish an independent Palestinian state enjoying full sovereignty on the basis of the 1967 borders with East Jerusalem as its capital, and ensure the right of the Palestinian people to statehood, their right to existence and their right of return . . .

Document 8. China's Position on the Iran Nuclear Issue

(*Source*: Ministry of Foreign Affairs, China, March 14, 2025, https://www.mfa.gov.cn/eng/wjbzhd/202503/t20250314_11919.html)

On 14 March 2025, Member of the Political Bureau of the CCP Central Committee and Foreign Minister Wang Yi met with Deputy Foreign Minister Ryabkov Sergey Alexeevich of the Russian Federation and Deputy Foreign Minister Kazem Gharibabadi of the Islamic Republic of Iran who attended the Beijing Meeting Between China, Russia and Iran, and proposed the following five points on the proper settlement of the Iranian nuclear issue.

First, stay committed to peaceful settlement of disputes through political and diplomatic means, and oppose the use of force and illegal sanctions. All parties should uphold the vision of common, comprehensive, cooperative and sustainable security, work actively to create conditions for the resumption of dialogue and negotiation, and refrain from actions that might escalate the situation.

Second, stay committed to balancing rights and responsibilities, and take a holistic approach to the goals of nuclear nonproliferation and peaceful uses of nuclear energy. Iran should continue honoring its commitment to not developing nuclear weapons, and all other parties should fully respect Iran's right to peaceful uses of nuclear energy as a State Party to the Treaty on the Non-proliferation of Nuclear Weapons (NPT).

Third, stay committed to the framework of the Joint Comprehensive Plan of Action (JCPOA [the 2015 nuclear deal]) as the basis for new consensus. China hopes that all parties will work toward the same direction and resume dialogue and negotiation as early as possible. The United States should demonstrate political sincerity and return to talks at an early date.

Fourth, stay committed to promoting cooperation through dialogue, and oppose pressing for intervention by the U.N. Security Council (UNSC). Under the current situation, hasty intervention by the UNSC will not help build confidence or bridge differences among the relevant parties. Initiating the snapback mechanism would undo years of diplomatic efforts, and must be handled with caution.

Fifth, stay committed to a step-by-step and reciprocal approach, and seek consensus through consultation. History has proven that acting from a position of strength would not lead to the key to resolving difficult issues. Upholding the principle of mutual respect is the only viable path to finding the greatest common ground that accommodates the legitimate concerns of all parties and reaching a solution that meets the expectation of the international community.

As a permanent member of the UNSC and a party to the JCPOA, China will stay in communication and coordination with all relevant parties, actively promote talks for peace, and play a constructive role in realizing early resumption of talks.

5

China's Relations with Its Near Neighbors

Introduction

In April 2025, Xi Jinping convened a high-level conference on what was billed as "neighborhood work"—that is, China's policies and aims in Asia's several regions. A Chinese report on the conference "highlighted that China's vast territory and long borders make its neighborhood a vital foundation for national development and prosperity, a key front for safeguarding national security, a priority area in the country's overall diplomacy, and a crucial link in building a community with a shared future for humanity."[1]

In this chapter we consider China's relations with the two Koreas, Japan, India, and Myanmar (the former Burma)—countries chosen because each relationship reveals features of China's foreign policy. The Democratic People's Republic of Korea (DPRK, North Korea), a socialist country, has been strategically and economically supported by China ever since the Korean War (1950–53). In more recent years, Beijing has stood by the DPRK in confrontations with the United States over the North's nuclear weapons. Yet Chinese leaders have always had to worry about the steadiness of the DPRK's leader, Kim Jong Un, whose aggressive posturing and missile buildup might bring on another war that would risk dragging China in. That concern is complicated by North Korea's "strategic partnership" with Russia that was declared in 2024 (**Selections 1, 2**).

US policy has not been able either to create a breakthrough in relations with North Korea or take advantage of China-DPRK tensions (**Selection 3**). North-South Korea tensions also impact China's substantial trade with the Republic of Korea (South Korea), which began in the early 1990s when they established diplomatic relations. China has become the top trading partner of the ROK, displacing the United States.

China's relations with Japan have been heavily influenced by Imperial Japan's horrific occupation during the Second World War. Those memories have created persistent Chinese mistrust in Japan's rearmament and tight alignment with US security policies (**Selections 4–5 and Documents 1–2**). Yet, in keeping with the notion of "hot economics, cold politics," the Chinese and Japanese economies are highly interdependent: They are each other's largest trading partner (**Selection 7**). Japan faces new challenges in the second Trump term—pressure from both the United States and China over trade and defense (**Selection 6**).

Mistrust is a central issue in China's relations with India, specifically over their border, scene of a war in 1961 and territorial conflict that continues to the present. China's close ties with Pakistan, India's defense ties with the United States, and India's dependence on imports from China have also contributed to mutual suspicion—all abetted by the brief Indo-Pakistan fighting over Kashmir in May 2025. Countries that sit between India and China are inevitably drawn into the competition (**Selection 9**). India's refusal to join the BRI, in contrast with the China-Pakistan Economic Corridor, now in its tenth year, is indicative of another source of tension: the competition for leadership among Global South countries (**Selection 8 and Document 3**).

In Southeast Asia, China has become the central player in the ten ASEAN economies. Beijing claims several major contributions to regional commerce and infrastructure building (**Document 4**). Myanmar is the weak link; civil war has gravely weakened the military junta's rule, raising questions for Beijing about how to secure its interests in that country. China appears to be working with both the rebels and the junta, ignoring the latter's appalling human rights record (**Selection 10**).

(1) Renewed Tensions on the Korean Peninsula (2023)

A Profitable Visit, and Nuclear Threats Reemerge

Alarm bells rang in Tokyo, Seoul, and Washington over North Korean leader Kim Jong Un's transactions during his six-day stay in Vladivostok in 2023. He visited a full range of Russian military installations—bases, missile sites, ports, and a space port. Kim seemed to have a particular interest in space technology, no doubt due to the failure of two recent space launches. From various reports, the transactions were two-way. Russia promised to provide North Korea with help on missile technology, notwithstanding UN sanctions on the North's ballistic missile tests. Russia may also have agreed to provide food assistance to offset North Korea's always troubled agriculture sector, and it may have increased the number of workers it sends to North Korea to reinforce industrial development. North Korea probably provides Russia with a variety of weapons, including multiple rocket launchers, artillery shells, sniper rifles, drones, and missiles.

North Korea suddenly has become the darling of Russian and Chinese diplomats. In July 2024, Russia sent its defense minister, Sergei Shoigu, to visit North Korea, the first time since Soviet days that a Russian defense minister had visited North Korea. Following on Kim Jong Un's trip to Vladivostok, China's foreign minister Wang Yi went to North Korea, and Russia's foreign minister Sergei Lavrov did the same. The substance of those visits was not revealed, but they probably involved more than just a reinforcement of cooperative ties. Most likely is that the visits were also in response to three developments: the recent trilateral agreement of South Korea, the United States, and Japan to deepen security cooperation; a new round of meetings of United States and South Korean defense officials on deterring North Korea through the recently created Nuclear Consultation Group; and high-level talk in South Korea, though restrained by Washington, about developing its own nuclear weapons.

Thus, implicit nuclear threats were being made by *both* Koreas—by the North, in expanding its nuclear and missile arsenal, and by the South in hinting at going nuclear. Consider this report in the South Korean press on a joint US-ROK statement after a visit by a US Defense Department official: "the U.S. side reaffirmed its 'ironclad' commitment to the defense of South Korea, leveraging the 'full range' of its military capabilities, and reiterated that any nuclear attack by the North against the U.S. and its allies will result in the 'end of the Kim regime.'"[2]

Alternative Views

Will new North Korean ballistic missile tests or even a long-awaited seventh nuclear test be in the offing? Has the threat from the North risen to a new level? Most US and South Korean analysts seem to think so, but here are some other ideas.

Two people with considerable experience dealing with North Korea, Robert Carlin and Siegfried Hecker, went deeper into the Kim visit to Russia. They wrote that "it is the result of a fundamental shift in North Korean policy, finally abandoning a 30-year effort to normalize relations with the US." Contrary to the conventional view of North Korea, these experts argued that even as Kim invested heavily in nuclear weapons and missiles, he also looked to use them as bargaining chips with the United States, hoping he could win security assurances as part of normal relations. But Kim finally concluded after his dealings with Trump and lack of attention from Biden that normalization wasn't achievable. At that point, he moved closer to Moscow and Beijing. A missed opportunity for the United States? Perhaps;

as with US relations with Iran, the war in Ukraine so absorbed Washington policymakers that creative diplomacy aimed at keeping nuclear weapons in their silos just didn't occur.

From another angle, Kim's Russia visit may have posed problems for China. Russia may have gained an advantage over China by becoming the key weapons supplier to Pyongyang. Kim used the occasion to reiterate support of Russia's war on Ukraine, saying for instance that Russia would "win a great victory in the sacred struggle to punish the band of evil that aspires to hegemony and feeds on expansionist illusions." An expected tribute to Russia, to be sure, but perhaps something more. Greater Russian influence in North Korea might lead to more missile tests by Kim and further tension on the Korean peninsula. Putin might find that helpful as the Ukraine war moves along, but the Chinese have always been concerned about a crisis on their doorstep precipitated by a North Korean weapons test. Given their domestic problems and tensions with the US today, a crisis on the Korean peninsula would seem particularly unwelcome in Beijing. I would have to think that view has been communicated to Kim Jong Un and the Russians more than once. If US relations with China were better, China's cooperation in restraining Kim Jong Un might be obtainable. That's not the case, and thus another missed opportunity for lowering tensions.

(2) The Russia-North Korea "Strategic Partnership": Implications for China (2024)

In the fall of 2024, North Korea sent around 10,000 special forces troops to the Russian Far East, apparently in preparation for their deployment to fight in Ukraine. This deployment took place after Russian President Vladimir Putin's visit to Pyongyang in June 2024 for the first time in twenty-four years. Putin signed a "comprehensive strategic partnership" and a mutual defense treaty with Kim Jong Un.

What the "Strategic Partnership" Might Involve

The "strategic partnership" expanded on Russia's security relationship with North Korea in two ways. First, North Korea would be increasing its supplies of artillery shells and short-range missiles it sends to Russia for use against Ukraine. Most analysts saw those supplies as being crucial to Russia's prosecution of the war. Second, the partnership would now include a mutual defense treaty, which stipulates that the two countries should "immediately provide military and other assistance using all available means" if either side is in a state of war. What that means in practice is far from clear, however. For example, would Moscow invoke this defense promise if North Korea were to precipitate a crisis with South Korea? That might well lead to a nuclear-level confrontation with the US.

After Putin's 2024 visit to the DPRK, the United States and South Korea worried, correctly as it turned out, that Russia would no longer vote in the UN Security Council to sanction North Korea for its missile and nuclear testing—a major shift in Russia's long-standing policy on nuclear nonproliferation. In April 2024, Russian vetoed continuation of the UN Panel of Experts on North Korea, its sanctions compliance regime. Additionally, the United States and the ROK also had to be concerned that Kim Jong Un might become even bolder in his missile tests, to the point where he could make a major miscalculation of US and South Korean reactions. In fact, just a week before the US presidential election on November 5, 2024, the North launched an intercontinental ballistic missile, which had a flight time longer than any previously tested ICBM. (In February 2025, eleven countries—including the United States and South Korea, but not Russia or China—formed a Multilateral Sanctions Monitoring Team to monitor North Korean nuclear and missile tests in place of the UN Panel of Experts.[3])

For South Korea, the Putin-Kim alliance raised still another issue: whether to continue the policy of not sending arms to Ukraine. Until then, South Korea had limited aid to Ukraine to humanitarian assistance and non-lethal military supplies. But Seoul reacted strongly to the new Russian arrangement with the North, saying it represented a national security threat. Putin warned South Korea that it would be a "big mistake" to change its policy. Moscow "will. . . [make] decisions which are unlikely to please the current leadership of South Korea," strongly implying that Russia would make new arms shipments to the North in retaliation. Putin said: "Those who supply these weapons believe that they are not at war with us. I said, including [when I visited] in Pyongyang, that we then reserve the right to supply weapons to other regions of the world." Chances are he and Kim had already made plans for the North Korean troops.

Sending military personnel to fight abroad is not unprecedented for North Korea; they served in the Vietnam War and fought on the side of the Assad regime in the Syrian Civil War in 2016. What North Korea probably got from Russia in return for its support in the Ukraine war was technical assistance for its nuclear and missile programs—and the opportunity for battlefield experience. But for South Korea, the troop deployment was worrisome: It came at a time when North-South Korea tensions had escalated. The North cut road and rail links between North and South as part of an official designation of South Korea as an enemy state, essentially writing off the long-term possibility of reunification. Kim may have thought he had bought Russia's backing for a bold move against the South. That possibility had to worry China's leaders too.

The China Factor

What does this tightening of the Russia-North Korea military relationship mean for China? Some analysts are talking about a Moscow-Pyongyang-Beijing axis that would complicate America's already overloaded security agenda. But "axis" suggests an alliance, which would not be entirely in China's interest. For one thing, China's 1951 mutual defense commitment with North Korea lapsed years ago, so Russia is the only official security partner of the North. The Chinese, long aware of Kim Jong Un's tendency to saber-rattling, are not about to put themselves in the position of one day being forced to make decisions about supporting Kim in a war. It was only about a decade ago that Chinese leaders and Korea experts, wary of North Korea's nuclear brinkmanship, debated the value of having close relations with the North.

Second, Beijing would probably strongly oppose Russia's endorsement of any kind of aggressive move against South Korea, since that would have a major impact on China's security, not to mention undercut China's strong economic ties with the South. Third, for China to identify too closely with the Moscow-Pyongyang alignment would only strengthen US-South Korea-Japan security ties for dealing with the "China threat." And fourth, China, along with Brazil, was touting a peace plan to end the Ukraine war. Since that plan rested on no further expansion of the fighting, Putin's invitation to Kim undermined China's effort to be a peacemaker.

In short, China may have had the most to lose from this latest Putin-Kim gambit. Beijing has always had some leverage with Kim—North Korea's dependence on China for food, fuel, and (in defiance of UN sanctions) goods such as machine tools that can be used to manufacture weapons.[4] In theory, North Korea's serious economic problems, such as inflation, a weak currency, and low energy production, added to China's leverage.[5] China also has had potential leverage with Putin—its critical economic and military aid in the Ukraine war. But all that leverage seemed unlikely to be sufficient to deter Kim, with Russia's support, from continuing to emphasize missile and nuclear weapon capabilities. At best, China might be able to prevail on Kim not to engage in highly provocative behavior with the South. (North Korea did not do so at the end of 2024 when South Korean politics was thrown into chaos by a president's declaration of martial law, which ended in his impeachment and resignation.) Still, having somewhere between fifty and sixty nuclear weapons can create the illusion of absolute security in Pyongyang. It would not be the first time a North Korean leader has tried to manipulate relations with Moscow and Beijing.

(3) US-China Relations and US Policy on North Korea (2025)

Years ago, the United States had an opportunity to make inroads in North Korea's international relations that might have avoided the current alignment of the DPRK with Russia and China. First, the United States could have concluded an agreement with North Korea aimed at freezing its nuclear arsenal and subjecting it to international inspection. In return, the United States would have provided assurances of the North's regime and state security. Second, the United States could have made engagement with China a top priority, giving Beijing incentives for using its influence with North Korea to prevent the kind of polarizing alignment with Russia that has taken place. To be sure, those two US actions would have aroused considerable hostility within the political establishment. But when we consider what has happened in the last few years—the increasingly tense US-China relationship, China's nuclear weapon buildup, North Korea's expanded and improved nuclear and missile arsenal, and North Korean soldiers fighting in Ukraine—an early emphasis on diplomacy with Beijing and Pyongyang looks like it would have been well worth trying.

Strains are appearing in North Korea's relations with China. China still supports North-South Korea unification and denuclearization, positions Kim Jong Un has discarded. In economic policy, North Korea is closing markets, reducing tourists and students visiting China, and in other ways moving away from a tight attachment to Beijing. On broader policy, China does not take the strong anti-imperialist stance that North Korea takes, and China rejects the North Korea-Russia argument that we're in a new Cold War in which all three countries square off with the United States and its security partners. To take such a position, the Chinese seem to be thinking, would only raise tensions even further in Northeast Asia, risking a major blowup on the Korean peninsula. Yet the United States has given China no incentives to break or lessen its partnership with Russia and the DPRK.

Donald Trump may again try to strike a deal with Kim Jong Un, his aim probably being to wean North Korea away from both Russia and China. Trump's statement early in 2025 that North Korea is a nuclear power surely caught Kim's attention. His comment suggests that denuclearization is no longer US policy, a position that would surely alienate South Korea and Japan, probably embolden pro-nuclear forces in the South, and cause considerable anguish in Beijing. Even so, it is hard to imagine that North Korea would jettison its mutual defense and aid agreements with Russia. That ship has sailed. North Korea has made the strategic choice to abandon hope of normal relations with the United States. And with US-China relations likely to go further downhill, Trump can expect no support from Xi Jinping.

(4) Risky Business as Japan Steps Out

Background to a Changing Strategic Perspective

When Japan's Prime Minister Kishida Fumio visited Washington in April 2024, he drew attention to how Japan was remaking its national security policy. He won applause from Washington and heard anguish in Beijing. Here's the background:

Ever since the American occupation of Japan after the Second World War, that country's national security has been constructed under the US umbrella. Japan's pacifist constitution, the size and budget of its armed forces, and its security strategy were all shaped in accordance with American preferences. The 1960 mutual defense treaty stipulates US defense of Japan from attack, the right of the United States to base forces in Japan, and US consultation with Japan on how American forces there will be used. Japan kept its military spending at about 1 percent of GNP and officially called its military Self-Defense Forces.

During the Korean War, Japan provided logistical and supply assistance to US forces. Questions have arisen since about the extent of Japanese support of the United States in a crisis that might involve war with North Korea or a direct Chinese threat to Taiwan. Washington was always pressing Japan to "do more" in the name of collective security. Tokyo accepted that "collective security" allowed for a stronger commitment to the alliance but typically restricted its action abroad to UN peacekeeping missions. Japan's hesitancy was due mainly to wanting to avoid becoming a target in a war, most likely with China.[6]

Despite constitutional limits, Japan has one of the world's most technologically advanced armed forces (around 261,000 troops) and one of the world's highest military budgets (around $54 billion, which ranks ninth). Under Prime Minister Abe Shinzo, Kishida's predecessor, constitutional strictures were stretched to allow for Japanese military involvement abroad—not frontline combat, but in supportive roles, such as in Afghanistan. Abe had also hoped to revise Article 9 of the constitution, under which Japan renounces war as an instrument of its foreign policy. He sought to revise the article specifically to allow Japan to deploy its military in combat overseas. Abe failed, though constitutional revision has always had US support.

New Threat Perceptions

Prime Minister Kishida, a former defense minister, seemed to take advantage of Japan's increasing vulnerability to North Korean missiles and an assertive Chinese military, especially near Taiwan, to push for all the things

Abe dreamed about. The 2023 Japanese national security strategy paper made the chief target clear: China. The paper said China is "the greatest strategic challenge that Japan has ever faced." It called for a doubling of Japan's military budget over the next five years and for assembling a so-called counter-strike capability, all geared to an upgraded regional threat assessment.[7] In practice, the new strategic perspective allowed Japan to target North Korean or Chinese bases if attacked. In light of North Korea's record-setting missile tests in 2023, with some missiles landing in waters near Japan, and its new doctrine of preemptive nuclear attack, Japan's strategic change was based on more than a hypothetical threat.

The war in Ukraine also shaped the new Japanese strategic perspective. The Japanese, said Michael Green, a Japan expert at the Brookings Institution, would have been taken aback had the United States not stepped up in support of Ukraine. It then became Japan's turn to step up: "Japan is choosing, not being forced by America, but is choosing to reinforce the international order that America helped to create after [World War II]."[8] Two other important upgrades in Japan's security partnerships resulted. First, Japan announced that, for the first time, it would have a "Reciprocal Access Agreement" with a European country, Great Britain, that will permit both to station troops on each other's soil and carry out extensive military exercises together. Japan already has the same arrangement with Australia.

Second is improved US-Japan military coordination. As summarized by one writer: "the United States and Japan are both updating their command-and-control arrangements. Tokyo has announced that it will create a permanent joint headquarters in Japan to command the Japanese Self-Defense Forces during a crisis."[9] In addition, at least one and probably more US marine regiments will have upgraded capabilities for rapid regional deployment, a further indication that deterring China is the centerpiece of US-Japan security cooperation. No wonder President Biden told Kishida: "I don't think there's ever been a time when we've been closer to Japan."

Tokyo thus sent a message to Pyongyang and Beijing: Another North Korea nuclear test, or a missile launch that threaten Japanese territory, might prompt a retaliation. The aim would be to deter the North. Beijing would need to be aware of the extent to which its military modernization, particularly in air and sea power, and its air maneuvers near Taiwan, were prompting public support in Japan for a new defense outlook focused on the China threat. Japan's hyping of the China threat might strengthen any voices in Xi Jinping's inner circle calling for caution on attacking Taiwan.

Cold War Alignments

There are two important upshots of Japan's latest national strategic thinking. It coincides with a strategic trend in Asia Pacific, led by the United

States, toward anti-China multilateralism. Several of China's neighbors—Japan, South Korea, the Philippines, India, Vietnam, and Australia—are either US security treaty partners, members of US-backed security groups (AUKUS and the Quadrilateral Security Dialogue), or countries that have granted access to US ships and planes. China would surely consider such a Cold War-style lineup threatening enough to make a military response. So far the response has been a continual expansion of its regional air and sea capabilities, as noted in Chapter 2. The other and opposite implication is that neither Japan nor any of the other countries aligned with the United States was suggesting or constructing peaceful, stabilizing steps that would discourage a confrontation with China.

We're headed back toward an "either you're for us or against us" alignment in Asia, with no middle ground—an uncomfortable strategic position that many countries in Southeast Asia have experienced before. Does anyone really think Japan's new security profile is more likely to deter rather than incite armed conflict?

(5) US-Japan Security Ties Strengthen (2024–2025)

The Biden-Kishida Summit

An "historic" summit meeting April 10–11, 2024 between President Biden and Prime Minister Kishida resulted in major changes in US-Japan security ties that are said to have smoothed relations but probably added to tensions with China. The two leaders shared a common evaluation of the threat posed by China, North Korea's increasing missile potential, and Russia's invasion of Ukraine. Prior to the summit, Kishida said: "The current security environment is tough and complex, and we are at a turning point in history. Cooperation between Japan and the United States and like-minded countries is a very important issue." Among the agreements reached by the two leaders were:

- An improved military common command-and-control system.
- Co-production of certain missiles for air defense.
- Japanese participation in US space missions.
- Major new private investments in each other's country, including an investment by Toyota of nearly $8 billion for electric car battery production in Greensboro, NC, which was expected to create 3,000 jobs. US and Japanese corporations will also invest in AI research at both countries' universities.

- "New high-level dialogue" on ways to meet climate change objectives.
- US support of Japan's restarting of nuclear reactors—a rather surprising addition given the unpopularity in Japan of nuclear power since the Fukushima tragedy.

One sensitive issue that was not mentioned, understandably, in an election year: the controversy over Nippon Steel's bid to take over US Steel. (Months later, the Biden administration rejected the deal, a slap in the face to Japan.)

Japan's Expanding Security Picture

Japan's changing strategic perspective is the kind the US has long wished for. Its military spending has jumped, its weapons modernization program has advanced, and it has joined with the United States in various security coalitions, such as the Quad. A US-Japan-Australia-Philippines joint naval exercise in disputed waters of the South China Sea also took place. The US, Japan, and Philippines held a first-ever joint White House security conference on April 11, 2024, with China's "coercive and unlawful" (Biden's words) actions in the South China Sea the main topic. And as part of the Biden-Kishida summit, Japanese involvement with the AUKUS security group was under discussion. Clearly, Japan was investing a great deal in a US strategic vision centered on an exaggerated notion of the China threat in the Asia Pacific.

Further steps toward China-oriented strategic cooperation took place later in 2024. During the US-Japan "2+2" security talks (talks led by each country's defense chief and top diplomat), both sides affirmed upgrading the command and control of US forces, as well as strengthening American-licensed missile production. The commander of the roughly 50,000 US troops stationed in Japan was granted expanded authority. When Ishiba Shigeru became the prime minister in the fall, he added a personal wish: that the Status of Forces Agreement with the US be changed so that Japanese would have access to US bases and other military facilities, such as when US soldiers break the law. It's a matter of Japanese sovereignty, Ishiba said, though he also said it's a complicated business that he would not pursue right away.

But US-Japan security relations became complicated in the second Trump term. Japan's compliance with US wishes for increased military spending proved insufficient. The Pentagon announced that the Trump administration had set a "global standard" in military spending by US allies of 5 percent of GDP. For Japan, that figure would be risky given its history, its economic situation, and most recently Trump's tariffs on Japanese autos and steel. The figure was also far more than Japan's planners had in mind, which was

2 percent of GDP by 2027. Tokyo responded by abruptly scrapping the annual 2+2 security talks with the US.

(6) Japan and China in the Trump Era

Like South Korea, India, and the European Union, Japan is struggling to find a way to keep relations with the United States on an even keel with Donald Trump as president again. Tokyo's challenge is to deflect the worst effects of Trump's tariffs and defend its decision on military spending. At the same time, Japan has to keep tensions with China from boiling over. The diplomatic challenge for China is how to take advantage of Japan-US trade tensions without adding to Japan's mistrust and threat perceptions of China.

Strategic Concerns

Meeting with Donald Trump in February 2025, Prime Minister Ishiba Shigeru proposed to resolve the Nippon Steel-US Steel issue by having Nippon make a substantial investment to upgrade US Steel's technology. The final deal calls for Nippon Steel to invest about $15 billion in US Steel, make it a subsidiary, but allow the US government to play a key role in the new company's decisions. Subsequently, Japan announced that it would tighten defense relations with the Philippines. Japanese and US officials agreed that China is the reason for these changes. As Kamikawa Yoko, Japan's foreign minister under Kishida, said: "We are standing at a historic turning point as the rules-based, free and open international order is shaken to the core. Now is a critical phase when our decision today determines our future."

Not addressed was how expanded military arrangements around China's periphery might impact Chinese strategic thinking.[10] Ishiba surely rankled Beijing when he said on February 7 that Japan and the United States "opposed any attempts to unilaterally change the status quo by force or coercion" in relation to Taiwan. For Japan, that was a step up from previous comments on Taiwan by Japanese leaders, who were prone to use the same ambiguous language used by US officials—urging "stability" in the Taiwan Strait while avoiding a commitment to act if China threatened Taiwan.

Lingering Mistrust

Two other issues complicate Japan-China relations in 2025. One is that four Chinese professors teaching in Japan have been unable to return to Japan after visiting home. The most recent such case occurred in 2024 when a Chinese professor who taught at the Hokkaido University of Education for twenty-five years vanished after returning to China to attend his mother's funeral. In all four cases, contacting these professors proved impossible. The Hokkaido University professor was charged with espionage. His Japanese colleagues started a petition drive in protest, but the case was dealt with behind a veil of secrecy until a sentence was handed down. The case is important not just for its likely impact on educational exchanges between China and Japan but also because it reflects the worsening of their relations in general. Ken Suzuki, a professor of Chinese law at Meiji University in Tokyo, told *University World News* that "Professor Yuan was not a political activist." "Japanese and Chinese professors have begun rejecting offers to conduct research in China to avoid a similar fate," Suzuki said. "I see the risk facing this sector as only escalating in the future."[11]

The second lingering issue is the discharge of the Fukushima nuclear power plant's contaminated water following the nuclear accident in 2021. China has opposed Japan's decision to discharge the water without consulting Beijing. A China-Japan High-Level Economic Dialogue in March 2025 revealed that the issue remains alive and needs continual monitoring. Until then, China has indicated it will not accept Japan's seafood exports, which is a heavy blow to Japanese fishers.

Damage Control

As **Documents 1 and 2** at the end of this chapter make clear, Chinese officials involved in exchanges with Japan urge the Japanese to put aside strategic rivalry and focus on trade and other areas of cooperation. That means not only papering over historical animosities but also minimizing China's growing military power, particularly in areas of security concern to Japan. Besides Taiwan, the East China Sea continues to be a point of contention, centered around a territorial dispute over islands that China calls Diaoyutai and Japan calls Senkaku. The islands are uninhabited but are valued for the fishing around them.[12] The United States supports Japan's claim to the islands. Chinese diplomats may cite an old saying that "distant relatives are not as good as close neighbors," but sending heavily armed coast guard vessels to protect claimed territory undermines proffers of friendship.

Nevertheless, we can expect that if Japan's "distant relative" in Washington pressures Tokyo on trade and defense spending, the "close neighbor" China will keep up the diplomatic appeals and might even provide Japan with lower tariffs on its exports to China. Trump didn't act like an ally when, in April 2025, he imposed a 24-percent tariff and repeated one of his long-standing criticisms of the US-Japan alliance, calling it "one-sided." At a cabinet meeting, Trump said, erroneously: "We defend them, but they don't have to defend us." And: "We pay hundreds of billions of dollars to defend them . . . they don't pay anything."[13] Trump chose to forget Japan's hosting of US bases, participation in US security groups, and increased military spending. Yet Trump seems to expect that Japan will follow the United States in decoupling its economy from China's, a highly unlikely prospect given their extensive commercial ties and China's importance in the global supply chain.

China has already warned Japan and others of retaliation if they respond to US threats by reducing trade with China in hopes of getting a tariff rate reduction from Trump. "Seeking so-called exemptions by harming the interests of others for one's own selfish and shortsighted gains is like negotiating with a tiger for its skin," the Chinese commerce ministry said. "In the end, it will only lead to a lose-lose situation."[14] A more positive diplomatic approach by Beijing came early in 2025 when representatives of Japan's ruling party, the Liberal Democrats, and its coalition partner, Komeito, met with Chinese Communist Party leaders for the first time in six years. And in March 2025, the Chinese, Japanese, and South Korean foreign ministers met to reinforce a common commitment to a stable and peaceful Asia Pacific. China may be hoping that the Trump administration will follow up its critique of Japan by reducing the US military presence and defense support in East Asia. But in any case, Japan-China economic relations will remain significant, as Chart 5.1 below shows.

(7) China-India Diplomacy Seeks Improvement (2024–2025)

Late in 2024, high-level dialogue resumed between China and India. Among the most important issues is the tense border situation, which has been the subject of numerous military and diplomatic meetings for several years.[15] The two sides reached agreement on a "disengagement from friction points," as the Indian external affairs minister put it, which would seem to include the creation of buffer zones. Fighting in April-May 2020 along the long-disputed Line of Actual Control had caused a major disruption in relations. When the Chinese and Indian foreign ministers—S. Jaishankar and Wang Yi—met in November 2024, the wording of their respective readouts revealed subtle but important differences.

The readout of India's Ministry of External Affairs (EAM) included these statements (my italics):

2. The Ministers recognized that the *disengagement in our border areas* had contributed to the maintenance of peace and tranquility. The discussions focused on the next steps in India-China relations. It was agreed that a meeting of the Special Representatives and of the Foreign Secretary-Vice Minister mechanism will take place soon.

CHART 5.1 *A Snapshot of Japan-China Economic Relations*

	Exports to China (2024)	**Imports from China (2024)**	**Total Japan-China trade (2024)**	**Foreign Direct Investment in China (2022)**	**Japanese companies in China (2022)**	**Chinese tourists visiting Japan (2023)**
JAPAN	$144.5 billion	$188.8 billion	$333.3 billion	$9.2 billion	31,324	2.4 million
CHINA	Share of total=19.3%. Rank: #1	Share of total=21%. Rank: #1	Rank: #1; Share of Japan total=19.3%	Japan ranks #3	China ranks #1	China ranks #3

Sources: Ministry of Foreign Affairs, Japan, January 2024, https://www.mofa.go.jp/files/100540401.pdf; World Bank, 2022, https://wits.worldbank.org/countrysnapshot/en/JPN

4. On the global situation and international issues, EAM noted that India and China have both *differences and convergences*. We have worked constructively in the BRICS and the SCO [Shanghai Cooperation Organization] framework. Our cooperation in the G20 has also been evident.

5. EAM said that we are strongly committed to a multipolar world, *including a multipolar Asia*. Where India is concerned, its foreign policy has been principled and consistent, marked by independent thought and action. *We are against unilateral approaches* to establish dominance. India does not view its relationships through the prism of other nations.[16]

The Chinese readout included this statement:

The two sides should implement the important consensus reached by the two heads of state, *respect each other's core interests*, enhance mutual trust through dialogue and communication, handle differences properly with sincerity and integrity, and bring the bilateral relationship *back on the track* of stable and sound development at an early date. The two sides should send more positive signals and engage in actions that facilitate bilateral exchanges, create more mutual trust and less suspicion, and have more cooperation and less depletion. The two sides should strive to make practical progress in such issues as resuming direct flights, exchanging journalists and easing visa procedures as soon as possible.[17]

Early in 2025, Indian and Chinese diplomats took additional steps to normalize relations. They reached an agreement on exchanges that would test the waters on improved relations. The exchanges involved media and think tank personnel, resumption of direct air service, and renewal of cross-border river communications. Xi Jinping, writing in the Indian newspaper *The Hindu* on April 2, stressed partnership over rivalry, indirectly acknowledging that mutual senses of threat will not be easy to overcome. "We should uphold the principles of mutual respect, mutual understanding, mutual trust, mutual accommodation and mutual accomplishment," Xi wrote. "We should properly handle differences through dialogue, and never allow bilateral relations to be defined by the boundary question, or let specific differences affect the overall picture of bilateral ties."[18]

Prime Minister Narendra Modi may agree, but he balanced agreements with China by strengthening ties with the US. On an official visit in February 2025, President Trump promised Modi that the United States would increase military sales to India by "many billions" of dollars. Modi said India and the United States will develop a framework for long-term defense and advanced technology cooperation.[19] But later in the year, all the goodwill evaporated when Trump imposed high tariffs on India to stop it from buying Russian oil. China suddenly looked like a better bet to Modi. He also said that the two countries will collaborate to develop semiconductors, quantum technology, and artificial intelligence.

The significance of that agreement became apparent in May 2025 when India and Pakistan exchanged fire for four days after a terrorist attack occurred in India's part of divided Kashmir. The conflict showed how the pattern of arms suppliers to the two countries has reversed over the years. India is mainly using Western-supplied arms, in contrast with the Cold War era when Russia was the main arms supplier. The United States now provides about 10 percent of India's arms; France is the main supplier. China is by far the main arms seller to Pakistan—over 80 percent. The United States, once a major arms supplier to Pakistan, most conspicuously during the war in Afghanistan, now provides nothing.[20] The fighting tested China's resumption of high-level diplomacy with India, since Pakistan was using Chinese weapons. China did not criticize Pakistan for the initial attack, called India's retaliation "regrettable," and urged both sides to "remain calm, exercise restraint." They did, agreeing to a US mediation that helped secure a ceasefire.

(8) India's Strategic Headaches on Land and Sea

Indian strategists worry not only about the ever-present potential for armed conflict with China along disputed parts of their border. They also have concerns about political developments in the small states that sit between China and India and in the Indian Ocean. Bhutan falls into the first category, the Maldives into the second.

Bhutan

The tiny kingdom of Bhutan borders Tibet to the north and India to the west. In terms of geopolitics today, Bhutan's location poses serious problems for its diplomacy. On one hand, Bhutan has long relied for security on India. On the other, Bhutan must reckon with China's economic and political power, as well as with China's determination to exert tight control over Tibet. Bhutan does not yet have diplomatic relations with China, nor does it have forces that can defend its border from Chinese encroachments. Bhutan's vulnerability illustrates the delicate balancing of power and diplomacy that South Asian countries, including India and Nepal, must practice when dealing with Beijing.

Specialists on Bhutan observe that in recent decades, the country has managed to keep China at bay, resisting diplomatic ties but increasingly relying on its commerce, while maintaining security and trade relations with India. But those days may be ending. Bhutan's value to China in the competition with India and fear of unrest in Tibet may force Bhutan, like Nepal, to recognize Beijing in return for greater economic benefits. As two writers conclude, once normalization of relations with China takes effect, "Bhutan will then be faced with a challenge identical to that which confronted other small states, namely, how to manage a significantly asymmetrical relationship without losing either agency or sovereignty."[21]

Complicating Bhutan's decision on ties to China is China's steady aggrandizement of Bhutan's border areas, as documented by Robert Barnett, a leading scholar of China-South Asia affairs, in his 2024 book, *Forceful Diplomacy: China's Cross-border Villages in Bhutan*.[22] Over the years, the Chinese have moved into unpopulated areas within Bhutan's territory, brought several thousand settlers in, and turned those areas into villages complete with administrative and security officials. Barnett identified twenty-two villages and settlements that China had thus occupied, the most important ones being in the west, where a strategic plateau looks into India. China has sought without success to trade its occupied northeastern land for that strategic western area. Bhutan has maintained that India's security concerns must be considered, a position that, as explained above, is eroding.

The Maldives

The Maldives are an archipelago in the Indian Ocean that has long had tight relations with India but at times has been neglected by New Delhi. The election of a new president in September 2023 changed all that as he made Beijing one of his first overseas stops. There, he secured a "comprehensive strategic cooperative partnership" and, subsequently, a "military assistance" agreement from China. The agreements put an end to what the new Maldivian leadership considers excessive dependence on India for security and economic support. Leaning toward China is in hopes of the same. The Maldives now belong in the same camp as nearby Sri Lanka, which has become heavily indebted to China while participating in the Belt and Road Initiative. Yet from another angle, the tilt to China affords the chance to play both sides, much like Bhutan.

Strategically, Indian observers worry that China is building a network of partners across the Indian Ocean that begins with China's first overseas base in Djibouti on the Horn of Africa. The United States must also take notice, since it also has a base in Djibouti and one in Diego Garcia, in the Indian Ocean. Exactly how, and whether, the Chinese will take military advantage of their diplomatic successes remains to be seen. For India, the Maldives turnabout means it now must worry about a maritime frontier as well as a land frontier.[23]

(9) The Problematic Situation for China in Myanmar

Myanmar's (Burma) military dictatorship, which seized power in 2021, in 2024 has become vulnerable to attack from the hodgepodge resistance forces loosely aligned under a National Unity Government. These forces are of two kinds: ethnic minority armies, sometimes referred to as the Three Brotherhood Alliance, that have a long history of opposition to the military government, and pro-democracy groups backed by the NUG that have come together since the 2021 coup. (A publication of Myanmar journalists in exile in Thailand lists thirty armed groups in all, ten of which are ethnic armies.[24]) What makes the resistance so threatening to the military is that the various armies are coordinating and becoming increasingly successful in the north and northeast, areas that border China as well as Thailand and India. The opposition has captured towns, seized arsenals, and obtained the surrender of some government units, including an entire battalion in 2024. Thousands of people have fled the fighting, mainly into India.

The Myanmar junta has superior forces on the ground and in the air, yet a BBC report says: "After two and a half years of battling the armed uprising it provoked with its disastrous coup, the military is looking weak, and possibly beatable." A Council on Foreign Relations study suggests that another coup by disgruntled army officers is possible.[25]

China's Position

China seems to be playing both sides, no doubt because of the security implications of backing just one. On one hand, it has consistently supported the junta's repression. The Myanmar leadership pretends that all is well in relations with China. It insists that ties are strong, and that the strategic partnership is firm. For example, on November 27, 2024, three Chinese vessels, including a destroyer, made a port visit in preparation for joint naval maneuvers. Behind the scenes, however, reports indicate displeasure within the junta over China's relations with the rebel groups, in particular sales of weapons to them. That displeasure led to a first-ever anti-China demonstration outside the Chinese embassy in Yangon on November 17. China's foreign ministry spokesman had to issue a formal statement reassuring the protesters that China never interferes in Myanmar's internal affairs.[26]

But China *is* interfering, though not necessarily to good effect. Chinese authorities are in close touch with the rebelling ethnic groups, which have promised to protect Chinese investments in areas the groups control. The northeast border area is the site of criminal activity—drug trafficking and cyberscam operations—that concerns China because of its impact on Chinese nationals and the capacity for border unrest. Beijing has neither condemned the opposition forces nor endorsed the junta's efforts to quash them. According to a report by the US Institute of Peace (USIP), "Beijing almost certainly approved the offensive after the junta generals ignored its appeals to crack down on lucrative crime centers along the border that prey on China nationals."[27] That has probably gotten the generals' attention: The junta reported in 2024 that China was brokering peace talks between the main armed opposition group and the government.

China's policy toward Myanmar is purely self-interested. The criminal activity is important to Beijing only because it puts a crimp in China's border security and its mineral investments in Myanmar. The junta's widespread repression of human rights, including genocidal actions against the Rohingya people (see Chapter 8), does not seem to be of concern to China. When the European Union and nine governments released a joint statement in January 2025 condemning the humanitarian crisis in Myanmar, China was not among the signers. (The United States was a signer, as were Britain and Australia.) The statement cited:

> credible reports of human rights violations and abuses and international humanitarian law violations committed against civilians. These include: abduction and forced recruitment of children and members of ethnic and religious minorities; the Myanmar military's indiscriminate aerial bombardments that kill and injure civilians and damage civilian infrastructure; sexual and gender-based violence; the burning of homes; attacks on humanitarian workers and facilities; and restrictions on humanitarian access by the military regime and various armed groups. We have also seen disturbing reports of dismemberment and burning of civilians.[28]

Ongoing repression of the Rohingya, the forced displacement of 3.5 million people, and food insecurity for 15 million people were also mentioned in the statement. UN Security Council Resolution 2669, passed in December 2022, had called for an end to the violence, de-escalation of tensions, release of "arbitrarily detained prisoners," and respect for human rights and the rule of law. But China, as well as Russia and India, abstained from the vote.

A Criminal State

While the civil war rages, Myanmar is now the biggest nexus of organized crime on the planet, according to the Global Organized Crime Index. The *New York Times* reports: "It is now the world's largest producer of opium and one of the world's largest manufacturers of synthetic drugs, including methamphetamine, ketamine and fentanyl. Concocted with precursor chemicals from neighboring China and India, tablets made in Myanmar feed habits as far away as Australia. With factories in overdrive and international law enforcement overwhelmed, street prices of these drugs are alarmingly cheap."[29]

The country's northern borderlands are largely the domain of Chinese criminal syndicates. "Production in Myanmar intensified after a crackdown on the assembly of drugs in China. The chemical precursors instead found their way to Myanmar, and Chinese lab technicians taught locals how to craft crystal methamphetamine, also known as ice, in jungle redoubts. Chinese kingpins brought in pill presses to make yaba." The *New York Times* report cited above says that the syndicates "are operating with impunity and monopolistic ambition in the region, despite occasional crackdowns by Beijing. Chinese weapons flow both to the ruling junta and to the resistance forces that are fighting it. In Myanmar's borderlands, criminal networks that unite Chinese kingpins with ethnic warlords are kidnapping people from all over the globe to toil in factories that scam people online." Beijing would seem to have limited influence over its border with Myanmar.

Documents

Document 1. Foreign Minister Wang Yi Says China-Japan Relations are at a Critical Stage (November 2024).
(*Background*: Wang Yi, who is also a member of the Chinese Communist Party's politburo, met in November 2024 in Beijing with Takeo Akiba, special adviser to the Japanese cabinet and secretary general of Japan's National Security Secretariat. *Source*: Xinhua, November 4, 2024, https://english.news.cn/20241104/1a4c39664bc14ac9ae1f224bb09fdb24/c.html.)

Wang Yi said the two sides should follow the consensus reached by the leaders of the two countries, stick to the right direction of improving and developing bilateral relations, and build a constructive and stable China-Japan relationship that meets the requirements of the new era.

Wang said the Japanese side should establish an objective and rational understanding of China, honor its political commitment on the Taiwan question and earnestly safeguard the political foundation of China-Japan relations, urging the Japanese side to take concrete actions to implement the important consensus of "being each other's cooperation partners rather than threats," and promote the steady and long-term development of bilateral ties.

The two sides reiterated that they will abide by the principles and consensus set out in the four political documents between China and Japan and commit to comprehensively advancing the strategic relationship of mutual benefit between the two sides, reaching agreement to maintain high-level intercourse, dialogue and exchanges in various fields, and send more positive signals to the outside world. [The "four political documents" refers to the 1972 China-Japan Joint Statement that restored diplomatic relations, the signing of a peace treaty in 1978, the China-Japan Joint Declaration of 1998, and a joint statement on advancing strategic and mutually beneficial relations signed in 2008.]

The two sides believed that China and Japan, as two important neighbors with development closely linked to each other and highly complementary economies, should not and will not decouple, pledging to jointly promote the healthy development of economic and trade cooperation and the stable and smooth production and supply chain.

On the discharge of nuclear-contaminated water from the Fukushima Daiichi Nuclear Power Station, the two sides agreed to accelerate the follow-up and implementation of the bilateral political consensus [i.e., the four documents noted above].

Stressing that China is firmly committed to the path of peaceful development, pursues a national defense policy that is defensive in nature, and is a major country with the best record of peace and security, Wang said China will continue to uphold fairness and justice to prevent war or chaos in the region.

It is hoped that all parties will jointly resist non-regional forces inciting confrontation in the area and take concrete actions to safeguard regional peace and stability, Wang added.

Document 2. Xi Jinping Meets Japan's Prime Minister Ishiba Shigeru (Chinese report)
(*Source*: Xinhua, November 16, 2024, https://english.news.cn/20241116/0f24e4af311f45739bf3c1ed1f150bbc/c.html)

[Xi] noted that China is willing to work with Japan, in accordance with the principles and directions established in the four political documents between China and Japan, to uphold the important consensus that the two countries should "be partners, not threats," comprehensively advance the strategic relationship of mutual benefit, and endeavor to build a constructive and stable China-Japan relationship that meets the requirements of the new era.

Xi stressed that China's development is an opportunity for the world, and this is especially true for neighboring countries like Japan. He expressed hope that Japan will work with China to develop a correct mutual understanding, steer the bilateral relationship in the right direction from a strategic perspective and with a broad view of the overall situation, and translate the important political consensus reached by both sides into concrete policies and actions.

Xi called on the Japanese side to face history squarely, look to the future, and properly handle major issues of principle such as history and Taiwan, manage differences in a constructive manner and maintain the political foundation of bilateral relations.

Both sides should deepen and expand cultural and local exchanges, promoting mutual understanding between the people of the two countries, especially the younger generation, said Xi.

As China's and Japan's economic interests and production and supply chains are deeply integrated, both sides should adhere to mutual benefit and win-win cooperation, safeguard the global free trade system as well as stable and smooth production and supply chains, said Xi.

He also called on the two countries to strengthen coordination on international and regional affairs, practice true multilateralism, promote open regionalism, and jointly address global challenges.

For his part, Ishiba said that Japan and China are responsible for regional peace and prosperity and it holds great significance to the region and the world that the two sides work together to comprehensively advance the strategic relationship of mutual benefit between the two sides and build constructive and stable bilateral ties.

Japan's position on the Taiwan question, based on the Japan-China joint communique in 1972, remains unchanged, he said, adding that the Japanese side remains committed to the principles and consensus established in the four political documents between Japan and China, and adheres to the path of peaceful development.

The Japanese side is willing to engage in candid dialogue with China at all levels in the spirit of facing history squarely and looking to the future to enhance mutual understanding and trust, he added.

Japan-China economic cooperation holds immense potential and Japan has no intention of decoupling from China, Ishiba noted.

Japan hopes to strengthen people-to-people and cultural exchanges between the two sides and promote cooperation in various areas, including trade, green development, as well as medical and healthcare, to achieve more tangible results that will better benefit the two peoples, he said. Japan is willing to work closely with China within frameworks such as APEC, he added.

The two sides agreed to maintain high-level exchanges, make good use of high-level dialogue mechanisms in the fields of economy, people-to-people and cultural exchanges and other fields, and translate the consensus reached on the discharge of nuclear-contaminated water from Fukushima into action as soon as possible.

Document 3: Xi Jinping and Narendra Modi Comment on China-India Relations (2024)

(*Background*: This document is the Chinese readout of a meeting between Xi and India's Prime Minister Narendra Modi in October 2024.

Source: Huanqiu, October 23, 2024, https://hqtime.huanqiu.com/article/4Jxgf2gFyBh)

Xi Jinping pointed out that China and India are both ancient civilizations, major developing countries, and important members of the Global South. They both are in a key period of national modernization. China and India are correctly moving with the historical tide and the development of bilateral relations. That fits with the basic interests of the two countries and their peoples. Both countries should strengthen cooperation, increase strategic mutual trust, and together use their successes to realize the development dream. The two sides also shoulder international responsibilities, provide a standard for the unified self-strengthening of the many developing countries, and make contributions to advancing international multilateralization and the democratization of international relations.

Xi Jinping emphasized that the essential issue in China-India relations is how two neighboring major developing countries with over 1.4 billion people can get along. Development is the "greatest common denominator" that China and India now face. The two sides should continue to uphold an important Sino-Indian consensus: "opportunities for mutual development, not being a threat to each other, partners in cooperation and not competitive rivals," etc. They should uphold correct strategic understanding and work together on the bright path to achieve peaceful coexistence among major neighboring countries and develop together. . . .

The two leaders positively evaluated the important advances made in resolving the border area issues in the recent period through intense communication. Modi raised ideas and suggestions for improving and developing relations between the two countries. Xi Jinping expressed approval in principle on that.

The two sides agreed to give full play to the mechanism of meetings of the bilateral border problem special representatives, so as to protect together peace and tranquility in the border area and seek measures to resolve it peacefully and reasonably. The two sides agreed that their foreign ministers and officials at various levels should open dialogue and promote putting the development of stable relations back on track at an early date.

Document 4. Chinese Vice Premier Ding Xuexiang's Speech at the Opening Plenary of the Boao Forum for Asia Annual Conference, March 2025
(*Background*: The speech marked the tenth anniversary of Xi Jinping's call for "building an Asian community with a shared future." The excerpts below speak to China's view of ASEAN's accomplishments and future agenda.
Source: Xinhua, March 27, 2025,
 https://english.news.cn/20250327/dc20e6d004324c4c8a2210cb42c6b60f/c.html)

- China and ASEAN have established a comprehensive strategic partnership.
- The Regional Comprehensive Economic Partnership (RCEP) has entered into effect. [The RCEP is a fifteen-nation free trade agreement that includes ASEAN members as well as China, South Korea, Japan, Australia, and New Zealand.]
- Connectivity networks among Asian countries are improving, boosted by the implementation of landmark Belt and Road projects such as the China-Laos Railway, the Jakarta-Bandung Railway, and the China-Pakistan Economic Corridor.
- The Asian Infrastructure Investment Bank (AIIB) has been launched and is making more impact through providing active financing support for relevant projects.

"We should champion the Asian values built around peace, cooperation, inclusiveness and integration, uphold and carry forward the Asian Way of mutual respect, consensus building, and accommodating the comfort levels of all parties, respect each other's core interests and major concerns, keep building common ground and mutual trust, and jointly create a big Asian family of solidarity and progress.... We should jointly safeguard the free trade system, uphold open regionalism, and firmly oppose trade and investment protectionism. We should make full use of regional cooperation mechanisms in East Asia and the Asia Pacific, push for high-quality implementation of the RCEP, work toward the signing of the China-ASEAN Free Trade Area, and promote regional economic integration and connectivity."

PART II

Inside China

6

Politics and Society

Introduction

Chinese officials often say that a country's foreign policy is mainly determined by its domestic circumstances. In China's case, the key domestic circumstance is rapid, state-led economic development. Foreign policy is largely shaped by the Chinese Communist Party's (CCP) plans for strengthening the economy, which is key to maintaining "stability"—that is, social and political order. The priority given to economic development has strong historical roots: *nei luan wai huan*—chaos within, catastrophe without. Today's Chinese leaders, no less than their predecessors, believe that economic weakness invites social instability, raises questions about the leadership's authority and legitimacy, weakens China's international influence, and exposes the country to foreign intrigue. Party control of economic planning, social movements, and the military is therefore essential. A successful leadership is one that provides security at three levels: for the overall economy, for leaders of the one-party state, and for China as it seeks great-power status while minimizing external threats.

Xi Jinping's views are thus more in accord with Mao Zedong's than is often assumed. On internal security in particular, Xi is more Maoist and Leninist than Marxist—committed above all to the maintenance of the one-party state and the CCP's rectitude (**Selection 2**). Xi is a party man. By 2007 he was a member of the CCP's innermost circle, the standing committee of the political bureau, after having served as party secretary of Shanghai. Once in full command in 2012, he made clear that collective decision-making and rule by consensus were out. Xi consolidated his and the party's authority over the military, all enterprises, and government organs. He became "core leader," his "thoughts" were elevated to Mao's level ("Xi Jinping Thought on Socialism with Chinese Characteristics for a New Era"), and his tenure as president was made indefinite in 2018. These moves became the backdrop to a widespread purge of political enemies and corrupt party leaders that is ongoing (**Selection 2**).

Yes, Xi is also an economic reformer, furthering the ambitions of Deng Xiaoping to make China a major international player. Market socialism is the rule, "getting rich" is lauded, and China is presented as a model of modernization (**Document 3**). But Xi insists, just as Deng and Mao did, that "democratic dictatorship" must prevail amidst economic changes—first, because those changes may cause social disruption; and second, because CCP officials may succumb to the lure of the market and enrich themselves, thus undermining the party's claim to an exclusive right to rule. Indeed, at the start of 2025, Xi explicitly said that "corruption is the greatest threat facing our party," requiring "continuously purifying the cadre ranks." Mao, too, preached party purification, but he was willing to launch mass movements to rectify behavior from outside the party—the Great Proletarian Cultural Revolution (1966–76) being the most costly and chaotic. Xi is dealing with inner-party problems in ways he hopes will not disrupt the economy or society.

The selections that follow offer insights to different aspects of political leadership that reflect Xi's chief concerns: the link between security and economic development (**Selection 1**); the importance of discipline, ideological commitment, and incorruptibility in the party's ranks (**Selection 2 and Document 1**); the necessity of social order, including religion, during political reform (**Selection 5 and Document 2**); and an educational policy that promotes scientific and technological expertise (**Selection 7**). Xi makes an emphatic case for the superiority of "Chinese-style modernization," thanks to the party's leadership (**Documents 3 and 4**). But for all the insistence on social order, important problems exist inside as well as outside the CCP, such as popular and elite concerns about the income gap, corrupt officials, and the scale of Xi's purges (**Selections 2 and 3**); Maoist-style repression in the name of political reform (**Selection 4**); the suppression of scientific evidence (**Selection 6**); and unethical behavior by intellectuals (**Selection 7**).

(1) Economic Development Requires Security

For China's leadership, internal security is essential for China's economic development. Sustained party leadership over all institutions and individuals is a prerequisite to security. And effective leadership requires absolute loyalty to Xi Jinping and the CCP. The overall implication for foreign policy is the need to strengthen party discipline in order to protect China's external interests, particularly at a time of setbacks in the economy and in leadership. The party must be unified under Xi, security in all areas must be strengthened, and the economy must get back on track for China to effectively carry out foreign affairs.

To illustrate, here is an opinion piece by Zhong Caiwen (possibly a pen name) that appeared in the official *Renmin ribao* on February 1, 2024, under the title "Firmly Adhere to a Positive Interaction of High-Quality Development and High Levels of Security." Zhong said that "only with high-quality development can we advance a high level of security. High-quality development is the primary task in the full establishment of a socialist country's modernization." He went on: "Security is the necessary environment and important protector of development. Security is the bottom line. Without security and stability, we cannot talk about development, and the achievements of development can be lost." Many countries have lost opportunities for development because of internal upheavals, Zhong wrote. Thus, there are many economic development issues that must be resolved, such as food security and the "problem of technology being subject to others."

(2) Xi Jinping's Anti-Corruption Campaign

Casting a Wide Net

Xi launched the anti-corruption campaign soon after taking office in 2012. The targets have been high-ranking party and military officials, past and present; provincial and other local officials; and a few tycoons. Among the so-called "tigers" who have been punished are Zhou Yongkang, head of internal security; General Xu Caihou, former vice-chairman of the Central Military Commission, which Xi heads; Liu Zhijun, onetime minister of railways; and Bo Xilai, the party leader in Chongqing who at one time was thought to be headed to the apex of Communist Party power, the Politburo's Standing Committee. Wu Guoguang at Stanford University draws particular attention to the purges that have taken place in the military since 2022. Besides General Xu, they included "the third PLA general in charge of political and organizational work ..., and the second of the six members of the 20th Central Military Commission," the military's top decision-making body. Also removed were two former PLA generals from the National People's Congress (NPC), a former deputy commander of the PLA Ground Force, and the former commissar of the PLA's Southern Theater Command Navy. Most recently, two more members of the Central Military Commission have been cashiered: Admiral Miao Hua in November 2024 and General He Weidong in early 2025.[1]

Wu also notes that CCP Central Committee members have not been spared. "Across the Party-state system, at least 58 high-ranking cadres lost their positions in the first three quarters of 2024 and 642,000 cadres at various levels were punished over the same time period"—in all, about 9 percent of the Central Committee. Thousands of local-level officials and senior military officers just below the top level have also been punished. Indeed, the scope of the anti-corruption campaign is staggering. A party work report in January 2025 noted that 12,000 individuals were sanctioned the previous year for violating political discipline. The report says that

> nationwide, 3,375 disciplinary and supervisory officials were placed under investigation [for corruption], and 3,917 were given Party disciplinary and administrative sanctions. A total of 107,000 cases of formalism and bureaucratism were investigated, with 156,000 individuals criticized, educated, or disciplined. Nationwide, discipline inspection and supervision organs have filed a total of 877,000 cases, detained 38,000 people, and imposed Party disciplinary and administrative sanctions on 889,000 people, including 17,000 in the financial sector, 94,000 in state-owned enterprises sector, 3,147 in the tobacco system, and 60,000 in the pharmaceutical sector.[2]

"Selective Punishment"

One prominent Chinese writer has called Xi's approach "selective punishment."[3] When he was writing in 2015, the crackdown generally targeted political rivals and people outside the official "family." It was "more of a Stalinist purge than a genuine attempt to clean up the government," often relying on extrajudicial means. But Wu Guoguang's later study, which also underscores the Stalinist aspect of the purges, points out that while they began with people outside Xi's circle, in recent years they have snared Xi's once-trusted proteges.

Purges of such broad scope suggest that Xi's leadership is not as secure as is often thought. Underlying regime insecurity are policy failures, such as "zero-Covid," and (see Chapter 7) structural weaknesses in the economy that have led to a slowdown in economic growth. The purges may be Xi's way of shifting blame to "corrupt" cadres. Some US military specialists think the purges of senior military officials show that Xi cannot trust the military high command, thus exposing weaknesses in military leadership that the United States can exploit. By way of comparison, however, the Trump administration, in its second term, also purged the top ranks of the military, starting with the chairman of the Joint Chiefs of Staff, his navy chief, and the judge advocates general of three services. Unlike Xi's purges, usually due to bribery, Trump's were for presumed disloyalty to his political agenda.

(3) The People and the Party

The rapid developmental pace of China's market socialism has aroused criticism of official policy from many different sources—intellectuals, think-tank experts, nongovernmental organizations (NGOs), even former senior party and government officials, not to mention ordinary people who experience the widening gap between rich and poor. Indeed, the income gap and official corruption are the major sources of people's disaffection with the one-party state. Many people hurt by new economic priorities have become upset to the point of hostility toward authorities: workers laid off from state-owned industrial enterprises, farmers whose lands have been seized without fair compensation, citizens whose lawsuits and petitions have been ignored or even led to their being jailed, and people forced from their homes by government and private construction projects (such as dams, urban renewal, and golf courses).

Ordinary Chinese probably understand the contradictions of the anti-corruption campaign. Xi's own family has amassed a fortune in the reform era, as the International Consortium of Investigative Journalists reported in 2014.[4] A long-awaited report released by the US Director of National Intelligence in March 2025 came to the same conclusion. The report, "Wealth and Corrupt Activities of the Leadership of the Chinese Communist Party," said corruption is endemic in a system where political power is so highly centralized and independent checks on high officials are virtually absent. It "highlighted that from 2012 through 2022, [the two organizations responsible for dealing with corruption] investigated almost five million people within the PRC government and the CCP and found 4.7 million officials guilty." Xi and family have accumulated enormous wealth, estimated at "over $1 billion in business investments and real estate." Most likely, Xi has someone manage these funds for him. The report does not directly link Xi or family members to specific investments, but it suggests that he and all other high party and government officials are well positioned to take advantage of privileged information about the economy's leading sectors.[5]

Chinese billionaires have been coopted (and protected) by being brought into the Communist Party's legislative organs.[6] Thus, whereas being a tiger can be risky, and watching one being caged may be popular with the Chinese masses, being a "princeling" as part of a prominent family or being part of the president's inner circle can be richly rewarding. It affords exceptional opportunities for lucrative investments, senior corporate and banking appointments, access to offshore tax havens, and education abroad. Politically attuned Chinese easily identify this privileged elite. They see that those officials who are toppled rarely include Xi's closest associates, and thus many conclude that cronyism often triumphs over justice.

Does all this upset mean the CCP is unpopular? CCP leaders say the answer to this question is clear: They are supported overwhelmingly, and they cite Western polling in which Chinese are asked directly if they support their government. Typically, 90 percent say they do. But now two survey experiments in China, reported in the journal *China Quarterly*, suggest that citizens conceal their opposition to the CCP for fear of repression.[7] "When respondents are asked in the form of list experiments, instead of being asked directly, CCP support hovers between 50 per cent and 70 per cent," these scholars say. By "list experiments," they mean letting respondents express sensitive opinions without stating them directly, and with greater anonymity. "On average," they write, "our list experiments suggest that respondents overstate regime support in direct questioning by 28.5 percentage points. Roughly 40 per cent of citizens decline to protest owing to fear of repression, quadruple the rate under direct questioning." This study also found that, contrary to existing literature, dissatisfaction with the government in China is not confined to urban elites.

(4) Reform and Repression

Western-style democracy is another threat to China's internal order. Here Xi has followed in the footsteps of his predecessor, Hu Jintao, who warned that "international hostile forces are intensifying the strategic plot of westernizing and dividing China." To combat this supposed threat, but at the same time to exploit it, Xi Jinping has engaged in what Elizabeth C. Economy terms a "power grab." Political reform to him means "consolidating personal power by creating new institutions, silencing political opposition, and legitimizing his leadership and the Communist Party's power in the eyes of the Chinese people."[8]

From Economy's article and other sources, here are some of the specific ways in which the Chinese leadership's anti-Westernism has manifested:

- Strengthening regulation of the Internet, not only by censorship and shutdowns of websites but also by arresting and humiliating popular bloggers.
- Cracking down on NGOs that might become an organized opposition.
- Restricting academic research and teaching that reflect Western ideas, such as civil society, judicial independence, and press freedom.
- Prosecuting newspaper editors and writers, lawyers, artists, professors, women's rights activists, and others who are too outspoken on behalf of individual or group rights, and/or who challenge the party-state's authority too vigorously.

- Responding forcibly to indications of ethnic or local independence, such as Hong Kong's pro-democracy demonstrations, Tibet's quest for autonomy, and separatist tendencies in ethnic minority areas.

The bottom line: Reform and repression are not contradictory trends in China. Rather, they are mutually reinforcing. Reforms, by meeting many people's material needs, sustain faith in Communist Party leadership. Selective punishment ensures that reforms do not lead to domestic chaos, unlike the Mao-era mass movements. But like Mao, Xi has endorsed a cult of personality. Party members participate in an extraordinary number of study sessions, inspection tours, and other activities to demonstrate fealty to Xi Jinping and ensure that his "thoughts" are put into action. How long such a commitment can be maintained is a frequent source of debate among China watchers.

(5) The Culture War in China

Patriotic Education

China has its own version of "woke" culture warfare: repression of "unpatriotic" cultural acts. In the name of national security, which is to say, the Chinese Communist Party's control, Xi Jinping has authorized a crackdown on cultural performances that don't conform with "revolutionary culture" or exhibit "sissy" (i.e., insufficiently masculine) behavior. LGBTQ groups that once were unofficially allowed to meet, and even hold gay pride parades, now are being driven underground. Performances that suggest nonconformity are being canceled. Xi may have a larger target in mind: young people who face great difficulty in finding jobs, with one in five unemployed. Xi was asked for advice he would give these discontented youth. He answered in a letter to students at an agricultural college in 2024. Referring to his own youth, Xi said: "The first demand I made of myself was, find my own bitterness to eat. Young people should do the same." The reference to "eating bitterness" goes back to the early days of the communist movement, when China's new leaders urged people to recall the bitter past to expose and eliminate class enemies and build a socialist society. That message is not likely to resonate with today's young Chinese, however. They're very materialistic and have their own ideas about what constitutes the good life.

Nevertheless, under Xi Jinping, education has become infused with study of his "thoughts," just as happened under Mao Zedong. Patriotic education is the ideological and political ingredient in every curriculum, as this example from Nankai University in the northern city of Tianjin shows[9]:

> Guided by patriotic education for the new era to uphold the "five educations"—moral, intellectual, physical, aesthetic, and labor—Nankai University has tightly focused on the fundamental task of cultivating morality and educating people, accelerated the construction of a first-class university and first-class curriculum, encouraged students to contribute their youthful energy where the motherland needs them most, and contributed Nankai's strength to the building of a strong nation and the rejuvenation of the Chinese people. . . . The course "Introduction to Xi Jinping Thought on Socialism with Chinese Characteristics for a New Era" is being offered according to the "golden course" standard. Each institution under the university has a dedicated team for this purpose. The leadership teams at both the school and college levels take the lead in the current affairs and policy course.

The report goes on to say that

> ideological and political courses should not only be taught in classrooms but also integrated into social life. . . . The university has carried out a series of patriotic education activities in various forms and made good use of patriotic education bases; there have been patriotic theatrical performances, such as "Zhou Enlai [the longtime former premier] Returns to Nankai," "Three Questions on Patriotism," and "Eternal Remembrance" using stories of predecessors like Zhang Boling [a founder of Nankai University], Yang Shixian [a former university president], and Guo Yonghuai [an aerospace engineer] to inspire young students . . .

What we see here is a return to Maoist times, when learning from socialist heroes was the fashion. But back then, the heroes typically were ordinary people or soldiers who displayed selfless dedication to the socialist cause and a spirit of sacrifice. Now many of the heroes are vanguards of science and technology.

The Covid Resistance

A social and political perspective imposed from above doesn't always work, as witness what happened in China in November and December 2022 after the leadership decided on a "zero-Covid" policy. The long lockdown sparked the most significant dissent in China since the Tiananmen uprising in 1989. It began innocuously enough: A fire in an apartment building in Urumqi, the capital of Xinjiang, killed ten people. The lockdown was blamed for the slow response to the fire, and sympathy for the victims spread to several of China's major cities.[10]

A "White Paper" movement evolved in which protesters displayed blank slips of paper to convey their displeasure with the Covid restrictions, with official censorship, and, in some cases, with the CCP and its leader. Western media tended to emphasize that last agenda, pushing the possibility of regime change to the top of the news when in fact that theme was not the dominant one among the demonstrators. Though young people were mainly the ones calling for freedom and for Xi to step down, most everyone else focused on easing quarantines and returning to something resembling normal life. Neither in size, breadth of support, geography, or political impact were these protests anything like those at Tiananmen in 1989.

Predictably, China's security apparatus responded by cracking down on anyone who seemed to be leading the protests. (In a closed-door trial in January 2025, a young filmmaker who created a documentary of the White Paper protest was sentenced to over three years in jail.[11]) But there really were no leaders, just fed-up people. The real question was how lasting the protests might be, and whether they would evolve into mass resistance. That seemed highly unlikely, especially once party leaders eased Covid restrictions, putting pressure on protesters either to keep going or claim a small victory and disperse.

"It's like some national subconsciousness that resurfaces," said Geremie Barmé, a New Zealand-based scholar. "Now it's resurfaced again, this projection of self and of rights and ideas." He was referring to comments on China's Internet about civil liberties, democratic values, and freedom of movement. For some time, amidst a repression that has become the hallmark of the Xi era, these ideas have rarely surfaced, confined to small discussion groups of intellectuals and students. But it's questionable how much the public shared such sentiments; their concern was more likely about the arbitrary rules governing zero-Covid that had forced them into isolation and disrupted their daily lives. They had been fighting those restrictions for a long time in their neighborhoods.

Not Quite Back to Business as Usual

The Xi Jinping leadership appeared finally to be listening to the complaints, though that was very much out of character. "Frustrated students," Xi said of the protesters, perhaps in recognition that he needed to respond to their anger. Most likely dictating Xi's response was the severe impact of the zero-Covid policy on people's lives and on China's economy. Professor Dali Yang at the University of Chicago has proposed that during the first three years of the Covid-19 pandemic, around 1.7 million excess deaths occurred, with 2023 the worst year (post of February 20, 2025 on X). Zero-Covid was abandoned in December 2022 as public health officials switched gears, saying the threat was fading and the policy was working. That allowed for an easing of the rules. New regulations were then issued that allowed for quarantining at home rather than in some horrendous camp. Lockdowns of businesses ended in some cities. Reduction of mass testing was promised. The Foxconn plant that produces Apple products resumed production after protests over wages and working conditions.

Even though the protests subsided, they did seem to have dented Xi Jinping's reputation and the durability of his leadership at the very moment of triumph in extending his rule at the twentieth Party Congress. It became apparent that many younger Chinese, faced with difficulty finding jobs and enjoying the material benefits of China's rise, did not approve of his rule. Their "lying flat" at home (*tang ping*) became a new expression of resistance to the pressures of work and the material culture. But the power of the surveillance state (see Chapter 8) prevailed. What the Covid protests did show is that, as in the Mao era, China's leaders most fear organized resistance that might challenge the party-state's monopolization of power. As Nicholas Kristof wrote in the *New York Times*, "Historically in China, mass protests have arisen not when conditions were most intolerable (like the famine from 1959 to 1962) but when people thought they could get away with them, such as the Hundred Flowers Campaign of 1956, the April 5 incident of 1976, the Democracy Wall easing of 1978–79, the student protests of 1986 and Tiananmen in 1989."[12] The Covid scare gave protesters space to make their case and, as in all previous mass protests, students were critical participants in them. But the protests did not rise to the level of a well-organized movement. Xi's zero-Covid policy was a strategic mistake, but he recovered.

(6) The Covid Coverup

"The battle against Covid-19 wasn't just a fight against a deadly virus, but also a struggle against the political suppression of scientific evidence," writes Professor Dali Yang, drawing on his magisterial study.[13] Yang's research reveals that for nearly three weeks—between late December 2019 and January 20, 2020—China's front-line respiratory doctors suspected human-to-human transmission and took appropriate precautions. Some of them made repeated efforts to submit new cases, only to be thwarted by higher authorities. Political imperatives took precedence, as the healthcare bureaucracy and prevailing organizational culture stifled professional communication and transparency. Critical information that could have helped halt the outbreak, including lessons learned from China's experience with SARS in 2003, was suppressed. The leadership's overriding concern for social stability shaped the response, leading Xi Jinping to admit in February 2020 to "shortcomings in public health" and "formalism and bureaucratism in epidemic prevention and control work."

Professor Yang also concludes that once the initial errors of judgment and organization were acknowledged, China's healthcare system, with the full backing of the national leadership, responded with remarkable effectiveness. The accumulated knowledge and expertise of the country's medical professionals were finally brought to bear, enabling the containment of the virus. This success, however, laid the groundwork for the protracted zero-Covid policy. As a result, China found itself both the first to confront the pandemic and the last to fully emerge from the zero-Covid lockdowns.

(7) Trends in China's Higher Education

The Reverse Flow of Chinese Students

As noted in Chapter 1, China had suffered from a brain drain as some of its most talented students in science, technology, engineering, and mathematics (STEM) went abroad, mainly to the US, Britain, and Australia. Many of them stayed abroad. But the trend has reversed. Two Chinese researchers reported in 2024: "Since 2012, more than 80% of overseas Chinese students have opted to return—a big increase from about 5% in 1987 and 30.6% in 2007." STEM students had been especially unlikely to return, since they believed their careers would be better served outside than inside China. Now those students have been lured back by "China's prospering economy, strategic talent policies and the large sum of funding it has poured into scientific research."[14] Taking care of family obligations, such as ill parents, has also factored into the decision on returning. Interestingly, gender also mattered: Female Ph.D.s had less motivation to return because Western academia has become more focused on expanding opportunities for women and minorities. The researchers concluded that despite the general reverse flow, Chinese universities still had a long way to go when it came to gender equity and policy on faculty returning from abroad.

The attractiveness to students of returning to China has been complemented by several factors that have pushed them away from study and work in the United States. Trouble getting visas is one factor. The rise in US-China tensions since the first Trump administration is another. According to one study, *Building a Wall Around Science: The Effect of US-China Tensions on International Scientific Research*, racial profiling of Chinese researchers in the United States under the China Initiative and hostility toward ethnic Chinese during the Covid epidemic also alienated many Chinese students.[15]

Since the start of the second Trump presidency, international students in the United States, Chinese among them, have had new concerns for their future. One concern is for their safety as federal immigration control units have seized and tried to deport international students who, because of their participation in political events (mainly pro-Palestinian rallies), have been deemed to have engaged in "terrorism." Another concern is that the Trump administration has taken dead aim at Harvard, Columbia, Johns Hopkins, and other elite universities, seeking to undermine liberal education by imposing conservative guardianship over research, teaching, admissions, student life, and values. This attack on the independence of universities, carried out on the pretext of eliminating antisemitism on campus, has threatened billions of dollars in faculty research grants, universities' tax-exempt status, and research programs.

The impact of these developments on students has been profound. Foreign student enrollments in the US declined sharply by the start of 2025.[16] Nationwide, over 1,000 international students' visas were revoked by April. The *Chronicle of Higher Education* reported that over 4,700 international student records in the federal Student and Exchange Visitor Information System database had been terminated. As US universities struggle to maintain research programs and reassure students of support, we can expect that the decline in foreign study and employment in the US will accelerate. Two China specialists conclude: "international STEM students are increasingly reweighing their options in favor of countries outside the U.S. that are doing their best to take advantage of this unique recruiting opportunity. If visa revocations continue, the U.S. might lose some of the best and brightest minds the world has to offer—systematically undermining the future of American innovation at a time when China's homegrown engineers are already leapfrogging American competitors in key technologies."[17]

Expanding International Influence

The emphasis on science and technology is such that China's education minister declared late in 2024 that China aimed to be "an important education center with global influence" by 2035. Higher education, focused on science and technology, is the key, he and Xi Jinping said. Reference was made to a speech by Xi in September in which he said: "The education power we want to build . . . should have strong ideological and political leadership, talent competitiveness, scientific and technological support . . . [It should] safeguard people's livelihoods, [and have] social coordination and international influence." Xi indicated that rebuilding international exchange programs with leading foreign universities was essential to the educational plan. He pointed with pride to two developments that showed how quickly China had advanced in education: the doubling of the percentage of young Chinese moving into higher education (60 percent); and China's move up the international rankings in education overall, from forty-ninth in 2012 to twenty-third in 2024.[18]

Two developments in American education, in addition to the threats to visas and research funds mentioned above, may help China's ambition to expand its international influence. One is the Trump administration's virtual elimination of US programs that support education in developing countries, notably at the US Agency for International Development. "In 2023, the latest year for which federal data are available, 830 higher education institutions abroad received capacity-strengthening support from USAID... USAID provided assistance to approximately 130 countries in 2023, with Ukraine being the top recipient that year."[19] A second major budget cut was to the State Department's international exchange programs. Its budget was cut by 93 percent, leaving only $50 million for the department's educational and cultural affairs programs and operations. Might China offer those countries affected by the US retreat educational support under the Belt and Road Initiative?

The second (and somewhat more positive) development was unexpected: Some US joint venture universities in China, such as NYU Shanghai, and the Hopkins-Nanjing Center, have maintained their programs despite rising US-China tensions and sharp criticism from a Congressional study in November 2024 that claimed the partnerships were a "core channel" for China's acquisition of national security sensitive information. (Not all of them have survived, however: The University of Michigan ended its partnership with Shanghai Jiaotong University in 2025, and Duke Kunshan University was under pressure to terminate.) The surviving institutions are reported to have remained successful for several reasons, among them "careful leadership, innovative curricula, engaged communities."[20]

Questionable Behavior in Science

There's a downside to the rush to greatness in Chinese science. The newspaper *Caixin* reported in 2024:

> The Ministry of Education has asked the nation's colleges and universities to look into the retractions of academic papers by their researchers, as Chinese scholars produced three-quarters of the highest-ranking scientific papers pulled by journal publishers last year. The ministry also asked institutions of higher education to verify the reasons for the retractions and severely punish academic misconduct . . .

What is this all about? First, it's about fraudulent papers produced by so-called paper mills that journal reviewers manage to catch before publication. The British journal *Nature*, for example, has tracked "a flood of sham medical papers emanating from hospitals."[21] Second, this scandal also included papers that used human subjects without permission, mainly research based on the DNA of Uyghurs in Xinjiang, the victims of China's genocide (see Chapter 8). The co-authors of such papers often were military researchers. Foreign journals usually forced the retraction of these papers, though some journals did not do so to stay on the good side of China. Third, these fraudulent papers, produced by ghostwriters for Chinese scholars and doctors who paid a substantial fee, were then frequently sent to fraudulent journals. "Publish or perish" is alive and well in China.

Documents

Document 1. Xi Jinping on Continuing Reforms (2024)
(*Background:* Xi's speech was at a study session for senior provincial and ministerial-level CCP officials. *Source*: *China Daily*, October 31, 2024, https://www.chinadaily.com.cn/a/202410/31/WS67233a6ea310f1265a1cab0e.html)

Xi emphasized that maintaining the right political orientation and breaking new ground is a major principle that must be firmly upheld in further comprehensively deepening reform. China's reform has direction and principles to follow. We must uphold the Party's overall leadership, Marxism, socialism with Chinese characteristics, and the people's democratic dictatorship, with promoting social fairness and justice as well as enhancing people's well-being as our starting point and ultimate goal. These principles are fundamental, directional, and long-term, reflecting the nature and mission of the Party, conforming to China's realities, and tallying with the fundamental interests of the people. They must be firmly upheld on any occasion and at any time. We should continue to improve and develop the socialist system with Chinese characteristics, work hard to realize the reform's overall goal of modernizing the national governance system and governing capabilities, and consistently march forward in the direction guided by this overall goal, decisively reforming what should be reformed and never reforming what should not be reformed. In response to the new trends of the times, the new requirements for development, and the new expectations of the people, efforts should be made to advance reform in all aspects in a comprehensive and coordinated manner with an emphasis on economic structural reform, Xi said, urging vigorous work to promote innovations in theories, practice, institutions, culture, and other areas, so as to provide strong impetus and institutional support for Chinese modernization.

Noting that reform is a systematic undertaking, Xi said relevant work should be done through proper means and by carefully balancing concerns in various aspects. He underlined the need to adhere to the coordination between reform and the rule of law, advance the rule of law with reform measures, further deepen reform in the realm of law-based governance, and continuously better the system of socialist rule of law with Chinese characteristics. The role of the rule of law should be given better play in removing the obstacles in reform and consolidating the achievements of reform, and it is important to think in terms of the rule of law and adopt a law-based approach in advancing reform to ensure that major reforms are carried out in accordance with the law and the legitimate rights and interests of all citizens and legal entities are under equal protection, Xi said. . . .

Xi emphasized that officials, particularly senior officials, bear the crucial responsibility of advancing reform. They must cultivate a strong sense of political responsibility and historical mission, confront problems and challenges head-on with political courage to tackle difficulties, decisively address entrenched issues, face up to risks without hesitation, and strive to break new ground for reform and development. The right approach should be adopted to promote reform, arrangements must be made systematically, and actions should never be taken before decisions are made.

Xi noted that extensively building consensus and fully mobilizing all positive factors are quite important for smooth reform. It is imperative to do a good job in guiding public opinion, intensify efforts to conduct positive public communication, champion the overarching theme, and project positive energy. . . . It is imperative to timely address confusions, respond to the concerns of society, and extensively build consensus, so as to consolidate the intellectual foundation and public support for the whole Party and entire society to jointly promote reform. Officials and the general public should be guided to think with a broad perspective and have a correct understanding of the adjustment of interests and personal gains and losses in the reform.

Document 2. A Politburo Member Discusses Religious Conformity
(*Source*: "Wang Huning Chairs the Spring Seminar of Responsible Members of the National Religious Organizations," *Renmin ribao*, January 24, 2025. Wang Huning in a member of Xi Jinping's inner circle. The politburo (Political Bureau), with twenty-four members, is the key decision-making body of the CCP Central Committee, which has over 200 members.)

To systematically advance Sinicisation of our country's religions, we must adhere to the guidance of the socialist core values and immersion in Chinese culture and gradually form religious thought that conforms with the special points of our country's national spirit. We must strengthen the rule of law in religious affairs, push forward religious circles and the masses of believers to strengthen the national consciousness, popular consciousness, and consciousness of the rule of law, and make our work accord with laws and regulations. We must consistently advance completely strict teachings and encourage religious circles to raise up the capability and standards of self-teaching, self-regulating, and self-discipline.

Shi Taifeng, member of the Standing Committee of the CCP Political Bureau and the chief of the Central Committee United Front Bureau, attended the seminar. Speeches were made by the China Buddhist Federation, the China Taoist Federation, the China Islamic Federation, the China Catholic Patriotic Association, and the China Protestant Three-Self Patriotic Movement Committee's responsible person.

Document 3. Xi Jinping's New Year Address (December 31, 2024)
(*Source*: Ministry of Foreign Affairs, China, December 31, 2024, https://www.fmprc.gov.cn/mfa_eng/xw/zyxw/202412/t20241231_11948.html)

Greetings to everybody! Time flies fast, and the new year will be with us shortly. I extend my best wishes to you all from Beijing.

In 2024, we have together journeyed through the four seasons. Together, we have experienced winds and rains and seen rainbows. Those touching and unforgettable moments have been like still frames showing how extraordinary a year we have had.

We have proactively responded to the impacts of the changing environment at home and abroad. We have adopted a full range of policies to make solid gains in pursuing high-quality development. China's economy has rebounded and is on an upward trajectory, with its GDP for the year expected to pass the 130 trillion yuan [about $17.8 trillion] mark. Grain output has surpassed 700 million tons, and China's bowls are now filled with more Chinese grain. Coordinated development across regions has gained stronger momentum, and mutually reinforcing advances have been made in both new urbanization and rural revitalization. Green and low-carbon development has been further enhanced. Indeed, a more beautiful China is unfolding before us.

We have fostered new quality productive forces in light of actual conditions. New business sectors, forms and models have kept emerging. For the first time, China has produced more than 10 million new energy vehicles in a year. Breakthroughs have been made in integrated circuit, artificial intelligence, quantum communications and many other fields. Also for the first time, the Chang'e-6 lunar probe collected samples from the far side of the moon. The Mengxiang drilling vessel explored the mystery of the deep ocean. The Shenzhen-Zhongshan Link now connects the two cities across the sea. The Antarctic Qinling Station is now in operation on the frozen continent. All this epitomizes the lofty spirit and dreams of the Chinese people to explore stars and oceans. . . .

The concerns of the people about jobs and incomes, elderly and child care, education and medical services are always on my mind. This year, the basic pension has been raised, and mortgage rates have dropped. Cross-province direct settlement of medical bills has been expanded, making it easier for people to seek medical treatment across the country. And consumer goods trade-in programs have improved people's lives. All these are real benefits to our people.

In the Paris Olympics, Chinese athletes raced to the top and achieved their best performance in Olympic Games held overseas, fully demonstrating the vigor and confidence of young Chinese. The PLA Navy and Air Force celebrated their 75th birthdays, and our servicemen and women are full of drive. When floods, typhoons and other natural disasters struck, members of the Communist Party of China and officials stepped forward to lead disaster relief efforts, and our people were of one mind and reached out to each other. People in all fields—workers, builders and entrepreneurs, among others—are working hard to fulfill their dreams. I presented awards to recipients of national medals and honorary titles. The honor belongs to them; it also belongs to every hard-working person who has lived up to their responsibilities.

In a world of both transformation and turbulence, China, as a responsible major country, is actively promoting global governance reform and deepening solidarity and cooperation among the Global South. We are making deeper and more substantive advances in high-quality Belt and Road cooperation. The Beijing Summit of the Forum on China-Africa Cooperation was a full success. We put forward China's vision at the Shanghai Cooperation Organization, BRICS, APEC, G20 and other bilateral and multilateral forums. We have contributed greatly to the maintenance of world peace and stability. . . .

In 2025, we will fully complete the 14th Five-Year Plan. We will implement more proactive and effective policies, pursue high-quality development as a top priority, promote greater self-reliance and strength in science and technology, and maintain sound momentum in economic and social development. The Chinese economy now faces some new conditions, including challenges of uncertainties in the external environment and pressure of transformation from old growth drivers into new ones. But we can prevail with our hard work. As always, we grow in the wind and rain, and we get stronger through hard times. We must be confident.

Document 4. Xi Jinping on China's Modernization

(*Background*: "Through Chinese-Style Modernization, Comprehensively Promote the Construction of a Strong Country and the Great Cause of National Rejuvenation," was published in *Qiushi* (Seek Truth), the CCP Central Committee's theoretical journal, in December 2024. Originally, the article was a speech delivered by Xi in February 2023. No explanation of the time gap in publication was given. *Source*: Below is a translation of portions of Xi's speech from the Chinese text at https://archive.is/eTGeK.)

Our party from the beginning had a clear mind that they would not simply follow the Western countries like other developing countries did. They emphasized proceeding from Chinese realities and going on our own modernization road.

China's accomplishments are truly exceptional, in particular eliminating absolute poverty, completely establishing a well-off society, propelling party and country to make historical achievements and historical change, providing

Chinese modernization with an even more perfect systemic guarantee, even firmer material foundation, and an even more proactive spiritual strength.

It can be said that only by unswervingly adhering to the leadership of the Party can China's modernization have a bright future and prosper; otherwise, China's modernization will deviate from its course, lose its soul, and even make subversive mistakes.

Our Party has deeply realized that China-style modernization is the cause of hundreds of millions of people. The people are the main body of China-style modernization. We must rely closely on the people, respect the people's creative spirit, and gather the wisdom and strength of all the people to promote the continuous development of China-style modernization. We adhere to the Party's mass line, think about problems, make decisions, and do things. Pay attention to grasping the pulse of the people, responding to the people's concerns, reflecting the people's wishes, and improving the people's well-being, and strive to make the Party's theories, lines, principles, and policies wholeheartedly supported by the people.

Chinese-style modernization is deeply rooted in the excellent traditional Chinese culture, embodies the advanced nature of scientific socialism, draws on and absorbs all the excellent achievements of human civilization, represents the development direction of human civilization progress, and presents a new picture different from the Western modernization model. It is a brand-new form of human civilization. As the latest major achievement of scientific socialism, Chinese-style modernization has attracted widespread attention internationally.

Chinese-style modernization is a major transcendence of Western-style modernization theory and practice. Capitalist civilization is based on the capitalist exploitation system, and it cannot overcome and eliminate the barbaric nature of civilization. Fundamentally speaking, the contradiction between private ownership of the means of production and socialized mass production is an inherent contradiction that the capitalist system cannot overcome. Although the capitalist system and the Western modernization model are also constantly evolving, their inherent nature of capital supremacy—the law of the jungle, polarization, and hegemony—has not changed at all, and their drawbacks are becoming more and more obvious. The unique worldview, values, historical view, civilization view, democratic view, ecological view, etc. contained in Chinese-style modernization and its great practice are major innovations in the theory and practice of world modernization.

We have no intention or desire to export Chinese-style modernization or the "Chinese model," but Chinese-style modernization has set an example for the vast majority of developing countries to independently move toward modernization, and will inevitably be used as a reference by some developing countries. . . .

From an international perspective, the world is undergoing a major change that has not been seen in a century, the impact of the century-old epidemic is far-reaching, anti-globalization thoughts are on the rise, unilateralism and protectionism are rising significantly, the world economy is recovering sluggishly, the Ukrainian crisis is unresolved and its impact is spilling over, and the world has entered a new period of turbulence and change. From a domestic perspective, my country's reform, development and stability are facing many deep-seated contradictions that cannot be avoided or circumvented. The task of better coordinating epidemic prevention and control and economic and social development is arduous. Economic development is facing the triple pressure of demand contraction, supply shocks, and weakening expectations. There are a large number of risks and hidden dangers that affect social stability, and various "black swan" and "gray rhino" events may occur at any time. From the perspective of the party, some deep-seated problems within the party have not been fundamentally resolved, and the possibility of some old problems rebounding and resurfacing always exists. If they are relaxed a little, they will revive, and new problems are constantly emerging, . . especially the party's work style and clean government construction and the fight against corruption are still facing many stubborn and multiple problems. . . . We must never be complacent or sit back and relax.

7

The Economy and Environment

Introduction

China has become an economic behemoth, until recently posting extraordinary annual gains in production of goods and services. The economy lives on exports, and no country is a more fervent believer in economic globalization (**Selection 4**). Yet China can also claim great strides in poverty reduction. The economy compares quite well to the United States in several categories (**Selection 1**). But economic growth, which was 5.4 percent in the first quarter of 2025, has slowed, causing an uneasy dependence on international trade and investment (**Selection 3** and **Document 1**). If a lengthy trade war with the United States takes place, China's economy might be in need of a painful adjustment.

China's "market socialism" has "Chinese characteristics" that include endorsement of private capitalism, notwithstanding attacks on extremely successful individual entrepreneurs to bring them down to size (**Selection 5**). Perhaps it was only a matter of time, however, before the Chinese leadership would have to face the kinds of problems other major economies historically have faced: unemployment (5 percent in urban areas, notably among young people), an aging population (about 15 percent of the population is over 65), unmet consumer demands, and failures in certain sectors of the economy, starting with real estate. Thus, a debate has developed over whether China's economic growth has peaked (**Selection 2**). There are also questions about the value of measuring China's growth in terms of GDP now that China, according to Xi Jinping, has reached the stage of "high-quality development" (**Selection 6**). That conclusion seems to recognize that China's long-standing environmental problems—air and water quality, climate change, and significant reliance for energy on coal—can no longer be ignored, since they have to some extent undermined economic development as well as public health (**Selection 8, Documents 2 and 3**).

In 2020, Xi Jinping pledged that China would reach peak emissions "before 2030" and achieve net-zero emissions by 2060—that is, the greenhouse gases released would be balanced by the gases removed or absorbed. And in October 2025, Beijing announced it will reduce greenhouse gas emissions: 7 to 10 percent over the next 10 years. The "2024–25 Energy Conservation and CO_2 Reduction Plan" added specifics for high-carbon emission industries such as steel and petrochemicals, energy savings, and the proportion of non-fossil fuels (wind and solar) in energy consumption.[1] Still, even with the push for greater reliance on renewable energy for electricity—now close to 40 percent—some experts predict that China may already be close to peak emissions. (For comparison, the Biden administration's last projection in 2024 for carbon emissions was to reduce them by over 60 percent by 2035. The second Trump administration has shown no interest in reducing carbon emissions or even acknowledging the threat posed by global warming. The European Union in 2024 targeted reducing carbon emissions by at least 55 percent by 2030.)

How China's leadership responds to the negative consequences of rapid economic development affects not only China's 1.2 billion population but also global welfare. China is on track to be the world's leading carbon emitter (**Selection 7**). Its insistence on being classified as a developing country does not square with its wealth, which warrants more generosity toward environmental problems in the Global South (**Selection 9**).

(1) Comparative Economic Strength of the US and China

The chart below gives just a few comparisons as an introduction to China's economy. Figures can only provide a very partial picture, however. They do not, for example, tell us about creativity, innovation, and opportunity in the two countries. The comparison might imply that competition is the central feature of the US and Chinese economies, omitting interdependencies. China owns about $759 billion of US debt (as of the end of 2024), mainly in treasury bonds. (That is second only to Japan, which owns about $1 trillion in bonds.) Those holdings benefit both countries, helping the US finance its trade deficit with China and helping China maintain large foreign reserves and a low currency value that cheapens its exports. The fact that the United States and China combine to produce about 43 percent of global GDP and over 32 percent of global foreign direct investment suggests both competition and the necessity of coordination.

Finally, the chart can only partly convey the speed at which China is catching up to the US or, by some measures (such as GDP in PPP terms), surpassing it. The dynamism of China's economy can sometimes seem

CHART 7.1 *Comparative Economic Strength of the US and China (t=$US trillion)*

	GDP (2024)	GDP/PPP	GDP Per capita (2024)	National Debt	Debt: GDP Ratio (2025)	Inequality Index (0–100)	Percent of World Foreign Direct Investment (Cumulative 1990–2022)
US	$29t	$27t.	$86,600	$36t	124.1%	59.9	23.7%
China	$18.5t	$40t.	$13,870	$16.6t	93.8%	54.6	8.6%
Notes		Purchasing Power Parity (PPP) compares the different purchasing power of currencies for the same basket of goods.				Highest number is most egalitarian. For comparison: France-79.9, Australia-78.3	

https://www.statista.com/chart/33321/gross-public-debt-in-china-eu-and-the-us/#:~:text=This%20year%2C%20U.S.%20government%20debt,was%20written%20by%20Matthias%20Janson.&text=This%20chart%20shows%20public,%25%20of%20gross%20domestic%20product
https://www.visualcapitalist.com/the-worlds-largest-economies-comparing-the-u-s-and-china; International Monetary Fund, 2025, https://www.imf.org/external/datamapper/GGXWDG_NGDP@WEO/OEMDC/ADVEC/WEOWORLD/USA/EU/MAE/CHN; Statista, October 23, 2024, https://www.worldeconomics.com/Thoughts/The-Worlds-Biggest-Economy.aspx; *Visual Capitalist*, June 3, 2024, Sources: *World Economics*, n.d.,

breathtaking. As two China specialists, Jude Blanchette and Ryan Hass, write:

> Over the past three decades, China has indeed established itself as the factory of the world, dominating global manufacturing and taking the lead in some advanced technology sectors. In 2023, China produced close to 60 percent of the world's electric vehicles, 80 percent of its batteries, and over 95 percent of the wafers used in solar energy technology. That same year, it added 300 gigawatts of wind and solar power to its energy grid—seven times more than the United States. The country also exerts control over much of the mining and refining of critical minerals essential to the global economy and boasts some of the world's most advanced infrastructure, including the largest high-speed rail network and cutting-edge 5G systems.[2]

(2) Peak China

Signs of Peaking

China's economy has probably peaked in size and performance. The era of investment and credit expansion seems to be over. Factory output has slowed, unemployment has risen, and the stock market has experienced wide swings. China's share of the world economy has dropped. It peaked at 18.3 percent of global GDP in 2021, then dropped to 16.9 percent in 2023. (The US economy has averaged 26.2 percent of the world economy during all those years.) As of 2024, several key indicators showed that China's economic weakening was structural rather than cyclical. They included a declining workforce population, youth unemployment (17 percent according to the OECD—see **Document 1**), credit and investment drop-offs, failures in real estate and infrastructure, and the flight of multinational corporations to more accommodating locations.

All these problems suggest the need for significant reforms, but as 2025 began, the leadership did not seem ready to accept the idea of peaking. It very tentatively put major funds into propping up the weak sectors, starting with consumer spending. Economists outside China said it would take at least $1 trillion (7.1 trillion RMB) to make a difference. One prominent economic planner, Peng Sen, president of the China Society of Economic Reform, a think tank, said China should boost consumption as a share of GDP—household consumption plus social transfers in chart 7.2 below—from about 55 percent (in 2024) to 70 percent by 2035, which is roughly the level of consumption in the wealthiest countries.[3] But China's priority seems

Year	Household Consumption	Social Transfer in Kind	Government Consumption	Net Export	Gross Capital Formation
1993	~45%	~5%	~15%	~3%	~32%
2003	~42%	~6%	~16%	~4%	~32%
2013	~39%	~7%	~18%	~6%	~30%
2023	~38%	~8%	~19%	~7%	~28%

CHART 7.2 Estimated Breakdown of China's GDP Composition Over Time
Source: *National Bureau of Statistics, Bloomberg.* Note: *"Social transfers" includes government-provided benefits such as education and healthcare.*

to be major investments in exports, such as EVs, and high-tech areas that compete with the West, namely, renewable energy, AI, and semiconductors.

Real Estate and Youth Unemployment: A Closer Look

The real estate market is "the elephant in the room" according to a senior Chinese economist. Real estate once comprised 30 percent of China's GDP and 80 percent of household wealth. The economist says demand from China's consumers is there, but at present they don't want to buy property because of the risk that construction of the homes, which are paid for ahead of time, will not be completed. (Unlike Americans, the Chinese are savers, not spenders or stockholders.) Some 20 million pre-sold apartment units remain unfinished, according to one outside economic source. "Homebuyers of one such project told CNBC earlier this year [2024] they had been waiting for eight years to get their homes."[4]

China's property sector meltdown goes back to 2021 and the spectacular failure of Evergrande, the Shenzhen-based developer that lost almost $94 billion that year and reported substantial losses for the following two years. Another major property developer, Country Garden, reported losses in 2023 of $27.5 billion, one of the biggest in Chinese company history.[5]

If the Chinese leadership were serious about helping consumers, it might bail out unhappy property owners and take steps to stabilize the real estate market. China's central bank did try to help. In September 2024, it made loans easier to obtain and cut interest rates on existing mortgages. Commercial banks were told they could lend a good deal more money to companies and households. Early in 2025, the Bank of China and three other major banks were planning to raise up to $71.6 billion by issuing special bonds to investors, mainly the finance ministry. The plan was to increase loans to stimulate the economy at a time when the banks are saddled with bad loans and low earnings.[6]

(Here's a local example of insufficient effort to solve the problem: Xinhua, China's official news agency, reports that "Shanghai will allocate

500 million yuan from its municipal budget to issue consumption vouchers for the dining, accommodation, cinema and sports sectors." When you divide that amount among the city's 25-million-plus population, however, each Shanghai-ese will get only a few dollars to spend. Hardly the sort of allocation likely to stimulate consumption.)

Youth unemployment is a second serious economic problem to which China's leadership has not adequately responded. Unemployed young people can become a source of political protest, but meeting their needs has proved difficult for the Chinese government. It comes at a time when the population is fast aging and the workforce needs more bodies, in part so that enough people pay into the pension system to keep it viable. The government's decision in late 2024 to raise the retirement age will help keep the pension system afloat, but it will also mean that young working people will have to work longer to get to pension age. For them, the pension reform is bad news, a disincentive to work and save unless the government also provides higher-quality jobs, job security, and more opportunities for women.[7]

Not a Pretty Picture

Many observers therefore predict that the Chinese economy will continue to struggle, notwithstanding a jump in the stock market and in property sales right after the government announced stimulus plans. Bloomberg reported in 2024 on the World Bank's assessment of what China's economic slowdown means for the rest of Asia: "China's expansion is set to drop to 4.3% next year from an estimated 4.8% in 2024, the [Bank] said in its semi-annual economic outlook report. As a result, growth in East Asia and the Pacific—which includes countries like Indonesia, Australia and Korea—will slow to 4.4% in 2025 from about 4.8% this year." The Bank was not convinced that the Chinese government's various monetary stimuli would significantly jumpstart the economy. China needs structural reform, said the Bank.[8] A *Wall Street Journal* writer likewise warned that unless China boosted domestic spending, it might "slip into a damaging period of falling prices and subdued growth similar to Japan's decadeslong stagnation, or the painful debt workouts that followed past real-estate crises in Europe and the U.S."

In November 2024, the Chinese leadership responded to part of the economic problem with a $1.4 trillion stimulus plan designed to enable local governments to refinance high-interest debt. That debt has accumulated over years of overspending on infrastructure. The central government will now be borrowing more to offset some local debt. But experts doubt that the plan will be sufficient, since a great deal of local indebtedness is off the books. Besides, the stimulus looks more like a debt restructuring plan than one that will spark consumer spending.[9]

(3) China in the Global Economy: Setting Records, Facing Dilemmas

Trade and Foreign Investment Booms

Analysts of the Chinese economy point to exports as the lone bright spot. China's General Administration of Customs said as 2025 began that the country exported $3.58 trillion worth of goods and services the previous year, while importing $2.59 trillion. The resulting surplus of $990 billion broke China's record, which was $838 billion in 2022.[10] The trade surplus seems to be on a constant upward track. In 2015 it was about $600 billion, and in 2021 it was just under $700 billion. Exports are expanding at more than three times the rate of imports. But even that bright spot has problems, because China is viewed, especially in the US, Europe, and India, as exporting overcapacity in manufacturing, undercutting prices in those importing countries. Thus, as noted in Chapter 3, German automakers fought against electric vehicle imports from China, and the US and India imposed major tariff increases on Chinese goods in hopes of making local prices more competitive. (India in 2024 had a trade deficit with China of around $100 billion.)

The International Monetary Fund's managing director, Kristalina Georgieva, was quite direct in saying (in 2024) that "China is at the fork in the road. If they continue with their current model, which is export-led growth, there would be trouble. Why? Because the Chinese economy has grown to a point where China's exports are no more a minor factor in global trade." She, too, urged China to focus on stimulating domestic demand.[11] Such advice looked increasingly wise by early 2025 when, as noted in Chapter 1, the Trump administration imposed very high tariffs on China and on neighboring countries in Southeast Asia that also rely heavily on an export-led economy.

China's overseas investments also set records in 2023–2024. Investments in the ten ASEAN countries, which are nearly three times Chinese investments in North America and Africa, led the way. *Nikkei Asia* reported in 2025: "China's overseas investment was on track to hit an eight-year high last year, behind only the 2016 peak that marked the heyday of its foreign dealmaking, official data shows. Fueling the latest boom is a gush of Chinese money into developing-country markets. This 'greenfield' investment hit a new high of $162.7 billion in 2023, with Saudi Arabia, Malaysia and Vietnam being the top three recipients that year, according to fDi Markets."[12] These investments reflect an important shift away from the US and the European Union, both of which are tightening the rules around Chinese investments for security reasons, and toward the Global South. As the *Nikkei Asia* report pointed out: "By 2023, only 28% of China's outbound investment went to advanced economies based on the International Monetary Fund's classification, down from 80% in 2016 and 50% in 2021, data from the New York-based Rhodium Group shows."

Backlash

What we are witnessing is the revolutionary change in China's position in the world economy. From being an insignificant trade and foreign investment factor in Mao's time, China has risen to top-tier status. Its foreign economic policies have a major bearing on just about every country's economic well-being. Ordinarily, that might seem like good news for China's leaders, but the political reality is that several powerful players, such as the US and the EU, resent the fact that Chinese goods are flooding their markets. And the same resentment may also exist in some Global South countries that China is wooing, such as India. It's a two-edged sword: Chinese goods and investments stimulate some developing economies, but the export of overcapacity may contribute to the deindustrialization of others.

How China handles the political fallout poses a major problem given the structure of its economy, which is not consumer-oriented and which depends on keeping its factories humming. For now, its answer is a resounding plug for economic globalization, the next selection's topic.

(4) Two Chinese Commentaries on the Virtues of Economic Globalization

It is apparent that these and other commentaries appeared in reaction to Donald Trump's taking office, and the rise in tariffs on Chinese imports that he promised.

The first commentary, "Three Questions on Economic Globalization," appeared in *Renmin ribao* on January 17, 2025:

> Global trade has demonstrated strong resilience, particularly with the increasing dynamism of digital trade and service trade. Despite the spread of unilateralism and protectionism, and the enthusiasm of certain countries [meaning the US] for pursuing "decoupling and breaking chains" or building "small yards with high fences," the global picture shows that enterprises in various countries continue to coexist and thrive within global supply chains, industrial chains, and value chains. According to the World Openness Report 2024, global value chains have maintained an overall expansion trend in recent years, with digitalization, the green economy, and the service sector driving the process of global openness.[13]

A second commentary, under the byline of China's vice premier, Ding Xuexiang, also appeared in January 2025.[14] "With imminent tariff wars and trade wars, an ongoing tug of war between the forces for and against economic globalization, and intense rivalry between multilateralism and unilateralism, the global governance system is undergoing profound adjustments," Ding wrote. "Economic globalization is not a 'you lose, I win' zero-sum game, but a universally beneficial process where all can benefit and win together.... Protectionism leads nowhere. Trade war has no winners." For China, therefore, multilateralism, global governance, and "equal rules for all countries in international affairs" are critical to uphold. Ding pointed out that the developing countries' share of world trade has doubled in the last thirty years, not only to their benefit but to the benefit of the major trading countries as well.

Ding's speech, like other Chinese commentaries in recent years on the merits of economic globalization, begs the question: Does China's role in the world economy conform with the pledges of equal opportunity? When Ding says, for example, that digital access and information technology should be widely shared with developing countries, or that developed countries should "help [developing] countries strengthen emerging and future industries," or that food and energy security require "pooling global efforts," is China leading the way or taking advantage?

(5) Private Capitalism is OK

It's official: China endorses private capitalism so long as competition is fair. "Market access is the prerequisite for business entities to participate in economic activities, and fair competition is the basic principle of the market economy. General Secretary Xi Jinping emphasized that 'resolutely breaking down various obstacles to the equal use of factors of production and fair participation in market competition in accordance with the law' is to create more fair development opportunities for private enterprises." Fair competition, and breaking down barriers to competition, are essential to a stable and predictable economy—meaning that avoiding corrupt practices in government-business relations is also essential.

According to Xi, in 2025 there are more than 420,000 private enterprises among the national high-tech enterprises, accounting for more than 92 percent of the total. They are the "key drivers" of technological innovation. "In the new era and new journey, the private economy has broad prospects for development and great potential, and it is time for private enterprises and private entrepreneurs to show their talents," said Xi. Big-time entrepreneurs such as Jack Ma, the billionaire founder of the Alibaba Group, are appearing in public again, signaling that "getting rich" is acceptable but, more importantly, that wealthy entrepreneurs are critical to China's drive for world leadership in advanced technologies.[15]

(6) China's Rising GDP: Speedy Development or Quality Development?

Gross Domestic Product (GDP) is probably the most widely used indicator of a country's economy. China's GDP always gets attention because it seems to increase impressively every year. But many Chinese officials and economists seem to have concluded that rising GDP tied to the export of manufactured goods cannot fix the economy's weak points identified in **Selection 2**. Some of them believe that GDP figures are both unreliable and not the best measure of how the economy is doing. On the first point, former Premier Li Keqiang said in 2007 that GDP claims were "man-made" and actually for "reference only." That remark gibes with foreign criticism that China's GDP is inflated by large investments that are unproductive, such as housing and rail lines that go unused.[16] On the second point that questions the value of GDP itself, an article in the official *Renmin ribao* at the end of 2024, "How to View Economic Growth?" said just that: "General Secretary Xi Jinping has clearly pointed out that our economic development has entered a new normal of speed changes, structural optimization, and motivational transformation. He has offered the important thesis that our economy has shifted from high-speed growth to the high-quality development stage." Rapid growth was once fashionable, said the article, but it was also costly in terms of resources and the environment. Now, qualitative growth, which includes environmental protection, is said to be more important than quantitative growth.[17] Sounds very much in tune with what many Western economists have long said in criticism of their own country's as well as China's economic growth statistics.

(7) China is on Track to be the Leading Carbon Emitter—*and* Leader in Green Energy

Historically, the US and Europe have ranked 1 and 2 in total carbon emissions. But China, which is the leading annual emitter and has already surpassed the European Union in historical emissions, is on track to be number 1 in total carbon emissions as soon as 2030 (see chart 7.3 below).

The reason China is first in the carbon chart is, well, China's rise—its extraordinary and rapid economic growth, fueled in large part by coal and subject to far less regulation than in the other major economies. An

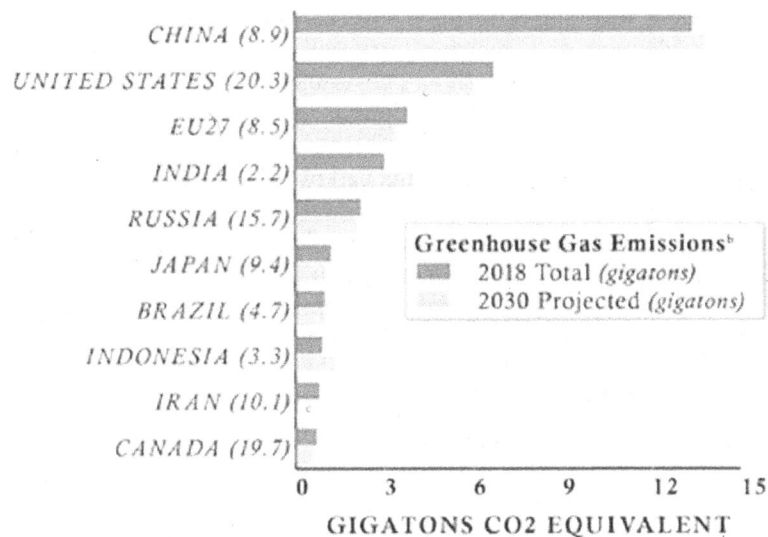

CHART 7.3 The Leading Greenhouse Gas Emitters *(Source: The National Security Archive, February 28, 2025, https://nsarchive.gwu.edu/briefing-book/climate-change-transparency-project-intelligence/2025-02-28/climate-intelligence)*

interactive data chart developed by James Eagle (https://lnkd.in/dNwaziVb) displays China's rise to the top of the list of carbon dioxide emitters over time: from number 8 in the world in the 1940s to fifth in the 1960s, third in the 1980s, second in the 1990s, and first around 2007. By 2022, China's carbon emissions were twice those of the US. However, account also has to be taken of emissions per person, and there the US is far ahead of China, as chart 7.3 shows (20.3 to China's 8.9).[18]

The flip side of the global warming debate is China's leadership in wind and solar power. As reported in the *Washington Post*,

> green energy is one arena where many analysts agree that China has pulled ahead of the United States in almost every key area, from electric vehicles to solar panels. That gap is likely to widen under President Donald Trump, analysts say. As Trump focuses on boosting fossil fuel production and cutting funding for clean energy projects, China is further increasing investment in renewable energy technologies. "It is difficult to overstate China's singular lead across clean energy technologies. The gaps are both enormous and historically unprecedented," said Milo McBride, fellow at the Carnegie Endowment for International Peace, a think tank.[19]

If global warming is to have any chance of reaching a plateau before heading downward, China's efforts will have much to do with it. "A recent spate of data from China's government, as well as reports by energy analysts," the *New York Times* reports, "have provided positive signs that while China's emissions may not decrease significantly, they also may not grow. China's president, Xi Jinping, had pledged to reach that turning point by 2030."[20] The biggest reason for these positive signs is the change in China's electricity profile, from coal to solar and wind. Coal still accounted for 53 percent of electricity generation in 2023, but that figure represented a considerable reduction in coal consumption.

While China's energy picture is changing, consider where the US is. "Last year alone," the *Times* article observes, "China installed more solar panels than the United States has in its entire history, and connected most of them to its electricity grid. Almost two-thirds of big wind and solar plants under construction globally are in China." Experts, however, caution that the trend may only be temporary, since a good deal of the decline in energy use has been due to the real estate and construction industry collapses. Moreover, China continues to invest heavily in coal; it is by far (around 60 percent) the world's largest user. "China alone accounted for two-thirds of the world's newly operating coal plants last year. In 2023, new coal-plant construction hit an eight-year high in China." In short, it is not yet time to celebrate.

(8) Some Contradictions of Development

Rapid, unregulated economic development often has serious downsides. In China's case, those downsides include air and water pollution, declining public health in the major cities, drought and other weather impacts, and reduced agricultural output. Two of these are explored briefly below.

Most of China's major cities, starting with Beijing and Tianjin, are slowly losing elevation. A study in *Science* shows that "In 100 years, a quarter of China's urban coastal land could sit below sea level because of a combination of subsidence and sea level rise . . . " Subsidence refers to the weight of buildings, pumping of water from aquifers, and oil drilling, all of which weaken underground soil and rock. Climate change and consequent rising sea levels may combine with subsidence to increase the pressure on cities. Unless China takes remedial action such as the Netherlands is known for, cities will face cracks in the earth on a major scale, such as happened in Tianjin in 2023, when thousands of high-rise residents had to be evacuated.[21]

Food security has historically been a major concern of Chinese leaderships. In more recent years, as supply chains have become less reliable and tensions with the West have increased, Chinese in farm areas have been drawn to the cities. Water supplies have become scarcer, putting food security high up on the political agenda. That was clear from a visit Xi Jinping paid to Hunan Province. He emphasized the province's key role in China's food security. "With a population of over 1.4 billion, China's food security must be ensured by ourselves," he said. "Chinese people's rice bowls should primarily contain Chinese grain." Xi urged the kinds of measures familiar to Western farmers, such as increased scale of operations, improvements in seed quality and variety, increased grain yield, and (most difficult) attraction of more farmers to engage in modern agriculture.

(9) Who Pays? China's Role in Global Climate Financing

Since China insists on being treated as a developing country, yet has the world's second-highest GDP, should it pay other developing countries to fight global warming? From 2013 to 2022, China did provide $45 billion in climate aid for poor countries through mechanisms such as a South-South Climate Cooperation Fund, according to research by the World Resources Institute (WRI), an environmental think tank. But these mechanisms lack the transparency and accountability of the United Nations process, said Shuang Liu, China finance director at the WRI and lead author of the analysis. Given China's dominance in solar panels and batteries, you would think Beijing would see economic opportunity in being more generous with climate aid. After all, when China defends its electric vehicle exports to Europe from charges of exporting overcapacity, one of its arguments is that EVs are helping in the "green transition."

Money was the central issue at the November 2024 UN climate summit—COP29, held in Baku, Azerbaijan. How much money should be raised to help protect poor countries from climate change, and where the money should come from, yielded contending views. Past efforts to raise $100 billion took a great deal of time, and the discussion at COP29 was in terms of *trillions* of dollars. "For decades, wealthy nations pledged $100 billion annually to support vulnerable countries," said Prime Minister Gaston Browne of Antigua and Barbuda. "Yet these promises have largely gone unfulfilled." Many rich countries see climate finance as "a random act of charity," Browne said, "not recognizing that they have a moral obligation to provide funding, especially the historical emitters and even those who currently have large emissions." He didn't mention China, but he didn't have to.

Some leaders in the wealthier nations have suggested that in addition to new funds from countries like Saudi Arabia and China, much of the money should come from the private sector, not from governments. Anticipating US withdrawal (again) from the Paris Agreement on climate change once Donald Trump took office may have been behind that suggestion. But other world leaders have called for a new series of global taxes on fossil fuels and other polluting industries. President Emmanuel Macron of France, Prime Minister Mia Mottley of Barbados, and President William Ruto of Kenya have proposed levying a fee of 0.1 percent on stock and bond trades, which they said could raise up to $418 billion per year. They also suggested taxing the shipping industry and oil and gas producers, which they said could raise another $290 billion annually. The World Bank and other international development banks announced that they were on track to provide $120 billion per year for low-income and middle-income countries by 2030, up from $74.7 billion in 2023.

Such figures are far from what developing countries are demanding. And when the Baku meeting adjourned, those countries' representatives expressed their dissatisfaction. COP29 announced agreement on $300 billion in annual climate assistance by 2035—far short of the $1.3 trillion they had sought. China continued to insist on developing-country status, as did India, in effect reducing funds that might be available to the poorest countries.

Documents

Document 1. China's Economic Outlook, 2024-2025
(*Background*: These contrasting perspectives come from three groups: the Organization for Economic Cooperation and Development (OECD), the financial firm J.P. Morgan, and the economic analysis group China Briefing. *Sources*: OECD, December 2024, https://www.oecd.org/en/publications/2024/12/oecd-economic-outlook-volume-2024-issue-2_67bb8fac/full-report/china_da81a082.html; J.P. Morgan, May 20, 2025, (https://www.jpmorgan.com/insights/global-research/economy/china-economy; *China Briefing*, January 17, 2025, https://www.china-briefing.com/news/chinas-gdp-expands-5-percent-fast-facts-key-drivers/)

OECD

Growth has slowed

[China's] year-on-year growth in the first three quarters of 2024 slowed to 4.8%. Property investment is still declining due to continuing weakness in real estate markets, weighing on growth, but at a slower pace. Infrastructure investment has been growing at a steady but moderate rate, while manufacturing investment has been robust on the back of strong export demand. Industrial production has been robust, driven by high-tech industries. Consumption growth is sluggish due to on-going high precautionary saving.

CPI inflation was 0.3% year-on-year in October 2024 with declines in some services prices, such as transportation and telecommunications. Lower input prices have been a key driver of falling producer prices in upstream industries. Productivity improvements, quality upgrades and innovation are helping to keep prices low, alongside a relatively weak consumption recovery. The urban youth unemployment rate has edged down in three successive months, but at 17.1% in September still remains high.

The rebound of external demand has spurred Chinese exports, especially in high-tech industries. Lower input prices keep Chinese exports competitive. Goods imports have also strengthened slightly, but reduced reliance on imported inputs and the low import content of consumption prevent a stronger rebound. A weak recovery of tourism imports has limited total import growth and boosted the current account surplus. . . .

The Chinese economy will continue to slow gradually with falling potential growth due to unfavourable demographics [referring to a rising elderly population] and slower productivity growth. Ongoing adjustment in the real estate sector will continue to weigh on residential investment and on related items of consumption, such as furniture sales. However, infrastructure investment will pick up, helped by greater local special bond issuance. There are pressing needs related to the green transition, urban village redevelopment and other environmental and social targets. Consumption growth is expected to remain stable and unlikely to pick up as long as the lack of social security reforms keeps precautionary savings high. Technological upgrading and competition in the domestic markets will likely keep exports competitive, despite faster rising unit labour costs than in other countries. Tourism imports, the largest single component of imports, may not recover to pre-COVID-19 levels. The current account surplus is projected to rise further. Inflation will return to more normal, but still low levels. . . .

J.P. Morgan

The intensifying [China-US] trade tensions are set to lead to a deceleration in China's economic growth in coming quarters, according to J.P. Morgan Research current forecasts. "The 34% reciprocal tariff led us to revise down full-year GDP growth forecast. First, regarding the trade channel, the larger-than-expected tariff increase from the U.S. implies a larger decline in China's exports to the U.S. and a weaker global economic outlook that will lead to a modest decline in China's exports to the rest of the world," said Haibin Zhu, chief China economist and head of Greater China Economic Research at J.P. Morgan.

The higher-than-expected U.S. tariffs on China and the rest of the world are expected to drag China's economic growth by about 0.7 percentage points, according to J.P. Morgan Research. After taking into account additional fiscal stimulus later this year, the full-year growth forecast is marked down marginally from 4.6% prior to the tariff announcement to 4.4%.

China Brief

China's economy in 2024 at a quick glance:

- **GDP growth:** China's GDP reached RMB 134.91 trillion (US$18.80 trillion) in 2024, the second-largest in the world, trailing only the United States, whose 2024 GDP is projected at approximately US$29 trillion.

- **Manufacturing sector:** China's manufacturing sector above the designated size (companies with an annual main business income of above RMB 20 million) grew by 6.1% year-on-year. Notably, equipment manufacturing expanded by 7.7%, while high-tech manufacturing rose by 8.9%. In terms of products, production in new energy vehicles, integrated circuits, and industrial robots grew by 38.7%, 22.2%, and 14.2%, respectively.

- **Services sector:** The services sector saw a 5.0% year-on-year growth in 2024. Key sub-sectors included: Information transmission, software, and IT services (10.9%), leasing and business services (10.4%), transportation, storage, and postal services (7.0%), accommodation and catering services (6.4%), financial services (5.6%), and wholesale and retail trade (5.5%).

- **Retail sales:** The total retail sales of consumer goods reached RMB 4.88 trillion (US$679.81 billion), growing 3.5% from the previous year. Online retail sales accounted for RMB 1.55 trillion (US$215.92), marking a 7.2% increase.

- **Fixed asset investment:** Total fixed asset investment (excluding rural households) amounted to RMB 5.14 trillion (US$716.03), rising by 3.2%. Excluding real estate development, fixed asset investment grew by 7.2%. Fixed asset investment in manufacturing grew by 9.2%. High-tech industries investment grew by 8.0%, with high-tech manufacturing and high-tech services growing by 7.0% and 10.2%, respectively. Notable sub-sectors of high-tech manufacturing included aerospace and computer manufacturing, with investment increases of 39.5% and 7.1%, respectively. In high-tech services,

investments in professional technical services and technology transformation services grew by 30.3% and 11.4%, respectively.
- **Unemployment Rate:** The national urban population surveyed had an unemployment rate of 5.1%, a slight decrease of 0.1 percentage points from the previous year.
- **Income growth:** The per capita disposable income of residents reached RMB 41,314 (US$5,755), a nominal increase of 5.3%. After adjusting for inflation, the real growth was 5.1%.

Document 2. 2023 Report on the State of the Ecology and Environment in China

(*Background*: This official report was issued by China's Ministry of Ecology and Environment in May 2024. Below is a portion of the report's summary. *Source*: Ministry of Ecology and Environment, China, May 24, 2024 https://english.mee.gov.cn/Resources/Reports/soe/SOEE2019/202408/P020240828593686591369.pdf)

. . . China's ecological and environmental governance achieved new progress [in 2023], and the overall ecological and environmental quality kept improving steadily. The ambient air quality across the country has been steadily improving. The concentration of fine particulate matter in cities at the prefectural level and above was . . . less than the annual target. The proportion of days with excellent or good air quality was 85.5%, and the figure was 86.8% after deducting the days with abnormally high dust levels, 0.6 percentage points better than the annual target. [The body of the report states that 203 of China's 339 major cities are said to have met the national air quality standard; 136 did not. 105 cities also failed to meet the standard for fine particulate matter.]

The quality of the surface water across the country continued to improve. The proportion of sections meeting excellent and good water quality (Grade I to III) was 89.4%, an increase of 1.5 percentage points from 2022; and the proportion of sections with water quality worse than Grade V was 0.7%, the same as that of 2022. The water quality of the main stream of the Yangtze River and the Yellow River remained stable at Grade II. The overall quality of ground water in China remained stable . . .

The water quality of sea areas under jurisdiction of China remained stable with an upward trend. The sea areas meeting Seawater Quality Standard Grade I accounted for 97.9% of the total sea areas under jurisdiction, an increase of 0.5 percentage points compared to that of 2022. . . .

Nationwide, soil environmental risks were largely brought under control, and the trend of aggravating soil pollution was preliminarily curbed. The soil environment of agricultural land was generally stable, and the safe use of key construction land was guaranteed.

The natural and ecological condition was generally stable in China. The Ecological Quality Index (EQI) value was 59.6, and the ecological quality met Grade II standard, showing no significant change compared with that of 2022. . . .

The condition of nuclear and radiation safety generally remained stable in China. The overall radiation environment quality across the country and that in the vicinity of key nuclear and radiation facilities was both generally good.

Document 3. China's Policies and Actions for Addressing Climate Change (2022)
(*Background*: This is a portion of the introduction and first chapter of the official report of China's Ministry of Ecology and Environment. *Source*: Ministry of Ecology and Environment, China, November 2022, https://english.mee.gov.cn/Resources/Reports/reports/202211/P020221110605466439270.pdf)

China has . . . established a new development paradigm and made efforts for high-quality development. It has implemented a national strategy of proactively responding to climate change by giving it higher priority in the national governance system . . .

Since 2021, China has actively implemented the [2015] Paris Agreement on climate change, updating its Nationally Determined Contributions (NDCs) goals, earnestly carrying out effective and well-conceived actions and making significant progress in meeting the targets of carbon dioxide peaking and carbon neutrality. China has put in place [a] policy framework for carbon dioxide peaking and carbon neutrality, developed a mid-term and long-term strategy for controlling greenhouse gas emissions, accelerated the development of a national carbon market, and formulated and implemented the National Strategy for Climate Change Adaptation. Based on preliminary calculations, in 2021, the carbon intensity of China dropped by 3.8 percent and 50.8 percent from the level respectively in 2020 and 2005, the share of non-fossil fuels in primary energy consumption rose to 16.6 percent, the total installed capacity of wind and solar power generation combined increase to 635 million kilowatts, the coal consumption per unit of GDP dropped significantly, and the forest coverage and stock have both risen over the past 30 consecutive years. By the first anniversary of the national carbon trading system, the cumulative volume of carbon emission allowances (CEA) was 194 million tonnes, and the cumulative turnover was 8,492 billion.

. . . [China's goal is to] strive to peak its carbon dioxide emissions before 2030 and achieve its carbon neutrality before 2060, lower its carbon dioxide emissions per unit of GDP by over 65 percent from the 2005 level and increase its share of non-fossil fuels in primary energy consumption to around 25 percent by 2030, and increase its forest stock by 6 billion cubic meters from the 2005 level and its total installed capacity of wind and solar power generation combined to over 1.2 billion kilowatts.

Document 4. Xi Jinping on Climate Change and Global Governance

(*Background*: UN Secretary-General António Guterres and Brazilian President Luiz Inácio Lula da Silva brought together a Leaders Meeting on Climate and the Just Transition. Seventeen national leaders from major economies and climate-vulnerable countries attended this virtual summit ahead of COP30, the next major international climate conference, to be held in Brazil in November 2025. Below are Xi's main points in his speech at the meeting, April 23, 2025. *Source*: Ministry of Foreign Affairs, China, April 23, 2025, https://www.fmprc.gov.cn/mfa_eng/xw/zyxw/202504/t20250423 _11660.html)

First, we must adhere to multilateralism. The more volatile and turbulent the international situation becomes, the greater the need for us to firmly safeguard the U.N.-centered international system and the international order underpinned by international law, and firmly safeguard international fairness and justice. The U.N. Framework Convention on Climate Change and its Paris Agreement are the legal cornerstone of international climate cooperation. It is important for all countries to champion the rule of law, honor commitments, prioritize green and low-carbon development, and jointly respond to the climate crisis through multilateral governance.

Second, we must deepen international cooperation. Solidarity and cooperation are needed more than ever as the world faces multiple, compounded challenges. We should rise above estrangement and conflict with openness and inclusiveness, boost technological innovation and industrial transformation through cooperation, and facilitate the free flow of quality green technologies and products, so that they can be accessible, affordable and beneficial for all countries, especially the developing ones. As a member of the Global South, China will vigorously deepen South-South cooperation and continue to provide help for fellow developing countries to the best of its capability.

Third, we must accelerate the just transition. . . . Green transformation is not only the essential way to address climate change, but also a new engine for economic and social development. . . . Developed countries are obliged to extend assistance and support to developing countries, help drive the global shift toward green and low-carbon development, and contribute to the common and long-term well-being of people of all countries.

Fourth, we must strengthen results-oriented actions. . . . All parties should do their utmost to formulate and implement their program of action for nationally determined contributions (NDCs) while coordinating economic development and energy transition. China will announce its 2035 NDCs covering all economic sectors and all greenhouse gases before the United Nations Climate Change Conference in Belém.

Harmony between man and nature is a defining feature of Chinese modernization. China is a steadfast actor and major contributor in promoting global green development. Since I announced China's goals for carbon peaking and carbon neutrality five years ago, we have built the world's largest and fastest-growing renewable energy system as well as the largest and most complete new energy industrial chain. China also leads the world in the speed and scale of "greening," contributing a quarter of the world's newly-added area of afforestation.

8

Human Rights

Introduction

President Xi Jinping would like everyone to pay attention to how China is exerting leadership in world affairs as a "responsible great power." China has, for example, loaned billions of dollars to developing countries under the Belt and Road Initiative, promoted energy conservation and solar power at home and abroad, and tried to play the honest broker in the North Korea-US dispute over nuclear weapons. China has contributed more personnel to UN peacekeeping missions than any of the other permanent Security Council members—mainly several missions in Africa—and is the second-largest contributor (after the United States) to the UN peacekeeping budget. Xi can certainly claim that China is a major player on the most pressing international issues, but when it comes to human rights and respect for the rule of law, how ethically and legally responsible a great power is it?

The short answer is that China's record on human rights has significant blemishes, as is true of virtually all countries to some degree. China's official position on human rights in China emphasizes the right of development, economic security, and constitutional guarantees enforced by the Chinese Communist Party (**Document 1**). China has signed and ratified most of the major United Nations human rights instruments—the Declaration of Human Rights and the conventions on economic, social, and cultural rights; discrimination against women; torture; racial discrimination; and the rights of children. (The United States has a poorer record in that regard, having signed but not ratified the UN covenants on economic, social, and cultural rights, the rights of the child, and discrimination against women.) China has greatly improved its citizens' human development, as defined by the United Nations and in comparison with other countries (**Document 3**).

As some of the readings below point out, ratifying rights and adhering to them are two different things. That is especially true when it comes to China's respect for civil and political rights—the one major UN convention it has not ratified. The readings and the documents reveal extremely serious violations among many social groups but particularly ethnic minorities—a common failing in numerous countries. Notably, when Chinese diplomats discuss the value of the UN, their focus is on the rights of states, not individuals (**Document 5**).

This chapter on China's human rights policies covers treatment of ethnic minorities (**Selections 1–3**), restrictions on democratic rights in Hong Kong (**Selection 4**), and repression of internal critics such as journalists, lawyers, professors, students, artists, and businesspeople (**Selection 10**). The mechanism used to sustain these policies is a nationwide surveillance and detention system (**Selection 5**). China consistently denies that systematic repression is occurring, but what keeps criticism from international and nongovernmental organizations, businesses, and governments in check is China's economic power (**Selections 3, 7, and 9**). China counters that outsiders have no right to interfere in its affairs, and that the US and other Western countries have their own record of curtailing civil liberties and paying lip service to social justice.

The selections below also include international responses to China's repression in Xinjiang (**Selection 6 and Document 2**); China's support of the Myanmar (Burma) military government's ongoing ethnic cleansing of the Rohingya minority (**Selection 8**); and the disruptive impact of China's hydropower projects, one of them the world's largest, on Tibetan culture and community (**Document 4**).

(1) Repression of the Uyghurs

Genocide?

The roundup of Muslim families in the Xinjiang Uyghur Autonomous Region, estimated at one million people and possibly more, has been widely reported and internationally condemned. Uyghurs and other Muslims in Xinjiang have been subjected to forced assimilation and other gross violations of human rights, leading some observers to charge China with *cultural* genocide. It could be more than that, depending on one's reading of the Genocide Convention (see box).

> Under the Convention on the Prevention and Punishment of the Crime of Genocide (the Genocide Convention, 1948), to which China is a party, the international crime of genocide may mean, besides killing members of a group, "(b) Causing serious bodily or mental harm to members of the group; (c) Deliberately inflicting on the group conditions of life calculated to bring about its physical destruction in whole or in part; (d) Imposing measures intended to prevent births within the group."

Mass detention and "reeducation" of Uyghurs, justified as counter-terrorism and counter-separatism, aims to change their language, religion, and way of life—in short, ensure that their primary identity and loyalty is to the Chinese party-state. Though the party's secret is now out, thanks to satellite photos and covert videos, some Chinese officials have maintained the view that all Uyghurs are potential enemies of the state who must be kept under surveillance at all times. It's an Orwellian situation, with face-recognition cameras everywhere, people's DNA samples taken without their approval, the rule of law entirely absent, and tens of thousands of Han Chinese minders dispatched to villages to live with and report on Uyghur families.

The Surveillance State

Initially, China's "reeducation" program in Xinjiang sought to replace Muslim culture with the dominant Han culture, in every way from language and religion to personal habits such as smoking. Hundreds of dissident Uyghur, Kazakh, and other indigenous writers and other intellectuals were whisked away, imprisoned, or simply "disappeared," according to anthropology professor Magnus Fiskesjö of Cornell University. At the same time, Chinese hackers were embedding malware in smartphones to track Uyghurs' movements and conversations, even when they left China, thus going far beyond anything George Orwell might have imagined. The surveillance campaign intensified with the deployment of a nationwide system of facial recognition technology, street cameras, and, most ominously, DNA collection. China's Ministry of Public Security announced plans to obtain the DNA via blood samples of tens of millions of male adults and children, starting in Xinjiang and Tibet. The resulting database is expected to cover virtually China's entire population, giving the police additional capacity to pressure the families of criminals, real and political.

There is also evidence that the Chinese authorities in Xinjiang are seeking to suppress the birth rates of Uyghurs through enforced birth control and forced mass sterilization. The decline in the birthrate for Uyghurs is several times the national average in parts of the province, leading some observers to call the situation outright genocide. Dr. Adrian Zenz, a leading German expert on the Uyghurs, is among them, having found that birth control is being vigorously enforced among Uyghur women. He draws an ominous conclusion: "These findings raise serious concerns as to whether Beijing's policies in Xinjiang represent, in fundamental respects, what might be characterized as a demographic campaign of genocide."[1]

China's surveillance system is not confined to the Uyghurs. It is a many-layered nationwide network designed to collect personal data for police and security units on every Chinese citizen whose behavior or personal characteristics might be troublesome to the authorities. Another piece of the network is the social credit system (*shehui xinyong tixi*), under which mass data collection is used to determine the trustworthiness of individuals and businesses, setting the basis for rewarding and punishing behavior.

In a word, no one is above suspicion. Facial recognition cameras are now installed in private as well as public places. They can collect voice and iris prints, and race and gender information for inclusion in an ever-expanding database. Phone tracking not only gives a person's location but also usernames and personal activities such as social connections and habits.

(2) China's Abuse of Biometric Data Collected in Minority Populations

In April 2023, the Citizen Lab at the University of Toronto submitted a highly critical report on China to the UN Special Rapporteur on counter-terrorism and human rights.[2] The report focused on two mass biometric data collection programs conducted by China's public security organs: a mass DNA collection program in the Tibet Autonomous Region (the TAR), and a mass iris scan collection program in Qinghai Province, which borders Xinjiang. Both regions have large populations of non-Han people—90 percent in Tibet and 49 percent in Qinghai. Far from being criminal investigations, the report said,

> these two programs appear to be part of broader public security surveillance and social control programs, without protection under any Chinese law. Mass biometric data collection programs in the TAR and Qinghai violate the human rights of those subjected to biometric data collection, in particular the right to privacy, freedom of expression, the right of peaceful assembly, and freedom from discrimination.

The Citizen Lab report noted that because the use of biometric data such as facial recognition surveillance is inherently intrusive and in violation of privacy rights, some civil society groups outside China have called for a halt in its use. Moreover: "Emerging digital technologies like biometric recognition systems are, according to the Special Rapporteur on contemporary forms of racism, capable of creating and sustaining racial and ethnic exclusion in systemic or structural terms." The problem is that under Chinese law, use of biometric data by public security agencies places no clear limits on when and how the data collection can be utilized in criminal and terrorism investigations. That leaves plenty of room for security authorities to use the law to cast a very wide net. "These programs appear to have been conducted without a clear basis in Chinese domestic law and in ways that may be at odds with China's obligations under international human rights instruments to which China is party," the report concluded.

(3) Forced Labor and "Reeducation" in Xinjiang and Tibet

Forced labor is an important feature of China's genocide in Xinjiang. A program with a seemingly innocent title, Vocational Skills Education and Training Centers, aims at more efficiently employing prison labor. The essence of the new program is intensive reeducation followed by assignment to profitable outside enterprises. Uyghurs have been systematically shipped off to other provinces and even put on board fishing vessels, all without pay.[3] How do the Chinese authorities justify forced labor? It's part of poverty alleviation! Labor, they say, is a constitutional obligation, and it gives poor, unskilled people opportunities to advance. Forced labor is justified as a release of surplus rural labor. An official Chinese government white paper on labor in Xinjiang, issued in September 2020, said:

> [China] fully respects the wishes of workers, protects citizens' right to work in accordance with the law, applies international labor and human rights standards, and strives to enable everyone to create a happy life and achieve their own development through hard work. In accordance with the country's major policies on employment and the overall plan for eliminating poverty, the Xinjiang Uygur Autonomous Region takes the facilitation of employment as the most fundamental project for ensuring and improving people's wellbeing. It has made every effort to increase and stabilize employment through various channels: encouraging individual initiative, regulatory role of the market, and government policies facilitating employment, entrepreneurship, and business startups. . . . [The local government] encourages the impoverished workforce to seek employment outside their hometowns.[4]

Forced labor poses a problem for multinational corporations. Global Rights Alliance, an NGO based in The Hague, Netherlands, reports that China, using forced labor, "has now invested significant resources to expand critical mineral exploration, mining, processing, and manufacturing in the XUAR [Xinjiang]. The region's rich mineral reserves and geographic proximity to China's trading partners have established it as a national extractive hub."[5] The report focuses on lithium, titanium, and two other minerals that are in global demand and are being intensely mined and processed in Xinjiang for export. The finding of labor abuse poses a major problem for foreign companies that depend on these minerals in advanced technology and clean energy.

Some international companies, either on their own or under public pressure, have decided not to produce goods assembled by forced labor in Xinjiang. Are you wearing a Calvin Klein jacket or a Tommy Hilfiger outfit, for example? PVH, the parent company of those clothing brands, has refused to buy the cotton for its garments from Xinjiang. Xinjiang accounts for about 90 percent of all the cotton grown in China. China has threatened retaliation, arguing (seriously) that it's discrimination. Its commerce ministry has given the company thirty days to respond to that charge. Beijing could sanction PVH's suppliers and factories in China. That poses a dilemma for other multinationals, including those not reliant on Xinjiang products, that want to keep doing business in China. Do they comply with China's implied threat to accept China's treatment of ethnic minorities or face sanctions on their businesses? Some do; many don't.

In Tibet, the Chinese are interested less in forced labor than in forced education—the kind of education that changes children's identity, language, and loyalties, from Tibetan to Chinese and from the Dalai Lama to the CCP. "Tibetan rights activists, as well as experts working for the United Nations, have said that the party is systematically separating Tibetan children from their families to erase Tibetan identity and to deepen China's control of a people who historically resisted Beijing's rule."[6] Around 800,000 children, or nearly 80 percent of Tibetan children, some as young as four years of age, have been placed in boarding schools without parental consent.[7]

What China has done in Xinjiang and Tibet is similar to what British, French, and Dutch colonial rulers did in their day. The horrific treatment of the children of Indigenous peoples recalls what has happened in the US, Australia, and Canada—treatment that has led to calls for official apologies and reparations.

(4) Destroying Democracy: China in Hong Kong

On July 1, 1997, the United Kingdom formally handed Hong Kong over to China under an agreement that was supposed to give Hong Kong fifty years of autonomy. "One country, two systems," Deng Xiaoping promised. That same year, students and professors at the University of Hong Kong erected a statue, called "Pillar of Shame," to commemorate the 1989 Tiananmen massacre. The tall sculpture by a Danish artist lasted until the end of 2021 when, in the dead of night, it was carved in half and removed. Two other sculptures of the same event at two other Hong Kong universities were also removed. The ongoing eclipse of civil society by the Chinese authorities could not have been more starkly demonstrated.

The Unexpected Happened

Many observers took the attitude of "it can't happen here"—that Hong Kong was immune to a Chinese authoritarian takeover—because massive protests in Hong Kong in 2019 and 2020, which started over an extradition bill and broadened to demands for greater autonomy, seemed to have the support of a clear majority of the city's 7.4 million people. Beijing surely wouldn't crack down on a highly visible and defiant uprising in an international trade and financial hub. The protesters, however, had no central leadership and no game plan, while Beijing controlled the police, the courts, and, if necessary, the People's Liberation Army bivouacked on the edge of the city. China's leaders had no interest in negotiating with the demonstrators, apparently believing that to do so would legitimize the protests and weaken its rule.

The new face of Hong Kong is direct Chinese intervention. It began with Beijing proclaiming the right to "supervise" Hong Kong's internal affairs, in violation of the Basic Law that was supposed to protect Hong Kong's autonomy. China's legislature passed a new National Security Law in 2020 and suspended legislative council elections in Hong Kong for a year. Then, in early 2021, what little remained of democratic governance in Hong Kong was obliterated by the imposition of a compulsory loyalty oath for candidates for district councils. The oath, to China and the Chinese Communist Party, was announced as a test of patriotism and "political reform." Hong Kong legislative elections in December 2021 under Beijing's new rules yielded predictable results. Only "patriots" were allowed to run. Turnout was a record low. Pro-China candidates won all but one seat, including all the directly elected seats previously held by opposition forces.

Democracy Obliterated

Virtually all elements of civil society, such as labor and student unions and NGOs, have been disbanded. Leaders of the protest movement who were unable to leave Hong Kong were arrested. Independent news sources have disappeared one by one, notably including the arrest in June 2021 of the editors of the newspaper *Apple Daily*, followed by its closure. *Stand News*, the last independent news outlet in Hong Kong, was forced to close in August 2024, its offices raided by the Hong Kong police and its files seized. A former member of the Hong Kong Legislative Council said: "Our freedom movement, our democratic movement, a large part of it relies on, for us, we have access to truth, we have access to a different narrative compared to the one the government is providing to us. And it's really difficult for us to find a really credible and well-read news media outlet for now." Difficult? I would say, impossible.

To make the point still firmer: On November 19, 2024, forty-seven Hong Kong pro-democracy activists were sentenced in Hong Kong for "conspiracy to subvert state power," a catch-all charge often used by pro-Beijing authorities to nab and try dissidents. In this case, the "Hong Kong 47" were guilty of running in a primary election in July 2020 that was not officially sanctioned but participated in by hundreds of thousands of Hong Kongers. It was following that election that Beijing imposed the National Security Law, which has provided a dragnet for jailing just about any critic of Chinese rule. Those convicted were sentenced to anywhere from 4 to 10 years. Probably the best known of the Hong Kong 47 is Jimmy Lai, the media baron and founder of *Apple News*. He was accused of sedition for colluding with "foreign forces." His sentencing, said Professor Ho-fung Hung at Johns Hopkins University, "sends a signal that HK's democratic movement, that freedom of the press and free elections, are done with."

Hong Kong's Future

Hong Kong is not going to become another Xinjiang, but neither will it be just another Chinese province. Hong Kong is a highly visible enclave, a dynamic center of international business with a well-educated Cantonese-speaking population that has its own diaspora. It has voluble supporters in the US Congress and in Australia, Canada, and the United Kingdom. Unlike Donald Trump, the Biden administration and members of Congress responded to China's policies in Hong Kong with vociferous criticism and sanctions. Trump reportedly told Xi Jinping in June 2019 that Washington would "tone down" its comments on the spiraling protests. "Very tough situation," Trump tweeted on August 12, 2019, "hope it works out for everybody, including China." Trump refused to weigh in on behalf of the pro-democracy demonstrators, saying "We have human rights problems too." His priority was a trade deal with China, and silence on human rights was the quid pro quo. Legislation such as the US Senate's Hong Kong Human Rights and Democracy Act appropriately sanctioned Chinese and Hong Kong officials, but to little effect. Not only did Beijing shrug off the criticism; it refocused Hong Kong's economy on those international investors and banks that didn't make an issue of political repression. Instead of experiencing capital flight, Hong Kong has seen a higher inflow of capital despite the implementation of the National Security Law.

Money talks, and China's enormous economic clout often silences international criticism. When the Hong Kong 47 were sentenced, for example, Britain's Prime Minister Keir Starmer would not express support for the dissidents. Asked for his opinion, Starmer would only cite "the opportunity for our economy" by staying engaged with China. A "pragmatic, serious relationship is the right relationship to have with China," he told the BBC. And that's a Labour government, mind you. The Conservative leader, Duncan Smith, derided Starmer for his remarks, which Smith said "means that he and his government are so desperate for trade, they will turn a blind eye to all future atrocities." Starmer was not alone in bowing to China's trade power. Australia's Prime Minister Anthony Albanese said he discussed human rights and several other controversial issues with Xi, but pointed out to reporters that "one in four Australian jobs are export dependent, and one in four of our export dollars comes from China." Like Starmer, Albanese stressed the importance of dialogue with China. He, too, heads the Labor Party. Only the European Parliament condemned the sentencing. It called for repeal of Beijing's National Security Law and urged the immediate release of the activists. The parliament also called on EU members to "warn China that its actions in Hong Kong will have consequences for EU-China relations," including "targeted sanctions" on Hong Kong officials.[8]

Western sanctions and direct dialogue with China's leader seem unlikely to be sufficient to derail Xi Jinping's aims. They will be considered impermissible interference in China's internal affairs. Hong Kong joins the ranks of countries and territories where democracy and social justice demanded by an overwhelming majority of the population have been denied by force. The sad reality is that the international community has very few means to protect these populations other than sanctions and shaming.

(5) China's Mass Detention System

A nationwide system of secret, extra-legal detention of regime critics has existed throughout the history of the People's Republic of China. Troublesome people have been sent into internal exile in faraway provinces, put into reform-through-work programs, or simply seized and interrogated for periods of time without legal representation. The aim of these practices is often to force people to confess their sins, which might lighten their sentences and give the appearance of a non-coercive system that merely seeks to correct behavior.

Now an even more pervasive detention system than any in the past, called *liuzhi* or retention in custody, is being reported.[9] It is taking place in the context of Xi Jinping's long-running anti-corruption campaign (see Chapter 6), which has become a dragnet for snaring people, especially but not exclusively Communist Party officials, who have violated norms of conduct or simply proven disloyal. Some 200 detention centers have been erected, all uniformly outfitted with "padded surfaces and round-the-clock guards in every cell, where detainees can be held for up to six months without ever seeing a lawyer or family members."

The *liuzhi* system has a legal basis, unlike past programs that operated in secret. It is under the Central Commission for Discipline Inspection, which deals with inner-party corruption, and the National Supervisory Commission, established in 2018. As reported by CNN: "The new liuzhi detention regime has kept many features of its predecessor, including the power to hold suspects incommunicado in custody and a lack of independent oversight." The system targets "not only party members, but anyone who exercises 'public power'—from officials and civil servants to managers of public schools, hospitals, sports organizations, cultural institutions, and state-owned companies. It can also detain individuals deemed to be implicated in a graft case, such as businessmen suspected of paying bribes to an official under investigation." Yet recent major construction of detention centers has also taken place in Xinjiang, where Uyghurs and other ethnic minorities are the victims.

No figures are available on the number of people being held in these detention centers.

(6) Crimes Without Punishment: International Attempts to Change China's Policies

The Bachelet Report

On August 31, 2023, Michelle Bachelet ended her tenure as UN high commissioner for human rights. She waited until her last moments in office to authorize the release of a damning report on China's treatment of Muslims in the Xinjiang Uyghur Autonomous Region. The report had been sitting in her office for over a year, and its release followed a much-criticized trip to Xinjiang that Bachelet undertook in May.

Little wonder that Bachelet delayed release of the report. Though it does not accuse China of genocide, it takes Beijing to task on numerous other counts of human rights abuses. It charges China with torture, forced medical treatment, and sexual violence. It says that Beijing has engaged in "far-reaching, arbitrary and discriminatory restrictions on human rights and fundamental freedoms, in violation of international laws and standards." The report "lays bare the scale and severity of the human rights violations taking place in Xinjiang," Amnesty International Secretary General Agnès Callamard said. "The inexcusable delay in releasing this report casts a stain on the [UN Human Rights Office's] record, but this should not deflect from its significance."

The significance can also be gauged by noting China's angry response, which was two-fold: a brief statement castigating the Bachelet report, and a lengthy document, "Fight Against Terrorism and Extremism in Xinjiang: Truth and Facts." For the most part, the Chinese defense borders on the absurd. It portrayed Xinjiang as a human rights paradise and China's policies toward ethnic minorities as empowering and economically advantageous. The document also contains more traditional Chinese defenses, such as rejecting foreign interference in China's internal affairs and upholding China's fight against terrorists and separatists. The defensiveness also reflected China's negative view of independent investigations, especially of its human rights policies.

China is not only defensive; it takes the offensive. The International Consortium of Investigative Journalists has found that the work of the UN Human Rights Council has been undermined by NGOs that have political and financial ties to China. The *Washington Post*, which took part in the investigation, reports that these NGO delegates

> seek to disrupt or drown out the testimony of legitimate NGOs on their findings about the detention of Muslim Uyghurs in internment camps in the Chinese region of Xinjiang, children separated from Tibetan families, or the targeting of democracy activists in Hong Kong. . . . The ICIJ analysis shows that nearly 60 Chinese-registered NGOs—more than half of the Chinese groups that have obtained privileged U.N. status—effectively function as extensions of the Chinese government or the Chinese Communist Party.[10]

The Politics of Human Rights

The international debate over China's treatment of the Uyghurs has as much to do with politics as with international law and human rights. Governments beholden to China, including those with substantial Muslim populations, have been silent; some have even extradited Uyghurs to China. (Thailand is in the latter category; see **Selection 7** below.) Resistance movements that receive Chinese support, such as the Palestinians, have praised China's policies toward minority peoples. In Donald Trump's first term, politics ruled on Uyghur rights. Though he signed a rights bill for Uyghurs, his admiration for Xi Jinping governed Trump's actual policy. A memoir (*The Room Where It Happened*) by a key national security adviser to Trump, John Bolton, revealed that Trump privately gave Xi a pass on Xinjiang as well as on Hong

Kong. At a meeting in Osaka in 2019, according to Bolton, Trump told Xi he should go ahead with building camps for the Uyghurs—"exactly the right thing to do." Bolton writes that these comments were really all about Trump's reelection hopes, "alluding to China's economic capability to affect the ongoing campaigns, pleading with Xi to ensure he'd win."

As for the Bachelet report, the UN did not recommend follow-up action, very likely out of deference to China. Neither did the G7 group of major economies recommend punishing China. In a statement in September 2022, the group said it "remained deeply concerned by the serious human rights violations in Xinjiang," but merely "took note" of possible "international crimes" being committed there.

Some Western governments have led the way in sharply criticizing Chinese human rights policies. They have supported forums on conditions in Xinjiang, prohibited imports from Xinjiang, sanctioned surveillance technology exports to China, and accused China of genocide, cultural genocide, or (as the Bachelet report suggests) crimes against humanity. The United States in the Biden administration, for example, sanctioned Chinese companies operating in Xinjiang under a 2021 law, the Uyghur Forced Labor Prevention Act, which bans the importing to the United States of products that are made in whole or in part in Xinjiang. By the time Biden left office in January 2025, 144 companies in real estate, mining, solar energy, and cotton production had been placed on the sanctions list.

A Cautionary Word

A further word of caution about criticism of China. Though it is fully warranted, we should not be self-righteous about repression there. Few countries are free of religious, political, or social oppression. Few have eschewed violent official responses to mass protest. Fewer still are the governments that have recognized, much less apologized and compensated for, the harm they have done to minority groups in the name of social stability. The US human rights record in that last regard is anything but exemplary.

The scale of China's human rights abuses may have no current counterpart, but it also falls within a depressing global pattern that embraces even the most "developed" and "democratic" countries. The struggle against abuses in one's homeland is also a struggle against abuses abroad. I suppose we should celebrate the fact that the UN's report on Xinjiang was not suppressed to mollify Beijing. But we're also reminded that, in an ideal world, the UN's human rights offices would be investigating and reporting on all countries' systematic repression of human rights and recommending meaningful ways to stop it.

(7) Thailand Extradites Uyghurs to China

A letter to Thailand's prime minister and other officials in January 2025, entitled "Urgent Researcher Statement on the Status of Uyghur Asylum Seekers in Thailand," called for the release and resettlement of forty-eight Uyghur refugees who had been detained in Thailand for more than eleven years. Would they be forcibly returned to China, contrary to the UN Convention Against Torture that Thailand ratified? Various sources reported that the men were asked to sign consent forms to return to China; they refused. All forty-eight applied for asylum to the United Nations High Commissioner for Refugees. The principle of non-refoulement guarantees that a person cannot be returned to a country where he or she would face torture, cruel, inhuman, or degrading treatment, or other forms of punishment.

The case brought reminders of how the forty-eight Uyghurs had come to be in detention. In 2014, over 350 men, women, and children were detained. 172 women and children were eventually sent to Turkey and 109 or more were forcibly returned to China. No news of their fate was ever received. Fifty-three Uyghurs remained in Thai custody. Five later died, including two children, leaving the disposition of the remaining forty-eight to a high-level Thai government decision.

When Thai Prime Minister Paetongtarn Shinawatra visited China in February 2025, Xi talked about China and Thailand being one family. Xi urged tighter cooperation on a range of issues, including law enforcement and the judiciary "to safeguard people's lives and property." He was referring not to the detained Uyghurs but to another thorny issue in China-Thai relations: the kidnapping of thousands of foreign tourists in Thailand, most of them Chinese, to work in internet scam compounds along the Myanmar border. Xi also said "China stands ready to work closely with Thailand to firmly defend the international system with the United Nations at its core and the international order based on international law," according to the Chinese report of the meeting.[11] Nothing was apparently said about the fate of the Uyghurs, whose lives were quite literally in the balance.

Paetongtarn was in a difficult position: China is Thailand's largest trade partner and foreign investor, whereas the United States, which opposed the deportation of the Uyghurs, is Thailand's principal security partner. The Thai government made the choice to accede to China's demands.[12] At the end of February, Thailand deported the Uyghurs to China under the cover of night. The decision was made despite official Thai assurances of their safety and Thailand's adherence to international law. A Chinese government statement said the Uyghurs would be "returned to normal life as soon as possible" after being "dealt with according to the law." Most likely that means the Uyghurs will be sent to concentration camps for "reeducation."

(8) China's Response to Repression in Myanmar

Repression and Resistance

In Myanmar, a United Nations investigation in 2018 cast the repression of the Rohingya minority as "an ongoing genocide." Over 700,000 Muslim Rohingyas had been driven from their homes into Bangladesh. Myanmar tried, with China's support, to block the lead investigator's briefing of the UN Security Council. The investigator said: "The Myanmar government's hardened positions are by far the greatest obstacle. Its continued denials, its attempts to shield itself under the cover of national sovereignty and its dismissal of 444 pages of details about the facts and circumstances of recent human rights violations that point to the most serious crimes under international law." The investigator suggested referring the matter to the International Criminal Court. "Right now, it's like an apartheid situation where Rohingyas still living in Myanmar . . . . have no freedom of movement. The camps, the shelters, the model villages that are being built, it's more of a cementing of total segregation or separation from the Rakhine ethnic community."

China's response has been shaped by Beijing's guidelines when dealing with its own ethnic minorities: First, don't make respect for human rights abroad a central issue, and second, don't "interfere" in another country's repression if that country is economically or strategically important to China. The latter point encompasses China's relationship with Myanmar's military dictatorship, which seized power in 2021. Repression of the Rohingya is a subset of nationwide repressive rule that resulted, in 2023 and 2024, in the formation of a hodgepodge resistance force loosely aligned under a National Unity Government (NUG). The resistance basically comprises two kinds of forces: ethnic minority armies, sometimes referred to as the Three Brotherhood Alliance, that have a long history of opposition to the military government, and pro-democracy groups backed by the NUG that have come together since the 2021 coup.

What made the resistance so threatening to the military in 2025 is that the various armies were coordinating and becoming increasingly successful in Myanmar's north and northeast, areas that border China as well as Thailand and India. The opposition captured towns, seized arsenals, and obtained the surrender of some government units, forcing China to deploy troops along the border. Thousands of people fled the fighting, mainly into India. The Myanmar junta, despite its vastly superior ground and air forces, has been unable to quash the resistance (see chapter 5, Selection 10).

China Plays on Both Sides

China seemed to be playing both sides, no doubt aware of the security implications of backing just one. On one hand, it consistently supported the junta's policies, invoking the noninterference principle. Criticism of the military is not "helpful" and the situation is "complicated," Chinese officials said at international gatherings. They called for "dialogue," as though the rampaging Myanmar military had the slightest interest in talking. "Dialogue" was China's alternative to UN Security Council and General Assembly resolutions critical of the junta that China regularly voted against.

The Myanmar leadership has pretended that all is well in relations with China. It has insisted that ties were strong and that the strategic partnership was firm. Behind the scenes, however, reports indicated displeasure within the junta over China's relations with the rebel groups, in particular sales of weapons to those groups. That displeasure led to a first-ever anti-China demonstration outside the Chinese embassy in Yangon, the capital, on November 17, 2023. China's foreign ministry spokesman had to issue a formal statement reassuring the protesters that China never interfered in Myanmar's internal affairs. Then, in October 2024, the Chinese consulate in Mandalay, Myanmar's second-largest city, was bombed.

Chinese authorities are indeed in close touch with the rebelling ethnic groups, which have promised to protect Chinese investments in areas the groups control. The northeast border area is the site of criminal activity—drug trafficking and cyberscam operations[13]—that concerns China because of its impact on Chinese nationals and the capacity for border unrest. Shan State on the northern border with China encompasses the China-Myanmar Economic Corridor, which has oil and gas pipelines that cross the border. Beijing has neither condemned the opposition forces nor endorsed the junta's efforts to quash them. According to a report by the US Institute of Peace, "Beijing almost certainly approved the [rebel] offensive after the junta generals ignored its appeals to crack down on lucrative crime centers along the border that prey on China nationals."[14] That approval probably got the generals' attention: They said China was brokering peace talks between the main armed opposition group and the government. That seemed to be the case in Shan State, reportedly to the military's advantage.[15] But the fighting continued into 2025, though interrupted in April by a devastating earthquake during which the military (according to eyewitness reports) obstructed international aid deliveries.

(9) Where is Peng Shuai?

In October 2024 the Women's Tennis Association held its China Open. A notable absence from the competition was a star Chinese player, Peng Shuai, whose disappearance three years earlier became international news and the focus of China's nascent #MeToo movement. The WTA suspended China-based competition in November 2021 after Peng posted on China's Internet that former Vice Premier Zhang Gaoli had sexually abused her. She then vanished from sight, and the Chinese apparently never investigated her charges. The WTA conditioned a resumption of China ties on a "full and transparent investigation—without censorship—into Peng Shuai's sexual assault accusation."

Yet in April 2023, the WTA boycott of tennis in China ended. No investigation, no charges against Zhang, and most importantly, no news about Peng Shuai's whereabouts.

Two great players who had started an online campaign for Peng no longer commented on the subject. The reason? Like many other international businesses that complained about China's human rights practices, professional tennis complied with the Chinese authorities' wishes. "The strong pull of the China market for international businesses" is the key, argued Yaqiu Wang, China research director at Freedom House.[16]

(10) Ai Weiwei and Freedom of Expression

Chinese leaders ever since Mao's time have insisted that art and literature must conform with the party's political program. Dissent is dangerous. Ai Weiwei (born in 1957) is China's most famous dissident artist, a man who has fearlessly used his art installations to challenge China's leaders, censors, and police. His father, the renowned poet Ai Qing, was constantly at odds with Mao's regime, and spent considerable time in "reform through labor" and imprisonment for his "counter-revolutionary" views. When his father died in 1995, Ai committed himself to fighting the status quo, "reaffirming, through the act of non-cooperation, my responsibility to take a critical stance." In Ai Weiwei's view, "Any artwork, if it's relevant, is political." After serving time in prison in China, Ai Weiwei was released in 2017 and moved to Berlin, where he still resides.[17]

Here is Ai's own account of how he came to produce a major work critical of the Chinese government's handling of the Sichuan earthquake, which occurred shortly after his return to China in 2008 from training as an artist in New York:

It was devastating: more than 80,000 lives disappeared. Many of the dead were young people at school and university. I'd been writing a daily blog—about modern Chinese society, the government and art—but I stopped suddenly. People asked me why but, faced with such a tragedy, I was silenced. I couldn't find the right vocabulary. . . .

I made hundreds of phone calls to the education department, the police and civil departments, to ask questions about the student casualties, but of course nobody would talk to me. So I used the internet to set up a citizen investigation team. On my blog, I said: "This is my question: Where are those lives?" A lot of young people began following me intensively online and we soon had a team of 100 people. We went out to the crisis area, to the ruins of the earthquake.... After almost a year of research, we had 5,219 names. Eventually, the government shut off the blog because there were too many people reading it and following us. This made me increasingly conscious of social and political issues relating to the internet.

I had a show coming up in Munich and decided to cover the Haus der Kunst museum's facade with one sentence from a victim's mother. She had written to me: "All I want is to let the world remember she had been living happily for seven years.... The work was called Remembering. Given all our social and political investigations, it was about how, in Chinese society, with censorship and control, individuals can still take action to defend their very, very fragile rights...."

The kind of authoritarian state we have in China cannot survive if it answers questions—if the truth is revealed, they are finished. So they started to think of me as the most dangerous person in China. That made me become an artist, but also an activist. So for Remembering, I covered the whole of the Haus der Kunst's facade with [9,000] children's backpacks, spelling out in Chinese what that mother had told me.... [18]

Documents

Document 1. The State Council Information Office, "The Communist Party of China and Human Rights Protection: A 100-Year Quest," June 2021 (excerpts).
(*Source*: State Council Information Office, China, June 24, 2021, http://english.scio.gov.cn/m/whitepapers/2021-06/24/content_77416.htm)

I. For People's Liberation and Wellbeing

The founding of the PRC in 1949 ushered in a new era for people's rights. It put an end to the exploitation, oppression and slavery that had shackled the Chinese nation for a century, and signified the beginning of substantial progress in human rights in a socialist country under the leadership of the Chinese Communist Party (CCP).

Since 1949, human rights in China have undergone three stages of development.

Stage 1: Beginning in 1949, the Chinese people committed themselves to socialist revolution and economic development under CCP leadership, establishing the basic systems of socialism, completing the most extensive and profound process of social change in Chinese history, and promulgating the first socialist constitution. All these laid the political and institutional foundation for human rights in China.

From a political perspective, the system of people's democracy was established and consolidated, with democracy of the people and socialism as the basic principles. With the implementation of the system of people's congresses, it was guaranteed that all rights of the state belonged to the people.

From an economic perspective, the completion of the land reform triggered a burst of great creativity among the people. Socialist transformation was completed in agriculture, individual craft industries, and capitalist industry and commerce, and the basic socialist system was formed to ensure equal access to economic development and the sharing of economic gains.

From a social perspective, the Marriage Law was promulgated, stipulating the free choice of spouses, the principle of monogamy, equal rights for men and women, and the protection of the lawful rights and interests of women and children. Efforts were made to promote education and health services, and medical and preventive care networks were established at every local level—village, township, county, city and province. Labor insurance was created and social relief was provided. The government stood firmly against ethnic oppression and discrimination, upheld equality among all ethnic groups, and introduced regional ethnic autonomy. In developing the legal framework, important laws were formulated and promulgated in line with the Constitution of the People's Republic of China to protect citizens' basic rights.

Stage 2: Beginning in 1978, when reform and opening up was introduced, the CCP led the Chinese people on a path of socialism with Chinese characteristics, unleashing an immense wave of social development and productivity. Thanks to tremendous progress in human rights, the people enjoyed better protection of their rights to subsistence and development and other basic rights. Reform and opening up is a great revolution on the part of the Chinese people under CCP leadership. The Party pursues development as its top priority in governance and as the key to solving the problems of China; it strives to promote social productivity and improve human rights protection through development. During this stage the people enjoyed better lives and grew more active economically and socially. Under CCP leadership, China upheld the rule of law in all areas, and included in the Constitution as an important principle of national governance respect for and protection of human rights. Human rights progress was included in national development strategies and plans, the mechanisms for ensuring human rights in the context of China's realities were improved, and the system for ensuring human rights with Chinese characteristics began to take shape.

Stage 3: Since the 18th CCP National Congress in 2012, socialism with Chinese characteristics has entered a new era. China has completed the mission of eradicating absolute poverty as scheduled under the strong leadership of the Party Central Committee with Xi Jinping at the core. Decisive success has been achieved in the final stage of building a moderately prosperous society in all respects, and human rights protection has been brought to new heights. Upholding people-centered development, the CCP is grounding its efforts in the new development stage, applying the new development philosophy, and creating a new framework of development. Focusing on high-quality development, it endeavors to meet the fundamental goal of satisfying the people's growing desire for a better life. . . .

II. The Principle of Respecting and Protecting Human Rights Embedded in Governance

In December 1982, the Fifth Session of the Fifth National People's Congress (NPC) adopted the current Constitution of the People's Republic of China, in which "The Fundamental Rights and Duties of Citizens" was moved forward and made second only to Chapter I, "General Principles". This adjustment highlighted the importance of citizens' rights. . . .

The amendment adopted at the Second Session of the 10th NPC, held in March 2004, added the line "The state respects and safeguards human rights" into the Constitution. Since then, respecting and protecting human rights has been a basic principle of the system of socialist rule of law with Chinese characteristics and a binding rule of conduct and a legal obligation of all state organs, armed forces, political parties, social organizations, enterprises and public institutions. No laws, regulations, rules and normative documents can be in conflict with the principle, and accountability must be enforced on all acts that violate it.

VII. Adding Diversity to the Concept of Human Rights

For China, there are no ready models to copy in respecting, protecting and developing human rights. China must proceed from its prevailing realities and go its own way. Applying the principle of universality of human rights to China's national conditions, the CCP has opened a new path of human rights protection, and added diversity to the concept of human rights with its own practices.

- Upholding CCP leadership and the socialist system in promoting human rights. We would not have socialism in China without the leadership of the CPC, nor could we protect the fundamental interests of the people without socialism as the basic system. The people as the masters of the country is the basic political principle of the CCP on human rights, realized by democracy, freedom, equality and other rights, which are also important core socialist values. By developing and protecting human rights, the CCP can strengthen its leadership and better develop socialism for long-term peace, stability, and prosperity.

- Promoting human rights through development. Development is the key to solving all China's problems; it drives human rights progress in the country. Based on its prevailing realities, the CCP considers the rights to subsistence and development to be the primary rights; this is the secret of China's progress in human rights. The right to subsistence comes before any other right, and the right to development is closely connected to the right to subsistence. The CCP believes that putting subsistence and development first and subsequently developing other rights is the only way to meet the people's expectation that their rights will be protected.

- Taking a people-centered approach to human rights. The CCP comes from the people and has its roots in the people. It serves the people and seeks to improve their wellbeing. Putting people first and ensuring their principal status have always been the core of the CCP's view on human rights. In his letter to the seminar on the 70th anniversary of the Universal Declaration of Human Rights, President Xi Jinping proposed that living a happy life is the primary human right, giving new meaning to China's progress in human rights in the new era. His thought on human rights highlights the position of the people and the essentials of human rights development in China. There is no end to human rights development and human rights protection is an ongoing cause. Human rights in China should be judged only by the Chinese people, and gauged by their sense of gain, happiness and security.

Document 2. The Australian Ambassador to the United States and Permanent Representative of Australia to the United Nations Makes a Joint Statement to the UN General Assembly's Third Committee on Human Rights in Xinjiang Province and Tibet.
Source: Mission of Australia to the United Nations, October 22, 2024, https://unny.mission.gov.au/unny/241022_UNGA79_Joint_statement_on_the_human_rights_situation_in_Xinjiang_and_Tibet.html)

I have the honour of delivering this joint statement on behalf of the following countries: Canada, Denmark, Finland, France, Germany, Iceland, Japan, Lithuania, Kingdom of the Netherlands, New Zealand, Norway, Sweden, United Kingdom, United States of America, and my own country, Australia.

These countries are all committed to universal human rights and have ongoing concerns about serious human rights violations in China.

Two years ago, the United Nations Office of the High Commissioner for Human Rights' assessment on Xinjiang concluded that serious human rights violations had been committed in Xinjiang, and that the scale of the arbitrary and discriminatory detention of Uyghurs and other predominately Muslim minorities in Xinjiang "may constitute international crimes, in particular crimes against humanity".

Subsequently, United Nations' Treaty Bodies have taken similar views and made similar recommendations . . . .

The Working Group on Arbitrary Detention has issued communications concerning multiple cases of arbitrary detention and enforced disappearances, and over 20 Special Procedure Mandate Holders have expressed concern about systemic human rights violations in Xinjiang.

Relying extensively on China's own records, these comprehensive findings and recommendations by independent human rights experts from all geographic regions detail evidence of large-scale arbitrary detention, family separation, enforced disappearances and forced labour, systematic surveillance on the basis of religion and ethnicity; severe and undue restrictions on cultural, religious, and linguistic identity and expression; torture and sexual and gender-based violence, including forced abortion and sterilisation; and the destruction of religious and cultural sites.

China has had many opportunities meaningfully to address the UN's well-founded concerns. Instead, China labelled the Office of the High Commissioner for Human Rights' assessment as illegal and void during its Universal Periodic Review adoption in July.

According to the Office of the High Commissioner for Human Rights' statement in August, the problematic laws and policies in Xinjiang continue to remain in place. The statement again called on China to undertake a full review, from the human rights perspective, of the legal framework governing national security and counterterrorism.

Mr Chair, as with our concerns for the situation in Xinjiang, we are also seriously concerned about credible reports detailing human rights abuses in Tibet. United Nations human rights treaty bodies and United Nations Special Procedures have detailed the detention of Tibetans for the peaceful expression of political views; restrictions on travel; coercive labour arrangements; separation of children from families in boarding schools; and erosion of linguistic, cultural, educational and religious rights and freedoms in Tibet.

We urge China to uphold the international human rights obligations that it has voluntarily assumed, and to fully implement all UN recommendations including from the Office of the High Commissioner for Human Rights' assessment, Treaty Bodies and other United Nations human rights mechanisms. This includes releasing all individuals arbitrarily detained in both Xinjiang and Tibet, and urgently clarifying the fate and whereabouts of missing family members.

Transparency and openness are key to allaying concerns, and we call on China to allow unfettered and meaningful access to Xinjiang and Tibet for independent observers, including from the UN, to evaluate the human rights situation.

No country has a perfect human rights record, but no country is above fair scrutiny of its human rights obligations. It is incumbent on all of us not to undermine international human rights commitments that benefit us all, and for which all states are accountable.

Thank you.

Document 3. China's Human Development Indices
(*Source*: United Nations Development Programme, *Human Development Report 2023/2024*, Tables 2 and 3, https://hdr.undp.org/system/files/documents/global-report-document/hdr2023-24reporten.pdf)

Overall Human Development Index Rank: China, 75 (of 193 countries)
  Comparisons: India, 134; Russia, 56; US, 20.

Life expectancy: China, 78.6 years
  Comparison: India, 67.7 years; South Korea, 84; Russia, 70.1; Brazil, 73.4; US, 78.2

Expected years of schooling: China, 15
  Comparison: India, 12.6; South Korea, 16.5; Russia, 15.7; Brazil, 15.6; US, 16.4

Gross National Income per capita: China, $18.025
  Comparison: India, $6,951; South Korea, $46,026; Russia, $26,992; Brazil, $14,616; US, $65,565

Average inequality in human development: China, 15.3
  Comparisons: India, 30.5; US, 10.7; South Korea, 9.3; Russia, 8.7; Brazil, 22.4

Rich-poor gaps in the population (Poorest 40%/ Richest 10%/ Richest 1%)

  China: 18.2 / 29.4 / 15.7
  India: 20.0/ 27.8 / 21.7
  Russia: 19.1/ 29.0 / 23.8
  US: 16.6 / 30.1 / 19.0
  SKorea: 20.5/ 24.0/ 11.7
  Brazil: 10.8/ 41.5 / 22.2

HUMAN RIGHTS

Note: The national figures are averages across the entire population, and therefore do not make distinctions such as between urban and rural areas, gender, and ethnicity. Nor does the UN Development Programme bring political criteria such as adherence to human rights into "human development" rankings.

Document 4. China's Hydropower and Dam Projects in Tibet (December 2024)

(*Background and Sources*: Following are excerpts from a report by the International Campaign for Tibet, "Chinese Hydropower: Damning Tibet's Culture, Community, and Environment," https://savetibet.org/chinese-hydropower/.)

The People's Republic of China's (PRC) hydropower and dam projects are increasingly leading to massive human rights violations and environmental damage in Tibet. Since Asia's largest rivers originate in the Tibetan plateau, the construction of hydroelectric dams in Tibet also threaten the water supply, livelihoods and health of up to 1.8 billion people across China, South and Southeast Asia.

This report draws on detailed regional research coupled with advanced Geographic Imaging Software (GIS) analysis and mapping based on a sample study of 193 hydroelectric dams constructed or planned in Tibet since 2000. It presents in-depth analysis and a clear picture of the impact each dam will have on the local population in Tibet, religious sites and the surrounding land. A striking example of the wide-scale impact of dams is the construction of the 2,240-megawatt Khamtok (Chinese: Gangtuo) hydroelectric dam project in the eastern Tibetan county of Derge, which will forcibly expel thousands of Tibetans, destroy their villages and irretrievably demolish valuable cultural assets, such as centuries-old Buddhist monasteries.

Given the breadth of environmental, climate, social, and geopolitical costs of hydropower dams in Tibet, the report also offers viable pathways for truly renewable energy and necessary considerations for improving regional knowledge and cooperation on water management.

KEY POINTS

Recognition of Tibet as a source of natural resources, such as minerals and water, is not new. The People's Republic of China's more than 70-year occupation of Tibet continues to inflict gross human rights violations on the Tibetan people, often directly linked to exploitation of Tibet's natural environment. Thus, the most essential investment the PRC must take to right the wrongs of its decades of resource plunder is to enter meaningful dialogue with Tibetan leaders to reach a political solution that also includes the Tibetan people's right to freely decide the use of their natural wealth and resources. The most politically marginalized communities should not pay the highest price of China's ambitious hydropower plan.

Perhaps the most prominent example of the People's Republic of China's exploitation is its accelerating construction of hydropower dams along Tibet's major rivers. The integrity of these rivers is fundamental to Tibet's rich environment and its unique civilization. Also, up to 1.8 billion people throughout China, South and Southeast Asia depend on their healthy flow for subsistence, health, and economic development. China's rampant, command and control hydropower plans put all this at peril. [Note: The dam will also affect water access in India and Bangladesh.[19])

Until this report, the scope and scale of China's single-minded push for ever more dams in Tibet has not been fully appreciated. The Chinese government has strategically obfuscated details of the hydropower expansion across Tibet, because the plans attract justified concern and scrutiny from environmental experts, local communities, and downstream countries.

Utilizing rigorous in-region research and advanced GIS analysis and mapping, of a sample study of 193 hydropower dams built or planned across Tibet since 2000, the analysis reveals the scale of hydropower expansion, as well as the impact each dam will have on local populations, religious sites, and surrounding land cover. In addition, an accompanying interactive map allows readers to explore individual dams, watersheds, and nearby settlements.

If completed, the 193 hydroelectric dams in the sample study would generate over 270 GW of hydropower. This is on par with Germany's energy production capacity in 2022. Of the 193 dams studied, almost 80 per cent of dams are large or mega dams (>100MW) which carry the most significant risk to the Tibetan civilization, environmental sustainability, and the climate. Over half the dams (59%) are either in proposal or preparation stage. This suggests that China's ambitious hydropower energy plan is still a long-term project. Fortunately, it also indicates that hope remains to alter this destructive course.

Particularly in the locations proposed by China, large scale dams suffer from a slate of environmental harms. Dams are both susceptible to and can cause an increased risk of earthquakes, landslides and flash floods. They also cause environmental damage to vulnerable and biodiverse ecosystems by inundating land, reducing water quality and flow, and interrupting aquatic life. Dams also block soil, water, and nutrient flows, which are essential for supporting life in downstream countries.

Dams routinely cause the expulsion of Tibetans from their traditional homes and lands, and often permanent exclusion from their land and water-based livelihood activities. From the 34 dams with public "relocation" figures, at least 144,468 people are known to be affected by hydropower dams, with 121,651 people already expelled since 2000 and a further 22,817 to be expelled. If we extrapolate from available data to all 193 dams in our database, we estimate a lower limit of 750,000 people have been and will be expelled due to hydropower dams in Tibet. Data analysis from available population data for residents living within a designated dam impact area for 134 dam sites with known geolocations estimates an upper limit of 1.2 million people potentially affected by the hydropower dams. When extended to capture all dams across Tibet (including the 45 dams without a known geolocation), this figure could be far higher.

China's dam building spree also stands to fuel South and Southeast Asia's existing water-related political instability. Climate induced water scarcity indicates that hydro-diplomacy is now more crucial than ever, especially given South and Southeast Asia's status as a hot spot for water scarcity. Unfortunately, the PRC's claims of absolute sovereignty over Tibet's water and adversarial approach to riparian policy actively thwarts progress toward a regional accord. Together with its economic and military power, the PRC wields its high ground, restrictions on sharing hydrological data, and refusal to pursue regional accords, as diplomatic weapons to reward, coax or punish downstream countries in service to its hegemonic agenda.

Hanging over all hydropower discussions is the specter of the advancing climate crisis and the urgent need to meet ambitious carbon emissions targets to mitigate the inevitable impacts of climate change. Chinese authorities regularly justify hydropower expansion as necessary to meeting the country's carbon pollution reduction targets. However, the scientific literature challenges this. Hydropower is not a carbon neutral energy source. Dams can release large amounts of methane, which is an extremely potent greenhouse gas. Dam emissions are often aggregated over long periods of time, obscuring the need to immediately reduce emissions. Lastly, once in place sunk costs, institutions, and norms threaten to lock in the greenhouse gas emissions lifespan of the initial dam despite better alternatives. Considering the shrinking window to address climate change, sustainable energy like solar and wind power options should be invested in.

Low impact renewable energy is critical to meet the moral and scientific imperative of reducing the pace of climate change, while limiting impacts on communities, not only on Tibet, but globally. This means China must radically shift course so the benefits of renewables like wind and solar can be captured while avoiding the detrimental effects of hydropower damming. However, how, where, and what is developed is crucial. Upfront environmental assessments and inclusive decision-making processes are essential, including free, prior and informed consent from affected communities. Location siting must consider sensitive ecosystems, wildlife needs, sacred sites, and local community priorities. Co-management should be prioritized. For example, installations combined with grazing have the potential to simultaneously support clean energy while facilitating traditional Tibetan pastoral rhythms. Portable solar also can support nomadic ways of life.

KEY RECOMMENDATIONS

- Cease all planning, proposing, and construction, including projects underway, of large-scale hydropower dams within Tibet.
- Protect the right of Tibetans to participate in all development projects as per the 1986 UN Declaration on the Right to Development the International Covenant on Economic, Social and Cultural Rights. . . .
- Invest in properly sited and inclusively developed solar and wind power, as they do not carry the demonstrable environmental, climate, and social costs of hydropower. These projects should prioritize co-management, co-benefits, and maintenance of traditional ways of life, and in particular they should correspond to the needs of the local Tibetan population. Co-benefits include employment opportunities for affected communities, as well as accessible technical education and training courses. . . .
- International financial institutions, including the World Bank and the Asian Development Bank, should refrain from all financial support for Tibet-based hydropower projects.
- The violation of the rights of Tibetans is a result of the occupation of Tibet. Therefore, as the Tibetan people have the right to self-determination, which includes the right to freely dispose of their natural wealth and resources, the negative implications of Chinese infrastructure projects, particularly hydropower, on the rights of Tibetans and Tibet's environment must be part of a political solution. This must be achieved through dialogue between the representatives of the Dalai Lama and the Chinese government. The international community should redouble efforts to urge the Chinese government to enter into a meaningful dialogue with the Tibetan side.

Document 5. Foreign Minister Wang Yi's Appraisal of the United Nations
(*Background*: This is a portion of the minister's press conference on March 7, 2025. *Source*: Ministry of Foreign Affairs, China, https://www.fmprc.gov.cn/mfa_eng/wjbzhd/202503/t20250307_11025.html)

This year marks the 80th anniversary of the U.N. Around the end of World War II, the most important decision the international community made was to establish the U.N. and make it the primary platform for maintaining world peace and promoting global governance. Facts have shown that the U.N. has withstood tests and has been instrumental.

Today there have been fundamental changes in the world situation. Unilateralism is on the rise, and power politics runs rampant. Some countries have voiced scepticism of one kind or another about the U.N. But China believes that the more complex the problems, the greater the need to accentuate the important status of the U.N.; the more pressing the challenges, the greater the need to uphold the due authority of the U.N.

All countries want to prevent the world from returning to the law of the jungle. To this end, the first thing to do is to cement the cornerstone of sovereign equality. All countries, regardless of their size and strength, should be recognized as equal members of the international community. Those with stronger arms and bigger fists should not be allowed to call the shots. Second, the principle of fairness and justice must be upheld. International affairs must not be monopolized by a small number of countries. Greater attention should be given to the voice of the Global South. The legitimate rights and interests of all countries should be fully protected. Third, multilateralism must be observed. Countries should stay committed to the principles of extensive consultation, joint contribution and shared benefit, replace bloc confrontation with inclusive collaboration, and shatter small circles with greater solidarity. Fourth, the authority of the international rule of law must be strengthened. Major countries in particular should take the lead in upholding integrity, embracing the rule of law, and opposing double standard and selective application. Still less should they resort to bullying, monopoly, trickery or extortion.

China is a founder and beneficiary of the post-World War II international order. Naturally, we are an advocate and builder of it as well. We have no intention to start all over again, nor do we support any country's attempt to overturn the current order. China is well aware of its international responsibility as a permanent member of the U.N. Security Council. It will firmly safeguard the central role of the U.N., come forward to be a pillar of the multilateral system, and speak up for justice for the Global South. Last month, at the U.N. Security Council, China chaired the high-level meeting on "Practicing Multilateralism, Reforming and Improving Global Governance." More than 100 countries signed up to attend, kicking off the commemorations of the U.N.'s 80th anniversary. China is ready to work with all sides to reflect on the founding vision of the U.N., observe the purposes and principles of the U.N. Charter, and build a more just and equitable global governance system.

PART III

9

For Further Reflection

China's world is in great flux. Internally, the leadership is trying to sustain an extraordinary period of economic growth while maintaining the party-state system that requires restrictions on social and political life. Externally, the country is in an intense rivalry with the United States that risks overt conflict. China and Russia are working closely together in a "comprehensive strategic partnership." Chinese economic competition with the United States, the European Union, and Japan, on one hand, and increasing Chinese political and economic influence in the Global South on the other, is reshaping the global order. Is stability in international affairs still possible? Is a new international order evolving, as some experts contend, between China-centered and US-centered groupings? And how does that new order compare with the earlier Cold War order?

Beyond those macro-level questions lie many more specific questions stemming from the reading selections and the documents. Any of these questions is worthy of debate.

US-China Relations

- What are the domestic and international factors that shape China's view of the world?
- How do those factors compare with those that shape US views of the world?
- How do the Biden and Trump administrations compare in their ways of dealing with China?
- When Xi Jinping asks for "mutual respect," what does he mean? What actions signify mutual respect?

- Which kinds of exchange programs with China seem most valuable? Should the US cut back on the number and types of exchanges with China?
- How do you evaluate the US policy of "strategic ambiguity" with regard to Taiwan?
- Is the US-China conflict over Taiwan avoidable? What would you advise Taiwan to do now that Trump is president?
- Is a US-China war possible, and if so, over what issues? What factors make war unlikely?
- What are the best ways to prevent a military miscalculation between the two countries?
- Is common ground on human rights possible?
- Is common ground possible on other issues, such as climate change?
- What do the Chinese mean when they say the United States has a "Cold War mentality?" Does it?
- The Chinese say the United States should choose between rivalry and partnership. Is that a reasonable depiction of the choice? Is a balance possible between rivalry and partnership?
- Some specialists think the United States is already in a new Cold War with China. Others argue that a new Cold War has not yet arrived. Still others dispute the comparison with the earlier Cold War altogether.
- Nationalism is central to the Chinese leadership's view of the world. Does that make China a threat to US national security?
- Is Trump's "America First" foreign policy a threat to China?
- What do you make of the US-Russia-China strategic triangle idea? Will it lead to greater or less stability in major-power relations?
- Is China right to regard US security arrangements in the Asia Pacific as threatening?
- Should China be regarded as the top threat to US national security? What is the basis for determining the leading threat?
- Trump imposed extremely high tariffs on Chinese goods in April 2025. Did his administration miscalculate China's reaction?
- Donald Trump is usually characterized as a transactional leader, one who is more concerned with making a good deal than with focusing on principles and values. How might those qualities affect Chinese perceptions of the US?

- The US and China are competing for influence among the Pacific Island states. What advantages and disadvantages does each country have in this competition?
- Evaluate the following quotations from two key US and Chinese policymakers in 2025:

  First, from Marco Rubio at his Senate confirmation hearing: "We welcomed the Chinese Communist Party into this global order. And they took advantage of all its benefits. But they ignored all its obligations and responsibilities. Instead, they have lied, cheated, hacked and stolen their way to global superpower status, at our expense."

  Next, from China's Foreign Minister Wang Yi, referring to Trump's tariffs on Chinese exports: "No country should fantasize that it can suppress China and maintain good relations with China at the same time. Such two-faced acts are not good for the stability of bilateral relations, or for building mutual trust."
- The former ambassador to China, Nicholas Burns, observed on leaving his post in January 2025 that the "central question is: how do you compete vigorously and at the same time keep the peace with China? That is what is at stake here for the United States and China." How might it be possible to do both?

China, Its Neighbors, and the Global South

- China's influence and development model are spreading rapidly throughout the Global South. What positive and negative outcomes can you foresee in that trend? Which factors might promote or retard the spread of Chinese influence?
- How does North Korea's "strategic partnership" with Russia affect China's interests in the Korean Peninsula?
- How might China strengthen its relations with Japan?
- What accounts for China playing both sides in Myanmar's civil war?
- What is your evaluation of China's "model for human advancement?"
- How would you compare China's BRI and Western aid programs?
- Why do you think China has become such a dominant player in Africa?
- Do you think China abides by its policy of noninterference in other countries' affairs?

China's Relations with the European Union and Russia

- Which factors bring China and Russia together, and which might drive them apart?
- Do you think warming US-Russia relations might be at China's expense?
- Does China have more in common with the EU than with the US?
- The EU stresses defense of "European values" in its diplomacy with China. What are those values, and how well do you think the EU is defending them?
- Might China be able to have more influence in Europe than Russia once the Ukraine war is over? What would a Chinese strategy to achieve that objective look like?
- Does China have a legitimate claim when it says that its EV exports to the EU should be seen as a contribution to fighting global warming?
- Should China's aid to Russia in the Ukraine war be regarded as an aggressive act? Or should China be regarded as a peacemaker in the war?

Chinese Politics, Economy, and Society

Thomas L. Friedman, an influential opinion writer for the *New York Times*, came away from a China trip in early 2025 expressing wonderment at China's achievements in advanced technology, particularly artificial general intelligence (AGI). He offered his observations in an op-ed on April 2, 2025. Friedman said he witnessed a sense of national purpose and a clear development strategy that seems to be missing in the US. Consider and discuss this quote:

> President Trump is focused on what teams American transgender athletes can race on, and China is focused on transforming its factories with A.I. so it can outrace all our factories. Trump's "Liberation Day" strategy is to double down on tariffs while gutting our national scientific institutions and work force that spur U.S. innovation. China's liberation strategy is to open more research campuses and double down on A.I.-driven innovation to be permanently liberated from Trump's tariffs.

- Do you think Friedman makes a fair comparison? If not, which characteristics of the US and China do you think would be fair to compare?
- China claims it has greatly advanced human rights in the country. How do you evaluate that claim?
- How do China's scientific and technological achievements rate alongside its serious social and economic problems?
- Is the way China is organized and motivated giving it an advantage over the US and other Western countries in dealing with economic problems?
- Which Chinese social and economic problems seem especially important in the years ahead? How do you think a regime still headed by Xi Jinping will handle those problems?
- Can you imagine a more liberal Chinese regime in power? How might it come to power? How might it differ from Western liberal governments in its treatment of (for example) human rights, economic globalization, private property, and gender equality?
- Would a more liberal Chinese government necessarily be a partner with the West on major international issues?
- We have read here that the Chinese leadership treats economic development and internal security as interconnected issues. How does that perspective affect (for example) research programs, military affairs, and the role of the party in everyday life, personal privacy, and ethnic minority rights?

NOTES

Chapter 1

1. Wang Jisi, "The Understanding Gap," *China-US Focus*, March 11, 2021, https:www.chinausfocus.com.
2. The White House, November 15, 2023, https://www.whitehouse.gov/briefing-room/statements-releases/2023/11/15/readout-of-president-joe-bidens-meeting-with-president-xi-jinping-of-the-peoples-republic-of-china-2/.
3. *Renmin ribao* (People's Daily, Beijing), November 16, 2023, http://politics.people.com.cn/n1/2023/1116/c1024-40119669.html.
4. CNN, June 2, 2023, https://www.cnn.com/2023/06/02/asia/austin-shangri-law-dialogue-speech-taiwan-intl-hnk/index.html.
5. CNN, October 17, 2023, https://www.cnn.com/2023/10/17/politics/us-china-risky-behavior-pilots.
6. *Washington Post*, April 12, 2025, https://www.washingtonpost.com/education/2025/04/12/international-students-visas-revoke-fear/.
7. *University World News*, November 22, 2024, https://www.universityworldnews.com/post.php?story=20241122101934576.
8. US Government Accountability Office, October 30, 2023, https://www.gao.gov/products/gao-24-105981.
9. US Congress, House Select Committee on the CCP, September 24, 2024, Research Security Report Final.pdf (house.gov).
10. *New York Times*, September 23, 2024, https://www.nytimes.com/2024/09/23/us/politics/us-china-research-military.html.
11. Harvard University, Belfer Center, "US and China Extend Science and Technology Agreement," January 21, 2011.
12. *Latitudes*, June 14, 2023, https://www.chronicle.com/newsletter/latitudes/2023-06-14.
13. *Axios*, August 5, 2023, https://www.axios.com/2023/08/05/china-us-tensions-science-technology-agreement-renewal.

14 *Voice of America News*, December 13, 2024, https://www.voanews.com/a/us-china-sign-5-year-amended-agreement-on-science-and-technology-cooperation-/7900132.html.

15 *South China Morning Post* (Hong Kong), June 10, 2023, https://www.scmp.com/news/china/science/article/3223515/xie-xiaoliang-latest-chinese-scientist-give-us-citizenship.

16 *PNAS* (National Academy of Sciences, US), June 27, 2023, https://www.pnas.org/doi/10.1073/pnas.2216248120.

17 *Los Angeles Times*, February 21, 2025, https://www.latimes.com/world-nation/story/2025-02-21/why-chinese-students-still-want-to-attend-u-s-universities.

18 *New York Times*, November 11, 2024, https://www.nytimes.com/2024/11/11/business/trump-china-trade-war.html.

19 CNN, December 2, 2024, https://www.cnn.com/2024/12/02/tech/china-us-chips-new-restrictions-intl-hnk/index.html.

20 "Fully Recognize the Nature of Mutual Benefit and Win-Win in Sino-US Relations," *Renmin ribao*, January 13, 2025.

21 *New York Times*, August 8, 2024, https://www.nytimes.com/2024/08/08/business/tsmc-phoenix-arizona-semiconductor.html.

22 *New York Times*, August 4, 2024, https://www.nytimes.com/2024/08/04/technology/china-ai-microchips-takeaways.html.

23 *Axios*, January 27, 2025, https://www.axios.com/2025/01/27/deepseek-ai-model-china-openai-rival; *Politico*, January 27, 2025, https://www.politico.com/news/2025/01/27/deepseek-freakout-us-ai-policy-00200820.

24 Ministry of Foreign Affairs, China, November 17, 2024, https://www.fmprc.gov.cn/mfa_eng/xw/zyxw/202411/t20241117_11527672.html?s=09.

25 *Politico*, March 27, 2025, https://www.politico.eu/.

26 A chart displaying China's major role in the processing of rare earth and other key minerals is at Datawrapper, 2024, https://datawrapper.dwcdn.net/joF6p/7/.

27 Xinhua, April 9, 2024, https://english.news.cn/20250409/7458b316f22944fe9059d229d4d22ed3/c.html.

28 *Renmin ribao*, April 17, 2025, http://paper.people.com.cn/rmrb/pc/content/202504/17/content_30068273.html.

29 *New York Times*, April 9, 2025, https://www.nytimes.com/2025/04/09/business/trump-tariffs-china-factories.html.

30 sinification@substack.com, May 12, 2025.

31 Tsinghua University Center for International Security and Strategy, April 2024, https://ciss.tsinghua.edu.cn/upload_files/atta/1727662169826_AD.pdf.

32 Chicago Council on Global Affairs, October 24, 2024, https://globalaffairs.org/research/public-opinion-survey/american-views-china-hit-all-time-low.

33 See Thomas Des Garets Geddes and Paddy Stephens, "China Reacts to Trump's Election," https://substack.com/home/post/p-151370528.

Chapter 2

1. *New York Times*, December 18, 2022, https://www.nytimes.com/2022/12/18/us/politics/defense-contractors-ukraine-russia.html.
2. Stephen Semler, December 22, 2022, https://stephensemler.substack.com/p/how-much-of-the-ukraine-aid-bill.
3. http://www.globalink.org/interview/view?cd=INT000035.
4. Henrik Stålhane Hiim et al., "The Dynamics of an Entangled Security Dilemma," Spring 2023, https://www.belfercenter.org/publication/dynamics-entangled-security-dilemma-chinas-changing-nuclear-posture.
5. *New York Times*, May 27, 2022, https://www.nytimes.com/2022/05/27/opinion/biden-taiwan-defense-china.html.
6. Thomas des Garets Geddes, Sinification.com, April 25, 2025, https://www.sinification.com/p/yan-anlin-on-the-drawbacks-of-a-timetable.
7. *Renmin ribao*, June 17, 2025.
8. Jude Blanchette and Ryan Hass, "Know Your Rival, Know Yourself," *Foreign Affairs*, January 7, 2025, https://www.foreignaffairs.com/united-states/know-your-rival-know-yourself-china.
9. Peter Robertson, "China's Military Rise," *VoxEU*, https://cepr.org/voxeu/columns/chinas-military-rise-comparative-military-spending-china-and-us.
10. *Washington Post*, August 8, 2022, https://www.washingtonpost.com/politics/2022/08/20/nancy-pelosi-biden-taiwan/.
11. Jordan Schneider and Lily Ottinger, "China Talk," January 13, 2025, https://www.chinatalk.media/p/amb-burns-reflects-from-beijing.
12. *South China Morning Post*, April 1, 2025, https://www.scmp.com/news/china/military/article/3304652/pla-launches-military-drills-around-taiwan.
13. Mareike Ohlberg, August 7, 2022, https://twitter.com/MareikeOhlberg/status/1556319180588187649.
14. Associated Press, July 30, 2024, https://apnews.com/article/united-states-philippines-antony-blinken-lloyd-austin-e8bc7af9b5a60f51cf60ffcf22748836.
15. BBC, October 26, 2023, https://www.bbc.com/news/world-asia-67224782.
16. DW, November 8, 2023, https://www.dw.com/en/philippines-drops-chinas-belt-and-road-as-tensions-flare/a-67344929.
17. Associated Press, March 5, 2025, https://apnews.com/article/philippines-south-china-sea-defense-secretary-gilberto-teodoro-air-defense-zone-4c63b28b674c63b1730a22dc9faa5f22.
18. Ulv Hansenn, "The Chinese 'Hypothetical Enemy,'" *Asia-Pacific Journal*, April 30, 2024, https://apjjf.org/2024/4/hanssen.
19. *Washington Post*, August 8, 2024, https://www.washingtonpost.com/world/interactive/2024/vietnam-south-china-sea-islands-growth/.
20. Zhang, "Great Power Competition in Associated States," *Asian Perspective*, Winter 2025, https://muse.jhu.edu/pub/1/issue/54346.

21 Ministry of Foreign Affairs, China, April 2, 2024 (in Chinese), https://www.fmprc.gov.cn/zyxw/202404/t20240402_11275431.shtml?s=09.
22 *Renmin ribao*, April 27, 2024.
23 Ministry of Foreign Affairs, China, September 23, 2024, https://www.fmprc.gov.cn/eng/xw/fyrbt/lxjzh/202409/t20240923_11495195.html.
24 *Japan Times*, March 22, 2025, https://www.japantimes.co.jp/news/2025/03/22/japan/politics/tokyo-trilateral-meeting/.
25 Schneider and Ottinger, "China Talk."
26 *Washington Post*, February 21, 2024, https://www.washingtonpost.com/world/2024/02/21/china-hacking-leak-documents-isoon/.
27 Ministry of Foreign Affairs, China, April 15, 2025, https://www.fmprc.gov.cn/mfa_eng/xw/fyrbt/lxjzh/202504/t20250415_11594942.html.
28 CNN, May 30, 2022, https://www.cnn.com/2022/05/30/asia/china-pacific-islands-unable-to-agree-security-pact-intl-hnk/index.html.
29 The Defense Post, May 30, 2022, https://thedefensepost.com/2022/05/30/pacific-nations-reject-china-pact/.
30 *New York Times*, November 30, 2024, https://www.nytimes.com/2024/11/30/world/asia/taiwans-president-pacific-islands-china.html.
31 War on the Rocks, March 2025, https://warontherocks.com/2025/03/the-south-pacific-is-the-new-frontline-in-the-rivalry-with-china/.
32 Congressional Research Service, Report R47589, https://crsreports.congress.gov.
33 *Washington Post*, February 14, 2025, https://www.washingtonpost.com/world/2025/02/14/china-cook-islands-pacific-deal/.
34 BBC, February 27, 2025, https://www.bbc.com/news/articles/cvg559y0803o.
35 *New York Times*, June 27, 2022, https://www.nytimes.com/2022/06/27/opinion/international-world/china-us-solomon.html.
36 *New York Times*, December 20, 2024, https://www.nytimes.com/2024/12/20/world/australia/australia-china-pacific-deals.html.
37 Bloomberg, July 16, 2024, https://www.bloomberg.com/features/2024-trump-interview-transcript/.
38 *New York Times*, February 25, 2025, https://www.nytimes.com/2025/02/25/world/asia/trump-ukraine-taiwan.html.
39 Breitbart, February 25, 2025, https://www.breitbart.com/politics/2025/02/25/exclusive-rubio-details-trump-offense-china-belt-road-initiative/.
40 *Washington Post*, March 29, 2025, https://www.washingtonpost.com/national-security/2025/03/29/secret-pentagon-memo-hegseth-heritage-foundation-china.
41 *New York Times*, March 22, 2025, https://www.nytimes.com/2025/03/22/us/politics/elon-musk-doge-china.html.
42 Quincy Institute, March 13, 2024, https://quincyinst.org/2024/03/13/only-credible-assurances-can-stabilize-u-s-china-relations/.

43 Ryan Hass and Jude Blanchette, "The Right Way to Deter China from Attacking Taiwan," *Foreign Affairs*, November 8, 2023, https://www.foreignaffairs.com/china/right-way-deter-china-attacking-taiwan.

44 Matt Pottinger and Mike Gallagher, "No Substitute for Victory," *Foreign Affairs*, April 10, 2024, https://www.foreignaffairs.com/united-states/no-substitute-victory-pottinger-gallagher.

Chapter 3

1 *New York Times*, April 5, 2023, https://www.nytimes.com/2023/04/05/world/europe/eu-china-embassador-russia-fu-cong.html.

2 Thomas des Garets Geddes and James Farquharson, Sinification, April 1, 2025, https://substack.com/home/post/p-159929963.

3 Thomas J. Christensen, "There Will Not be a New Cold War," *Foreign Affairs*, March 24, 2021, https://www.foreignaffairs.com/articles/united-states/2021-03-24/there-will-not-be-new-cold-war.

4 *Washington Post*, April 13, 2023, https://www.washingtonpost.com/national-security/2023/04/13/russia-china-weapons-leaked-documents-discord/.

5 *New York Times*, February 20, 2023, https://www.nytimes.com/2023/02/20/world/asia/china-russia-us-arms.html.

6 David Shambaugh, Eberhard Sandschneider, and Zhou Hong, eds., *China-Europe Relations: Perceptions, Policies and Prospects* (London: Routledge, 2008).

7 *Washington Post*, March 31, 2022, https://www.washingtonpost.com/world/2022/03/31/eu-china-summit-ukraine-war-russia/.

8 *Politico*, November 3, 2022, https://www.politico.eu/article/olaf-scholz-we-dont-want-to-decouple-from-china-but-cant-be-overreliant/.

9 Henry M. Paulson, "America's China Policy is Not Working," *Foreign Affairs*, January 26, 2023, https://www.foreignaffairs.com/china/americas-china-policy-not-working.

10 *New York Times*, March 25, 2025, https://www.nytimes.com/2025/03/25/world/europe/signal-jeffrey-goldberg-message-hegseth.html.

11 Thomas des Garets Geddes, Sinification, February 21, 2025, sinification@substack.com.

12 *New York Times*, May 15, 2024, https://www.nytimes.com/2024/05/15/opinion/putin-china-xi-jinping.html.

13 Ministry of Foreign Affairs, China, September 27, 2024 (in Chinese), https://www.fmprc.gov.cn/wjbzhd/202409/t20240927_11498584.shtml.

14 CNBC, January 20, 2023, https://www.cnbc.com/2023/01/20/china-must-be-in-france-says-its-diverging-with-washington-on-beijing-ties.htm.

15 *Politico*, April 9, 2023, https://www.politico.eu/article/emmanuel-macron-china-america-pressure-interview/.

16 *Wall Street Journal*, March 30, 2023, https://www.wsj.com/articles/china-wants-to-be-at-center-of-new-world-order-top-eu-official-says-22987030.

17 *New York Times*, February 24, 2025, https://www.nytimes.com/2025/02/24/world/europe/takeaways-germany-election.html.

18 *New York Times*, February 24, 2025, https://www.nytimes.com/2025/02/24/world/asia/xi-putin-call-russia-china-trump.html.

19 Ministry of Foreign Affairs, China, May 9, 2025, https://www.fmprc.gov.cn/mfa_eng/xw/zyxw/202505/t20250509_11617838.html.

20 Reuters, April 8, 2025, https://www.reuters.com/world/eus-von-der-leyen-calls-china-ensure-responsible-tariff-response-2025-04-08/.

21 *Politico*, June 17, 2025, https://www.politico.eu/article/donald-trump-china-ursula-von-der-leyen/.

Chapter 4

1 Christina Lu, "Washington Wants to Revive a Critical Minerals Mega-Railway Through Africa," *Foreign Policy*, February 28, 2024, https://foreignpolicy.com/2024/02/28/lobito-corridor-angola-critical-minerals-us-china-infrastructure-investment/.

2 China-Africa Research Initiative, Johns Hopkins University, 2025, http://www.sais-cari.org/data-chinese-global-foreign-aid.

3 CNN, November 7, 2023, https://www.cnn.com/2023/11/07/business/china-bri-developing-countries-overdue-debt-intl-hnk.

4 *PV Magazine*, January 27, 2025, https://www.pv-magazine.com/2025/01/27/china-installed-8-gw-of-solar-in-belt-and-road-countries-last-year/.

5 Business and Human Rights Resource Centre, July 2, 2022, https://www.business-humanrights.org/en/latest-news/africa-allegations-of-human-rights-violations-by-chinese-owned-firms-in-southern-africa-emerge-in-new-report/.

6 *The Guardian*, December 3, 2021, https://www.theguardian.com/us-news/2021/dec/03/us-electric-vehicle-car-sales-biden.

7 Yahoo.com, https://finance.yahoo.com/news/china-cash-flowed-congo-bank-220133166.html.

8 *Washington Post*, November 19, 2021, https://www.washingtonpost.com/national-security/us-africa-policy-biden-administration/2021/11/19/cc11c95c-4933-11ec-95dc-5f2a96e00fa3_story.html.

9 *New York Times*, March 26, 2025, https://www.nytimes.com/2025/03/26/health/usaid-cuts-gavi-bird-flu.html.

10 Pew Research Center, February 6, 2025, https://www.pewresearch.org/short-reads/2025/02/06/what-the-data-says-about-us-foreign-aid/.

11 *Washington Post*, March 31, 2025, https://www.washingtonpost.com/world/2025/03/31/myanmar-earthquake-thailand-usaid-trump/.

12 Korea Economic Institute, March 18, 2025, https://keia.org/the-peninsula/the-consequences-of-foreign-assistance-cuts-for-u-s-south-korea-cooperation/.

13 Johnson, "Can BRICS Finally Take on the West?" *Foreign Policy*, October 21, 2024, https://foreignpolicy.com/2024/10/21/brics-russia-china-kazan-summit-west-dollar/.

14 Bloomberg, February 20, 2025, https://www.bloomberg.com/news/articles/2025-02-20/us-dollar-s-use-in-global-transactions-tops-50-swift-says.

15 World Muslim Communities Council, https://www.twmcc.com/en/news/1673205895.

16 *Washington Post*, November 14, 2024, https://www.washingtonpost.com/world/2024/11/14/china-peru-port-latin-america/.

17 *The Economist*, February 9, 2025, https://www.economist.com/international/2025/02/09/chinas-stunning-new-campaign-to-turn-the-world-against-taiwan.

18 CNN, March 14, 2025, https://www.cnn.com/2025/03/14/business/panama-canal-sale-china-criticism-intl-hnk/index.html.

19 CBS News, February 6, 2025, https://www.cbsnews.com/news/panama-canal-president-mulino-denies-deal-free-passage-us-warships-rubio/?intcid=CNM-00-10abd1h.

20 *New York Times*, March 20, 2025, https://www.nytimes.com/2025/03/20/business/trump-panama-canal-china-hong-kong.html.

21 International Institute of Strategic Studies, October 2024, https://www.iiss.org/research-paper/2024/10/the-global-security-initiative-chinas-international-policing-activities/.

22 Ministry of Foreign Affairs, China, January 10, 2025 (in Chinese), https://www.fmprc.gov.cn/wjbzhd/202501/t20250110_11530248.shtml.

23 Africa Center for Strategic Studies, December 2, 2024, https://africacenter.org/spotlight/militarization-china-africa-policy/.

24 *New York Times*, March 11, 2023, https://www.nytimes.com/2023/03/11/us/politics/saudi-arabia-iran-china-biden.html.

25 *New York Times*, March 9, 2023, https://www.nytimes.com/2023/03/09/us/politics/saudi-arabia-israel-united-states.html.

26 *New York Times*, December 8, 2022, https://www.nytimes.com/2022/12/08/world/middleeast/china-saudi-arabia-agreement.html.

27 Trita Parsi and Khalid Aljabri, "How China Became a Peacemaker in the Middle East," *Foreign Affairs*, March 15, 2023, https://www.foreignaffairs.com/china-became-peacemaker-middle-east.

Chapter 5

1 Xinhua, April 9, 2025, https://english.news.cn/20250409/831119f64b2645aea0699bd6c42dbaed/c.html.

2. Yonhap News Agency, September 18, 2023, https://en.yna.co.kr/view/AEN20230918008151325?section=news.
3. 38 North, April 2025, https://www.38north.org/2025/04/the-new-face-of-north-korean-sanctions-monitoring-can-the-msmt-pick-up-where-the-panel-of-experts-left-off/.
4. *Lawfare*, January 12, 2025, https://www.lawfaremedia.org/article/cutting-north-korea-s-access-to-chinese-controlled-african-uranium.
5. KEI, January 12, 2025, https://keia.org/the-peninsula/kim-jong-uns-risky-year-of-the-snake/.
6. For further background, see Jennifer Lind, "Japan Steps Up," *Foreign Affairs*, December 23, 2022, https://www.foreignaffairs.com/japan/japan-steps.
7. *Japan Times*, January 11, 2023, https://www.japantimes.co.jp/news/2023/01/11/national/politics-diplomacy/britain-japan-troops-agreement-raa/.
8. *Washington Post*, December 23, 2022, https://www.washingtonpost.com/opinions/2022/12/23/japan-military-buildup-explained/.
9. War on the Rocks, January 2023, https://warontherocks.com/2023/01/japans-shift-to-war-footing/.
10. Associated Press, July 28, 2024, https://apnews.com/article/japan-us-military-command-missile-china-4e97f4cb01cfef7b6db8fb1a5df771e4.
11. *University World News*, May 16, 2024, https://www.universityworldnews.com/post.php?story=20240516140712575.
12. *New York Times*, March 27, 2025, https://www.nytimes.com/2025/03/27/world/asia/trump-china-japan-korea.html.
13. *Japan Times*, April 16, 2025, https://www.japantimes.co.jp/news/2025/04/16/japan/politics/japan-us-alliance/.
14. *New York Times*, April 23, 2025, https://www.nytimes.com/2025/04/23/business/trump-tariffs-japan-china.html.
15. Carnegie Endowment for International Peace, December 11, 2024, https://carnegieendowment.org/research/2024/12/negotiating-the-india-china-standoff-2020-2024?lang=en.
16. Ministry of External Affairs, India, November 2024, https://www.mea.gov.in/press-releases.htm?dtl%2F38543%2FExternal_Affairs_Ministers_meeting_with_Member_of_the_Communist_Party_of_China_CPC_Political_Bureau_and_Foreign_Minister_HE_Mr_Wang_Yi_on_the_sideline; Reuters, July 4, 2024, https://www.reuters.com/world/asia-pacific/india-china-foreign-ministers-agree-step-up-talks-border-issues-2024-07-04/.
17. Ministry of Foreign Affairs, China, November 19, 2024 (in Chinese), https://www.fmprc.gov.cn/wjbzhd/202411/t20241119_11528885.shtml.
18. *The Hindu*, April 2, 2025, https://www.thehindu.com/opinion/op-ed/china-india-ties-across-the-past-and-into-the-future/article69401052.ece.
19. *New York Times*, February 13, 2025, https://www.nytimes.com/live/2025/02/13/us/trump-news?smid=url-share#trump-modi-musk.

20 *New York Times*, May 7, 2025, https://www.nytimes.com/2025/05/07/world/asia/india-pakistan-weapons.html.

21 Passang Dorji and Nicholas Thomas, "Crafting Bhutan-China Ties: Small State Agency in Emergent Diplomatic Relations," *Asian Perspective*, Summer 2024, https://dx.doi.org/10.1353/apr.2024.a935485.

22 Turquoise Roof, October 15, 2024, https://turquoiseroof.org/forceful-diplomacy-china-cross-border-villages-in-bhutan/.

23 *Global Asia*, June 2024, https://globalasia.org/v19no2/feature/the-indian-ocean-chinas-new-strategic-marketplace_marwaan-macan-markar.

24 *The Irrawaddy*, December 12, 2023, https://www.irrawaddy.com/news/war-against-the-junta/whos-who-in-the-two-major-anti-regime-offensives-in-myanmar.html.

25 Council on Foreign Relations, November 30, 2023, https://www.cfr.org/blog/myanmar-army-could-actually-collapse-are-united-states-and-other-powers-ready-such-scenario.

26 *The Irrawaddy*, November 30, 2023, https://www.irrawaddy.com/specials/myanmar-china-watch/myanmar-junta-plays-up-strong-china-ties-a-week-after-anti-beijing-protests.html.

27 US Institute of Peace, November 2023, https://www.usip.org/publications/2023/11/we-shouldnt-fear-resistance-victory-myanmar.

28 Courtesy of Giles Raymond DeMourot, January 6, 2025, https://www.linkedin.com/feed/update/urn:li:activity:7282157403607830528/.

29 *New York Times*, December 31, 2024, https://www.nytimes.com/2024/12/31/world/asia/myanmar-drugs-crime.html.

Chapter 6

1 Wu Guoguang, "Xi Jinping's Purges Have Escalated," *China File*, February 25, 2025, https://www.chinafile.com/reporting-opinion/viewpoint/xi-jinpings-purges-have-escalated-heres-why-they-are-unlikely-stop.

2 Manoj Kewalramani, February 27, 2025, trackingpeoplesdaily@substack.com.

3 *New York Times*, January 17, 2015, www.nytimes.com/2015/01/17/opinion/murong-xuecun-xis-selective-punishment.html.

4 *New York Times*, January 22, 2014, http://sinosphere.blogs.nytimes.com/2014/01/22/report-details-overseas-accounts-of-chinese-elite/?hp.

5 *The Sunday Guardian*, March 23, 2025, https://sundayguardianlive.com/top-five/u-s-report-exposes-corruption-of-the-chinese-leadership.

6 *New York Times*, March 3, 2015, www.nytimes.com/2015/03/03/world/asia/in-chinas-legislature-the-rich-are-more-than-represented.html.

7 Erin Baggott Carter, Brett L. Carter, and Stephen Schick, "Do Chinese Citizens Conceal Opposition to the CCP in Surveys? Evidence from Two Experiments," *The China Quarterly*, January 10, 2024, https://www.cambridge.org/core/

journals/china-quarterly/article/do-chinese-citizens-conceal-opposition-to-the-ccp-in-surveys-evidence-from-two-experiments/12A2440F948D016E8D845C492F7D0CFE.

8   Economy, "China's Imperial President," *Foreign Affairs,* October 20, 2014, https://www.foreignaffairs.com/china/chinas-imperial-president.

9   *Renmin ribao,* October 18, 2024.

10 *New York Times,* November 27, 2022, https://www.nytimes.com/2022/11/27/world/asia/china-covid-protest.html?smid=nytcore-android-share.

11 *China Digital Times,* January 2025, https://chinadigitaltimes.net/2025/01/filmmaker-sentenced-to-more-than-three-years-in-prison-for-documentary-on-white-paper-protests/.

12 *New York Times,* November 30, 2022, https://www.nytimes.com/2022/11/30/opinion/china-covid-protests-xi-jinping.html.

13 Dali L. Yang, *Wuhan: How the Covid-19 Outbreak in China Spiraled Out of Control* (New York: Oxford University Press, 2024).

14 *University World News,* October 16, 2024, https://www.universityworldnews.com/post.php.

15 *University World News,* July 11, 2024, https://www.universityworldnews.com/post.php?story=20240711122935490.

16 Open Doors, n.d., https://opendoorsdata.org/data/international-students/enrollment-trends/.

17 *Washington Post,* April 21, 2025, https://www.washingtonpost.com/opinions/2025/04/21/trump-student-visas-china-crackdown/.

18 *University World News,* October 8, 2024, https://www.universityworldnews.com/post.php?story=20241008105010175.

19 Other top receiving countries, in descending order of funding amounts, were Ethiopia, Jordan, the Democratic Republic of Congo, Somalia, Yemen, Afghanistan, Nigeria, South Sudan, and Syria, *University World News,* February 8, 2025, https://www.universityworldnews.com/post.php?story=20250208071408604.

20 *University World News,* March 24, 2025, https://www.universityworldnews.com/post.php?story=2025032410162571.

21 *Nature,* February 19, 2025, https://www.nature.com/articles/d41586-025-00455-y.

Chapter 7

1   *China Briefing,* June 17, 2024, https://www.china-briefing.com/news/china-energy-conservation-and-co2-reduction-plan-compliance-considerations-for-businesses/.

2 Jude Blanchette and Ryan Hass, "Know Your Rival, Know Yourself," *Foreign Affairs*, January 7, 2025, https://www.foreignaffairs.com/united-states/know-your-rival-know-yourself-china.

3 Bloomberg, March 25, 2025, https://www.bloomberg.com/news/articles/2025-03-25/china-adviser-urges-boosting-consumption-to-70-of-gdp-by-2035/.

4 CNBC, September 22, 2024, https://www.cnbc.com.

5 *Statista*, January 20, 2025, https://www.statista.com/chart/33788/annual-net-profit-loss-of-chinese-property-developers/.

6 *Wall Street Journal*, March 30, 2025, https://www.wsj.com.

7 *The Hindu*, September 19, 2024, https://www.thehindu.com/news/international/china-piles-extra-work-on-weary-youth-to-ease-pension-crisis/article68655370.ece.

8 Bloomberg, October 7, 2024, https://www.bloomberg.com.

9 *New York Times*, November 8, 2024, https://www.nytimes.com/2024/11/08/business/china-stimulus-economy-debt.html.

10 *New York Times*, January 12, 2025, https://www.nytimes.com/2025/01/12/business/china-trade-surplus.html.

11 Reuters, October 17, 2024, https://www.reuters.com/markets/asia/imfs-georgieva-says-china-can-no-longer-rely-exports-growth-2024-10-17/.

12 *Nikkei Asia*, January 20, 2025, https://asia.nikkei.com/Politics/International-relations/China-FDI-trends-point-to-world-split-by-superpowers-as-Trump-comes-in.

13 Trans. Manoj Kewalramani, "Tracking People's Daily," January 16, 2025, https://trackingpeoplesdaily.substack.com/p/china-sri-lanka-joint-statement-huan.

14 World Economic Forum, January 21, 2025, https://www.weforum.org/stories/2025/01/davos-2025-special-address-ding-xuexiang-vice-premier-china/.

15 Trans. Manoj Kewalramani, "Tracking People's Daily," February 19, 2025, trackingpeoplesdaily@substack.com.

16 Stephen G. Brooks and Ben A. Vagle, "The Real China Trump Card," *Foreign Affairs*, February 20, 2025, https://www.foreignaffairs.com/united-states/real-china-trump-card-brooks-vagle.

17 *Renmin ribao*, December 4, 2024.

18 See also *New York Times*, November 19, 2024, https://www.nytimes.com/interactive/2024/11/19/climate/china-emissions-fossil-fuels-climate.html.

19 *Washington Post*, March 3, 2025, https://www.washingtonpost.com/climate-solutions/2025/03/03/china-renewable-energy-green-world-leader/.

20 *New York Times*, July 18, 2024, https://www.nytimes.com/2024/07/18/climate/china-greenhouse-gas-emissions-plateau.html.

21 *New York Times*, April 18, 2024, https://www.nytimes.com/2024/04/18/climate/china-sinking-sea-level.html.

Chapter 8

1. Zenz, "Sterilizations, IUCs, and Mandatory Birth Control," The Jamestown Foundation, July 21, 2020, https://jamestown.org/wp-content/uploads/2020/06/Zenz-Internment-Sterilizations-and-IUDs-REVISED-March-17–2021.pdf.
2. The Citizen Lab at the University of Toronto's Munk School of Global Affairs & Public Policy, April 21, 2023, https://www.ohchr.org/sites/default/files/documents/issues/terrorism/sr/cfis/cfi-gs-impact-ct-measures/subm-global-study-impact-cso-citizen-lab.pdf.
3. *The Globe and Mail* (Toronto), March 2, 2021, https://www.theglobeandmail.com/world/article-thousands-of-uyghur-workers-in-china-are-being-relocated-in-an-effort/.
4. State Council Information Office, China, September 17, 2020 (in Chinese), www.scio.gov.cn.
5. Global Rights Alliance, "Risk at the Source," June 2025, https://globalrightscompliance.org/wp-content/uploads/2025/06/GRC-critical-minerals.pdf?s=09.
6. *New York Times*, January 9, 2025, https://www.nytimes.com/interactive/2025/01/09/world/asia/tibet-china-boarding-schools.html.
7. Public Broadcasting System, "Frontline," February 18, 2025, https://www.pbs.org/wgbh/frontline/article/tibetan-children-boarding-schools-chinese/.
8. European Parliament, "Joint Motion for a Resolution on Hong Kong," November 27, 2024, https://www.europarl.europa.eu/doceo/document/RC-10-2024-0208_EN.html?s=0.
9. CNN, December 28, 2024, https://www.cnn.com/2024/12/28/china/china-liuzhi-detention-centers-dst-intl-hnk.
10. *Washington Post*, April 28, 2025, https://www.washingtonpost.com/world/2025/04/28/china-ngos-un-geneva/.
11. Xinhua, February 6, 2025, https://english.news.cn/20250206/98f381b658094a039ceaa8a3afae7c8d/c.html.
12. US Department of State, February 27, 2025, https://www.state.gov/on-thailands-forced-return-of-uyghurs-to-china/?s=09.
13. "Online scam compounds," mainly in Myanmar, Cambodia, and Laos, are a multibillion-dollar industry, run by gangs and a variety of other groups. They employ an estimated 220,000 mostly young and poor people in slave-like conditions. *Scam: Inside Southeast Asia's Cybercrime Compounds* examines this phenomenon, https://jacobin.com/2025/05/online-scam-industry-slave-labor.
14. US Institute of Peace, November 2023, https://www.usip.org/publications/2023/11/we-shouldnt-fear-resistance-victory-myanmar.
15. *Politico*, April 24, 2025, https://www.politico.eu/newsletter/china-watcher/pentagon-follies-beijing-jollies/.
16. *Politico*, October 31, 2024, https://www.politico.eu/newsletter/china-watcher/xi-jinping-and-the-us-election/.

17 *The New York Review*, March 10, 2022, https://www.nybooks.com/articles/2022/03/10/the-uncompromising-ai-weiwei/.

18 Ai Weiwei adds: "I have made many other works relating to the Sichuan earthquake, but this one had a profound impact on how I deal with social and political issues. It's about a real-life tragedy, the human condition, civil rights—an embodiment of my passion and imagination. If I hadn't engaged with that tragedy, I would not be the artist I am today." *The Guardian*, February 25, 2018, https://www.theguardian.com/artanddesign/2018/feb/15/ai-weiwei-remembering-sichuan-earthquake.

19 *New York Times*, January 27, 2025, https://www.nytimes.com/2025/01/27/world/asia/china-tibet-dam-india.html.